The Apology of Aristides

TEXTS AND STUDIES

CONTRIBUTIONS TO
BIBLICAL AND PATRISTIC LITERATURE

EDITED BY

J. ARMITAGE ROBINSON M.A.
FELLOW OF CHRIST'S COLLEGE CAMBRIDGE

VOL. I.

No. 1. THE APOLOGY OF ARISTIDES

THE APOLOGY OF ARISTIDES

ON BEHALF OF THE CHRISTIANS

FROM A SYRIAC MS. PRESERVED ON MOUNT SINAI

EDITED

WITH AN INTRODUCTION AND TRANSLATION BY

J. RENDEL HARRIS M.A.

FORMERLY FELLOW OF CLARE COLLEGE CAMBRIDGE
AND NOW PROFESSOR OF BIBLICAL LANGUAGES IN
HAVERFORD COLLEGE PENNSYLVANIA

WITH AN APPENDIX
CONTAINING THE MAIN PORTION OF
THE ORIGINAL GREEK TEXT

BY

J. ARMITAGE ROBINSON M.A.

FELLOW AND ASSISTANT TUTOR OF CHRIST'S COLLEGE CAMBRIDGE

Wipf and Stock Publishers
199 W 8th Ave, Suite 3
Eugene, OR 97401

The Apology of Aristides
on Behalf of the Christians
By Harris, J. Rendel
ISBN: 1-59244-847-X
Publication date 9/3/2004
Previously published by Cambridge, 1891

PREFACE.

THE first part of this tract contains the Syriac text of the lost Apology of Aristides, accompanied by such comments and elucidations as I have been able to give to the subject. It is my first venture in Syriac, and I am thankful to my learned friends who have from time to time assisted me with suggestions and criticisms for the elimination of some of the more glaring errors. Amongst them I may mention especially Professor Bensly, of Cambridge, and Professor Isaac A. Hall, of New York. In the attempt to give the Armenian fragments of the Apology, in such a form as may make them accessible for critical use, I have had the valuable aid of Mr Conybeare, of Oxford, who placed at my disposal the results of his own work at Edschmiazin.

When the pages were almost through the printer's hands, my friend Mr J. A. Robinson, of Christ's College, by one of those happy accidents, as we call them, upon which progress depends, discovered that substantially the whole of the Greek text was extant, and had been incorporated in that charming half-Greek and half-Oriental story, the Lives of Barlaam and Joasaph. Of course this means that, for the greater part of the Apology of Aristides, we have copies and versions in good number (Greek, Latin, Ethiopic, Arabic, Old French, etc.). This opens quite a new field before the student of Christian Apologetics. Need I say how gladly I make way for him in the Appendix, which will really be the text itself; and that I say in the language of the Acts of St Perpetua: "Hic ordinem totum Apologiae iam hinc ipse narrabit...manu sua et suo sensu."

J. RENDEL HARRIS.

NOTE.

WITH the aid of the photographs taken by Prof. Harris the Syriac text has been carefully revised by Prof. Bensly, who has taken special pains with the reproduction of the punctuation of the MS. There seems occasionally to be some deviation from the ordinary system in the use of the diacritical points: but as it is impossible to tell from the photographs to what date the punctuation belongs, it has seemed better to reproduce it without attempting to mend it.

The English translation was in the first instance made by Prof. Harris: but the discovery of the Greek made it necessary that it should undergo a complete revision, in order that scholars who do not read Syriac might be able to form a better estimate of the relation of the Syriac to the Greek, than could be given by a translation made without any reference to the latter. Moreover in several places the Greek cast new light upon the Syriac where it was obscure before. The task of revision would have been entirely beyond my power, but for the kind patience of Prof. Bensly, who allowed me to read the whole piece through with him. At his suggestion too I have added, within brackets, a few notes in addition to those made by Prof. Harris.

The Facsimile of a page of the Syriac MS. has been made from one of Prof. Harris's photographs. It corresponds with ܟܐ 5—ܟܒ 9 of this edition.

J. A. R.

TABLE OF CONTENTS.

INTRODUCTION.

THE present volume contains one of the earliest of the Apologies made to the Roman Emperors on behalf of the Christians, that, namely, which was said to have been presented to the Emperor Hadrian by an Athenian philosopher of the name of Aristides. Our information concerning this Apology has hitherto been of the scantiest kind, depending chiefly upon certain allusions of Eusebius in his *Ecclesiastical History* and in his *Chronicon;* as Eusebius did not, however, preserve any extracts from the book and presents only a most obscure figure in a philosopher's garb as its author, while subsequent writers have added little or nothing to what they found in Eusebius, it must be admitted that our ideas as to the character and scope of one of the earliest apologetic treatises on Christianity were about as vague as it was possible for them to be. It is true that there was a suspicion abroad which came from Jerome that the lost work of Aristides had been imitated by Justin in his Apology, and Jerome had also ventured the opinion that the Apology was woven out of materials derived from the philosophers: but it was almost impossible to put any faith in Jerome's statements, which are usually mere editorial expansions and colourings of what he found in the pages of Eusebius. Not that there was any *à priori* improbability in the opinion that one Christian Apologist had imitated another, for almost all the Apologies that are known to us are painfully alike, and it would not be difficult to maintain of any two of them selected at random that one of them had borrowed from or imitated the other. The difficulty lay in the want of literary faith in statements made by Jerome; but even if this confidence had not been wanting, we should not have been very much the wiser.

In the case of a companion Apology to that of Aristides, we were more happily placed for forming an opinion; since Eusebius not only describes an Apology presented to the Emperor Hadrian by a certain Quadratus, at the time of one of the imperial visits to Athens, but gives us also some striking and powerful sentences, just enough to convince one that the document was marked by argumentative force and spiritual insight, and could not have been a mere conventional tirade against paganism. Until recent times, then, all that could be said on the subject of these lost Apologies was that we had Eusebian tradition for their existence, Eusebian authority for their date, and a Eusebian extract from one of them as a specimen of sub-apostolic defence, a mere brick from a vanished house.

The mist, however, lifted some time ago, when the learned Armenians of the Lazarist monastery at Venice added to the obligations under which they have so often laid the scholarly and Christian world, by publishing an Armenian translation of the opening chapters of the lost Apology of Aristides; and although their document was received in some quarters[1] with incredulity, it will be seen, by what we have presently to bring forward, that the fragment which they printed was rightly entitled, and that they had at least made the way for a satisfactory conception of

[1] Especially by M. Renan, who in his *Origines de Christianisme*, vol. VI. p. vi., says: "Le présent volume était imprimé quand j'ai eu connaissance d'une publication des mékhitaristes de Venise contenant en Arménien, avec traduction Latine, deux morceaux, dont l'un serait l'Apologie adressée par Aristide à Adrien. L'authenticité de cette pièce ne soutient pas l'examen. C'est une composition plate, qui répondrait bien mal à ce que Eusèbe et S. Jérome disent du talent de l'auteur et surtout à cette particularité que l'ouvrage était *contextum philosophorum sententiis*. L'écrit Arménien ne présente pas une seule citation d'auteur profane. La théologie qu'on y trouve, en ce qui concerne la Trinité, l'incarnation, la qualité de mère de Dieu attribuée à Marie, est postérieure au IVe siècle. L'érudition historique ou plutôt mythologique est aussi bien indigne d'un écrivain du IIe siècle. Le second 'sermon' publié par les mékhitaristes a encore moins de droit à être attribué au philosophe Chrétien d'Athènes: le manuscrit porte Aristaeus: c'est une homélie insignificable sur le bon larron."

M. Renan was rightly opposed in this sweeping negation of authenticity by Doulcet, who pointed out relations between Aristides and the *Timaeus* as a justification of the philosophical character of the work. Unfortunately Doulcet

the dogmatics which underlay the apologetics. This was a great gain. Moreover their published fragment shewed traces of an interesting originality of method in the classification of the religious beliefs of the time.

Our contribution to the subject consists of a Syriac translation of the whole, or substantially the whole, of the missing Apology. We were so happy as to discover this text in a volume of Syriac extracts preserved in the library of the convent of St Catharine, upon Mount Sinai, during a delightful visit which we paid to those majestic solitudes and silences in the spring of 1889. Our copy has suffered somewhat in the course of time from successive transcriptions, and needs occasionally the hand of the critical corrector. The language and thought of the writer are, however, so simple and straightforward that the limits of error are much narrower than they would be in a document where the structure was more highly complicated; the unintelligible sentences which accumulate in a translation so much more rapidly than in the copying of an original document, are almost entirely absent. In fact the writer is more of a child than a philosopher, a child well-trained in creed and well-practised in ethics, rather than either a dogmatist defending a new system or an iconoclast destroying an old one: but this simplicity of treatment, so far from being a weakness, adds often greatly to the natural impressiveness of the subject and gives the work a place by the side of the best Christian writing of his age. But, before going further, it will be best to describe a little more closely the volume from which our text is taken.

Description of the MS.

The MS. from which we have copied is numbered 16 amongst the Syriac MSS. of the Sinaitic convent. The MS. may be

went too far, by trying to identify Aristides with the author of the Epistle to Diognetus.

Harnack (*Theol. LZ.* 1879, no. 16, col. 375 f.) was very favourable to the genuineness of the fragment, and made some excellent points in its defence.

M. Renan will now have the opportunity of verifying for himself that the term Theotokos, to which he objected so strongly as savouring of the fourth century, is not in the Syriac text.

referred to the 7th century, and is written in two columns to the page. The book is made up of a number of separate treatises and extracts, almost all of which are ethical in character. Thus on fol. 1 *b* we have

ܬܫܥܝܬܐ ܕܥܠ ܕܘܒܪ̈ܐ ܕܐܒܗ̈ܬܐ ܕܢܦܩܘ ܡܢ ܝܘܢܝܐ
ܠܣܘܪܝܝܐ

or, the history of the Lives of the Fathers, translated from Greek into Syriac.

On fol. 2 *b*

ܥܠ ܦܘܫܩ ܗܘ ܕܒܠܘܩܐ ܟܪܝܬܐ

Apparently we have here the *Liber Paradisi* or Lives of the Holy Fathers of the Desert, of which many copies exist in Greek, though it may be doubted whether there is any critical edition. Some portions of this Syriac version were published at Upsala by Tullberg and his disciples, in 1851, from MSS. in the Vatican and in the British Museum. In our MS. the current heading of the pages is

ܬܫܥܝܬܐ ܕܐܝܚܝܕ̈ܝܐ ܡܨܪ̈ܝܐ

or, History of the Egyptian Hermits.

After fol. 86 *b* two leaves appear to have been cut away.

Fol. 87 *b* bears the heading

ܕܩܕܝܫܐ ܢܝܠܘܣ ܝܚܝܕܝܐ

Of the holy Nilus the Solitary.

At the foot of fol. 93 *a* begins the Apology of Aristides.

On fol. 105 *a* begins

ܡܐܡܪܐ ܕܦܠܘܛܪܟܘܣ ܥܠ ܗܝ ܕܡܬܥܕܪ ܐܢܫ ܡܢ
ܒܥܠܕܒܒܗ

or, A discourse of Plutarch on the subject of a man's being assisted by his enemy.

At the foot of fol. 112 *a*

ܡܐܡܪܐ ܕܬܪܝܢ ܕܥܠ ܕܘܪܫܐ ܕܗܘ ܕܦܠܘܛܪܟܘܣ

or, A second discourse of the same Plutarch περὶ ἀσκήσεως.

Apparently this is the tract published by Lagarde in his *Analecta*, pp. 177—186, and translated by Gildemeister and Bücheler.

On fol. 121 *b* ܡܐܡܪܐ ܕܦܘܬܓܪܘܣ

A discourse of Pythagoras, probably the same as is published in Lagarde's *Analecta*, pp. 195—201.

On fol. 126 *a* ܡܐܡܪܐ ܕܦܠܘܛܪܟܘܣ ܕܥܠ ܪܘܓܙܐ

A discourse of Plutarch, on Anger, for which see Lagarde, *Analecta Syriaca*, pp. 186—195.

On fol. 132 *b*

ܬܘܒ ܡܐܡܪܐ ܕܠܘܩܝܘܣ ܥܠ ܕܠܐ ܩܠܐ ܕܢܩܒܠ
ܡܐܟܠ ܩܪ̈ܨܐ ܥܠ ܪ̈ܚܡܝܢ.

A discourse of Lucius (Lucianus), that we should not receive slander against our friends: περὶ τοῦ μὴ ῥᾳδίως πιστεύειν διαβολῇ.

Apparently the same as is given in Sachau, *Inedita*, pp. 1—16.

On fol. 140 *a*

ܬܘܒ ܡܐܡܪܐ ܕܥܒܝܕ ܠܦܝܠܣܘܦܐ ܥܠ ܢܦܫܐ

A discourse made by a philosopher, De Anima: probably the same as is given in Sachau, *Inedita*, as Philosophorum de anima sententiae.

On fol. 143 *a*

ܡܠܟܘܬܐ ܕܬܐܢܐ ܦܝܠܣܘܦܬܐ ܕܒܝܬ ܦܘܬܓܪܘܣ

or, the Counsel of Theano, a female philosopher of the school of Pythagoras: see Sachau, *Inedita*, pp. 70—75, as Theano: Sententiae[1].

On fol. 145 *b* a collection of Sayings of the Philosophers, beginning with

ܦܠܛܘܢ ܚܟܝܡܐ ܐܡܪ, (Plato the Wise said).

On fol. 151 *b*

ܡܐܡܪܐ ܩܕܡܝܐ ܦܘܫܩܐ ܕܩܘܗܠܬ ܕܥܒܝܕ ܠܡܪܝ.
ܝܘܚܢܢ ܐܝܚܝܕܝܐ ܠܘܬ ܬܐܘܓܢܝܣ ܛܘܒܢܐ

A first discourse in explanation of Ecclesiastes, made by Mar John the Solitary for the blessed Theognis. See Wright's *Cat. of the Syr. MSS. in the Brit. Mus.* p. 996.

[1] See Wright's *Catalogue*, p. 1160. The general contents of this MS. (Brit. Mus. 987) should be compared with those of the MS. here described: it contains e.g. the Apology of Melito and the Hypomnemata of Ambrose, and various Philosophical treatises.

And from fol. 214 *a* onward the volume is occupied with translations from the Homilies of Chrysostom on Matthew.

The above description will shew something of the value of the MS. It will also suggest that it was the ethical character of the Apology of Aristides that secured its incorporation with the volume. Let us now pass on to discuss the effect which this recovered document has upon our estimate of the Eusebiar statements concerning the earliest Church Apologists.

Aristides and Eusebius.

According to the *Chronicon* of Eusebius we have the following date for the Apologies of Quadratus and Aristides:

1. The Armenian version of the *Chronicon* gives under the year 124 A.D. as follows:

Ol.	A. Abr.	Imp. Rom.	
[d]226	2140	8[e]	[d] Adrianus Eleusinarum rerum gnarus fuit multaque (dona) Atheniensium largitus est. Romanorum ecclesiae episcopatum excepit septimus Telesphorus annis XI.

Codratus apostolorum auditor et Aristides nostri dogmatis (nostrae rei) philosophus Atheniensis Adriano supplicationes dedere apologeticas (apologiae, responsionis) ob mandatum. Acceperat tamen et a Serennio (*s.* Serenno) splendido praeside (iudice) scriptum de Christianis, quod nempe iniquum sit occidere eos solo rumore sine inquisitione, neque ulla accusatione. Scribit Armonicus Fundius (Phundius) proconsuli Asianorum ut sine ullo damno et incusatione non damnarentur; et exemplar edicti eius hucusque circumfertur.

One of the Armenian MSS. (Cod. N) transfers this notice about the Apologists to the following year, and it is believed that this represents more exactly the time of Hadrian's first visit to Athens (125—126 A.D.). With this agrees the dating of the Latin version of Jerome. We may say then that it is the intention of Eusebius to refer the presentation of both these

Apologies to the time when Hadrian was spending his first winter in Athens; and to make them the reason for the Imperial rescript to Minucius Fundanus which we find attached to the first Apology of Justin Martyr. And since Minucius Fundanus and his predecessor Granianus were consuls suffect in the years 106 and 107, it is not unreasonable to suppose that they held the Asian pro-consulate in the years A.D. 123 and 124, or 124 and 125. If then Aristides and Quadratus presented apologies to Hadrian, it is reasonable to connect these Apologies with his first Athenian winter and not with the second (A.D. 129—130).

But here we begin to meet with difficulties; for, in the first place, much doubt has been thrown on the genuineness of the rescript of the emperor to Minucius Fundanus; in the second place there is a suspicious resemblance between Quadratus the Apologist and another Quadratus who was bishop of Athens in the reign of Antoninus Pius, succeeding to Publius whom Jerome affirms to have been martyred; and in the third place our newly-recovered document cannot by any possibility be referred to the period suggested by Eusebius, and there is only the barest possibility of its having been presented to the Emperor Hadrian at all. Let us examine this last point carefully, in order to answer, as far as our means will permit, the question as to the time of presentation of the Apology of Aristides and the person or persons to whom it was addressed.

The Armenian fragment is headed as follows:

To the Emperor Hadrian Caesar, from Aristides, philosopher of Athens.

There is nothing, at first sight, to lead us to believe that this is the original heading; such a summary merely reflects the Eusebian tradition and might be immediately derived from it.

When we turn to the Syriac Version, we find a somewhat similar preface, to the following effect.

Apology made by Aristides the Philosopher before Hadrianus the King, concerning the worship of Almighty God.

But this, which seems to be a mere literary heading, proper, shall we say, for one out of a collection of apologies, is immediately followed by another introduction which cannot be anything else than a part of the primitive apology. It runs as follows:

...Caesar Titus Hadrianus Antoninus, Worshipful and Clement, from Marcianus Aristides, philosopher of Athens.

The additional information which we derive from this sentence is a sufficient guarantee of its genuineness; we have the first name of the philosopher given, as Marcianus; and we have the name of the emperor addressed given at length. To our astonishment this is not Hadrian, but his successor Antoninus Pius, who bears the name of Hadrian by adoption from Publius Aelius Hadrianus. Unless therefore we can shew that there is an error or a deficiency in the opening sentence of the Apology we shall be obliged to refer it to the time of the emperor Antoninus Pius, and to say that Eusebius has made a mistake in reading the title of the Apology, or has followed some one who had made the mistake before him. And it seems tolerably clear that if an error exist at all in such a precise statement as ours, it must be of the nature of an omission. Let us see what can be urged in favour of this theory. We will imagine that the original title contained the names both of Hadrian and of Antoninus Pius, his adviser and companion, much in the same way as Justin opens his first Apology with the words, "to the Emperor Titus Aelius Hadrianus Antoninus Pius Augustus Caesar and to his son Verissimus the Philosopher, and to Lucius the Philosopher, natural son of Caesar and adopted son of Pius....I Justin...have written the following appeal and supplication." In support of this theory we might urge the apparent dislocation of the opening sentence of our Apology. The Syriac version is clearly wrong in its punctuation, for example, since it transfers the expression ܐܚܝܕ ܟܠ (Almighty) to Caesar, by placing a colon after the word ܐܠܗܐ (God). This is clearly impossible, for that the writer did not attempt to translate, say, *αὐτοκράτωρ* as if it were *παντοκράτωρ* will be evident from his correct use of the Divine attribute later on in his work. But even if the translator had been guilty of such a mistake, the case would not have been bettered, because Antonine would now have been styled Emperor as well as Caesar.

But let us imagine if we please that the term Caesar or

Emperor Caesar belongs to a previous name which has dropped out and supply the connective necessary, so as to read, "To the Emperor Aelius Hadrianus Augustus Caesar and to Titus Hadrianus Antoninus." In support of this we may urge that the adjectives which follow are marked in the Syriac with the sign of the plural, as if the writer imagined himself to be addressing more persons than one. Supposing then that this is the case we should still have to face the question as to the name given to Antonine; if he is called Hadrian, this must mean that the Apology is presented at some time subsequent to his adoption, which is generally understood to have taken place in the year A.D. 138, only a little while before Hadrian's death. So that in any case we should be prohibited by our document from dating the Apology in question either in the first visit of Hadrian to Athens or in the second visit, and we should only have the barest possibility that it was presented to Hadrian at all. It would have, so to speak, to be read to him on his death-bed at Baiae. Seeing then the extreme difficulty of maintaining the Hadrianic or Eusebian hypothesis, we are driven to refer the Apology to the reign of Antoninus Pius, and to affirm that Eusebius made a mistake in reading or quoting the title of the book, in which mistake he has been followed by a host of other and later writers. If he followed a text which had the heading as in the Syriac, he has misunderstood the person spoken of as Hadrian the king; and if on the other hand he takes the opening sentences as his guide, he has made a superficial reference, which a closer reading would have corrected. All that is necessary to make the Syriac MS. intelligible is the introduction of a simple prepositional prefix before the imperial name, and the deletion of the *ribbui* points in the adjectives.

Nor is this all; for there can be no doubt that the two adjectives in question (ܣܒܣܛ̈ܐ ܘܡܪ̈ܚܡܢܐ) are intended to represent two of the final titles of Antoninus: ܣܒܣܛ̈ܐ standing for the Greek Σεβαστός, which again is the equivalent of the Latin *Augustus;* and ܡܪ̈ܚܡܢܐ being the equivalent of the title *Pius* which the Roman Senate gave to Antoninus shortly after his accession and which the Greeks render by εὐσεβής. And it is precisely in this order that the titles are usually found, viz. Augustus Pius, which the Syriac has treated as adjectives, and connected by a conjunction. Moreover this translation of εὐσεβής on the part of the Syriac interpreter shews that the meaning of the title is 'clement' or 'compassionate,' rather than that of mere filial duty, which agrees with what we find in a letter of Marcus Aurelius to Faustina; "haec (clementia) patrem tuum imprimis Pii nomine ornavit[1]."

Now how will this conclusion react upon the companion Apology of Quadratus? We could, no doubt, maintain that it leaves the question where it found it. The mistake made by Eusebius need not have been a double error, and the correct reference to Hadrian for Quadratus's Apology would have furnished a starting-point for the incorrect reasoning with regard to Aristides. On this supposition we should simply erase the reference to Aristides from Eusebius and his imitators.

But there is one difficulty to be faced, and that is the fact that we were in confusion over Quadratus before we reached any conclusion about Aristides. And our investigation has not helped to any elucidation of the confusion. Read for example the language in which Eusebius (*H. E.* IV. 3) describes the presentation of the Apology,

Αἴλιος Ἀδριανὸς διαδέχεται τὴν ἡγεμονίαν· τούτῳ Κοδράτος λόγον προσφωνήσας ἀναδίδωσιν, ἀπολογίαν συντάξας ὑπὲρ τῆς καθ' ἡμᾶς θεοσεβείας·

and compare it with the Greek of the *Chronicon* as preserved by Syncellus,

Κοδράτος ὁ ἱερὸς τῶν ἀποστόλων ἀκουστὴς Αἰλίῳ Ἀδριανῷ τῷ αὐτοκράτορι λόγους ἀπολογίας ὑπὲρ Χριστιανῶν ἔδωκεν·

and we naturally suspect with Harnack[2] that the title must have been something like the following,

λόγος ἀπολογίας ὑπὲρ τῆς τῶν Χριστιανῶν θεοσεβείας,

and we are confirmed in this belief by finding that the Aristides Apology was also headed

ἀπολογία ὑπὲρ τῆς θεοσεβείας·

at least its literary heading must have been very like this.

[1] Quoted by Eckhel, *Doctrina* vii. Pt. II. p. 36. This would seem to resolve the perplexity of Spartianus as to the origin of the name.

[2] *Die griechischen Apologeten* p. 101. I need not say how much I am indebted to Harnack's investigations. It will be apparent throughout these pages.

May we not also infer that the opening sentences of the Quadratus-Apology must have contained the dedication Αἰλίῳ Ἀδριανῷ which we find suggested above? But when we have made these suppositions the similarity between the two apologies in the titles is very great, for Aelius Hadrianus is also a part of the adopted name of the emperor Antoninus.

And let us look at the matter from another point of view. One of our early sources of information about Quadratus, *the bishop* of Athens, is found in a passage of a letter of Dionysius of Corinth preserved by Eusebius, and certainly Dionysius of Corinth ought to be good authority for Athenian religious history of the time immediately preceding his own. Eusebius does not actually quote the letter which Dionysius wrote to the church at Athens, but he tells us its scope and makes it easy to divine its contents: his language is as follows:

ἡ δὲ (ἐπιστολὴ) πρὸς Ἀθηναίους διεγερτικὴ πίστεως καὶ τῆς κατὰ τὸ εὐαγγέλιον πολιτείας· ἧς ὀλιγωρήσαντας ἐλέγχει, ὡς ἂν μικροῦ δεῖν ἀποστάντας τοῦ λόγου, ἐξ οὗπερ τὸν προεστῶτα αὐτῶν Πούπλιον μαρτυρῆσαι κατὰ τοὺς τότε συνέβη διωγμούς. Κοδράτου δὲ μετὰ τὸν μαρτυρήσαντα Πούπλιον καταστάντος αὐτῶν ἐπισκόπου μέμνηται· ἐπιμαρτυρῶν, ὡς ἂν διὰ τῆς αὐτοῦ σπουδῆς ἐπισυναχθέντων, καὶ τῆς πίστεως ἀναζωπύρησιν εἰληχότων.

From this it would naturally be inferred that the Quadratus mentioned in the letter was a contemporary of Dionysius of Corinth; for the latter writes to the Athenians at once convicting them of slackness in the faith, and congratulating them on their happy revival under the ministration of Quadratus. And since Dionysius writes letters also to Soter, the bishop of Rome, who belongs to the early years of Marcus Aurelius, we should probably say that Quadratus was not very much earlier than this, which would place him in the reign of Antoninus Pius. And the persecution at Athens which ended in the martyrdom of Publius must therefore fall in the same reign. Now Jerome (*de Virr. ill.* § 19) identifies this Quadratus, the bishop of Athens, with the Apologist[1], and consequently pushes back the persecution into the

[1] "Quadratus apostolorum discipulus, Publio Athenarum episcopo ob Christi fidem martyrio coronato, in locum eius substituitur et ecclesiam grandi terrore dispersam fide et industria sua congregat. Cumque Hadrianus Athenis exegisset

reign of Hadrian. We do not indeed attach any especial weight to Jerome's statement as to the time of the persecution, which is simply a combination made up out of passages from Eusebius concerning Quadratus and Dionysius with slight amplifications. He can hardly be right in placing the persecution under the reign of Hadrian, for, as Lightfoot points out[1], Eusebius, from whom he draws his facts, knows nothing about it: moreover we have information from Melito[2] that Antoninus Pius did actually write to Athens to suppress a persecution of the Christians. But, on the other hand, may he not be right after all in his identification of the bishop Quadratus with the Apologist, and do not the circumstances of the persecution suggested by Melito and testified to by Dionysius exactly suit the presentation of the Apology to the emperor?

While then we would readily admit that, as long as the Apology of Aristides was held to belong to the time of an Athenian visit of Hadrian, the Apology of Quadratus naturally remained with it, yet on the other hand when the Hadrian hypothesis is untenable for Aristides, will not the Quadratus-bishop and Quadratus-apologist naturally run together, and be one and the same person? Or is there anything to prevent the identification? The words 'apostolorum discipulus,' used by Jerome, and the corresponding words of Eusebius, *ἀποστόλων ἀκουστής*, can hardly be held to militate seriously against this hypothesis, for they are evident deductions from the passage which Eusebius quotes from the Apology of Quadratus about the sick people healed by the Lord, 'some of whom continued down to our times.' Jerome says boldly that Quadratus had seen very many of the subjects of our Lord's miracles; which is in any case a gross exaggeration. But if such persons, either many or few, had really lived into the age of Quadratus, it would be very difficult to place

hiemem, invisens Eleusinam, et omnibus paene Graeciae sacris initiatus dedisset occasionem his, qui Christianos oderant, absque praecepto imperatoris vexare credentes, porrexit ei librum &c."

[1] Lightfoot, *Ignatius*, ed. ii. II. 541.

[2] Euseb. *H. E.* IV. 26, ex apologia Melitonis, *ὁ δὲ πατήρ σου καὶ σοῦ τὰ σύμπαντα διοικοῦντος αὐτῷ, ταῖς πόλεσι περὶ τοῦ μηδὲν νεωτερίζειν περὶ ἡμῶν ἔγραψεν· ἐν οἷς καὶ πρὸς Λαρισσαίους καὶ πρὸς Θεσσαλονικεῖς καὶ Ἀθηναίους καὶ πρὸς πάντας Ἕλληνας.* This certainly looks like an outbreak of persecution in Greece.

the Apologist in the reign of Antoninus Pius. Unless, therefore, it can be maintained that the language quoted by Eusebius from Quadratus is an exaggeration or a misunderstanding we can hardly identify the bishop with the apologist. This is the furthest point to which the evidence carries the argument.

And now let us return to Aristides and see whether we can determine anything further concerning the time and manner of presentation of the Apology.

And first of all we may say that the simplicity of the style of the Apology is in favour of an early date. The religious ideas and practices are of an antique cast. The ethics shew a remarkable continuity with Jewish ethics: the care for the stranger and the friendless, the burial of the dead and the like, are given as characteristic virtues both of Judaism and of Christianity. Indeed we may say that one of the surprising things about the Apology is the friendly tone in which the Jews are spoken of: one certainly would not suspect that the chasm between the Church and the Synagogue had become as practically impassable as we find it in the middle of the second century. There is no sign of the hostile tone which we find towards the Jews in the martyrdom of Polycarp, and nothing like the severity of contempt which we find in the Epistle to Diognetus. If the Church is not in the writer's time any longer under the wing of the Synagogue, it has apparently no objection to taking the Synagogue occasionally under its own wing.

Such a consideration seems to be a mark of antiquity, and one would, therefore, prefer to believe, if it were possible, that the Apology was earlier than the Jewish revolt under Bar-Cochab. But since we have shewn that view to be untenable (and yet how attractive if we could place Aristides in the second visit of Hadrian to Athens, and Quadratus in the first!) we must content ourselves with seeking as early a date as is consistent with the superscriptions.

Another point that seems ancient about our Apology is that it contains traces, and very interesting traces, of the use of a creed, very similar to the Apostolic Symbol, but involving certain notable points of difference. We shall discuss the question more at length by and by; but at present it will be interesting to notice, especially in view of the obviously friendly attitude of the writer towards the Jews, that his creed contained a clause to the effect that

'He was crucified by the Jews,'

perhaps without the clause that was current in later times, 'under Pontius Pilate.' Now I am aware that there are some persons to whom this will seem an argument for a later date; for example M. Renan, *Origines* VI. p. 277, says: "les Chrétiens commençaient à faire retomber sur l'ensemble de la nation juive un reproche que sûrement ni Pierre ni Jacques ni l'auteur de l'Apocalypse ne songeaient à lui adresser, celui d'avoir crucifié Jésus." It would be interesting however to compare this statement of M. Renan with the language of Peter in Acts ii. 36, "Whom ye crucified;" of James in Ep. v. 6, "ye murdered the Just;" or with the writer of the Apocalypse where he describes Jerusalem as the spiritual Sodom and Egypt, "where also our Lord was crucified."

The very same charge is made by Justin in his dialogue with Trypho[1], who uses language very similar to that of the Epistle of James, and in discussing the miseries which have befallen the Jewish race, says pointedly "Fairly and justly have these things come upon you; for Ye slew the Just One." Why should we assume such a sentiment to be a mark of late date?

These references do not, however, suggest that the sentence in question was in the Creed. To prove that, we should have to go much farther afield, for the known forms of early creeds do not seem to contain it: if, however, we were to examine the Apocryphal Christian Literature of the early centuries, we should, no doubt, find many traces of the lost sentence. For example, it comes over and over in the Apocryphal Acts of John, a Gnostic document which Wright edited and translated from the Syriac. Here we find the sentence frequently in the very connexion which it would have with other Christian dogmatic statements if it had been incorporated with some actual form of the Symbol of Faith. When we find that these Acts give us as the staple of Apostolic teaching that

[1] *Dial.* 16.

"The Jews crucified Him on the tree,
And He died
And rose after three days,
And He is God,
And He ascended to Heaven
And is at the right hand of His Father"

we must admit that the sequence of ideas, and probably the very words, are from a Creed.

The same thing is true when we find the Apostle speaking, and saying

"In the name of Jesus the Messiah, God,
Whom the Jews crucified and killed in Jerusalem;
And He died and was buried
And rose after three days:
And lo! He is above in Heaven
At the right hand of His Father."

At all events we may maintain that there is evidence for the diffusion of the Creed in early times under a slightly different form to that generally received, and if so, we may call it a mark of antiquity to have the Apology of Aristides expressing itself to that effect; for certainly no such sentence in the generally received Creed existed in later times, however widely the sentiment against the Jews may have been diffused.

It is interesting also to compare the custom of the early Christians in the matter of fasting, that they might relieve by their self-denial the necessities of the poor. This is precisely what we find described so fully in the *Similitudes* of Hermas (*Sim.* v. 3), where the directions are given that on the day when we fast we are ourselves to eat only bread and water, and calculate the amount saved thereby and bestow it on the poor. Now very many of the later fathers teach the same doctrine, that fasting and alms are conjoined in duty and merit, and that it is proper, under certain circumstances, for the church to call for such an expression of religion. But what makes for the antiquity of the Apology is that the whole church fasts, not merely one day, but two or three days, and that not by direction or rule, but because they are poor and have no other way of meeting the needs of those who are poorer than themselves. It is a spontaneous, rather than a commanded charity, dictated at once by love and necessity. Can such a practice in such a form be other than early? But if the Apology is early in its doctrines and practices, where shall we place it? Must it not be at least as early as the first years of the reign of Antoninus Pius?

But here we are in difficulty again, for, if we assume that the Apology was presented to Antoninus Pius in person, we have no satisfactory evidence that Antoninus was ever in the East, or in Greece after his accession, and even the suspicions as to an Eastern visit belong to a later period of his reign, say A.D. 154. Did Aristides present the Apology at Rome or elsewhere? May we infer from his calling himself Marcianus Aristides, *Philosopher of Athens*, that he was in some city not his own natural dwelling-place? For that he came from Athens is deducible not only from his own statement but also from the fact to which we have already alluded that Antoninus wrote to Athens to suppress a persecution of the Christians. But this almost implies that Antoninus was not in Athens when he received the Apology, or where would be the need of writing a letter at all? He must have been out of Greece.

Only two solutions seem to present themselves, (i) that Aristides journeyed to Rome to present his apology; (ii) that Antoninus made some unrecorded visit to the East.

Now with regard to the second of these suppositions there is reason, outside of our argument and its necessities, to believe that some such visit must have taken place, and that Antoninus held court at Smyrna, some time after his accession to the throne.

In the celebrated letter of Irenaeus to Florinus (written probably later than A.D. 189) the writer speaks of having seen Florinus when he lived in lower Asia with Polycarp, when he was at the royal court, and rising in esteem there; he, Irenaeus, being at that time a boy. Now this seems to imply some kind of royal residence at Smyrna; but it has always been difficult to determine what is meant by such a royal residence. The problem is discussed by Lightfoot in his *Ignatius* (ed. ii. vol. I. p. 449). It cannot be Hadrian's visit in A.D. 129, which would be too early; and Lightfoot thinks that although there is some reason for believing

Antoninus Pius to have been in Syria, and presumably also in Asia Minor, somewhere about A.D. 154, 155, this date is too late, on account of the mention of Polycarp. Accordingly Lightfoot frames, with some hesitation, the following hypothesis: "About the year 136 T. Aurelius Fulvus was proconsul of Asia. Within two or three years of his proconsulate he was raised to the imperial throne, and is known as Antoninus Pius. Even during his proconsulate omens marked him as the future occupant of the imperial throne. ...Florinus may have belonged to his suite, and Irenaeus in after years might well call the proconsul's retinue the 'royal Court' by anticipation, especially if Florinus accompanied him to Rome, &c."

This ingenious hypothesis only fails to meet our requirement on one point, viz. that the name given to Antoninus in the Apology is the name given him after adoption, and so is subsequent to Feb. 25, A.D. 138.

But suppose we imagine a visit of Antoninus to Asia Minor some years later than this, we could find then some support for the theory that Aristides presented his Apology to the Emperor at Smyrna.

For we might say that the name of Marcianus is a conspicuous one in the Church at Smyrna. When the Church of the Smyrnaeans wrote for the Church of Philomelium the account of the martyrdom of Polycarp, they employed to compose the narrative a person whom they characterise as our brother Marcianus[1]. Now it is worthy of note that this person must have been conspicuous in the Church of Smyrna, for he is probably the same person to whom Irenaeus, whose relations with the Church at Smyrna are so intimate, dedicated one of his treatises[2]. Moreover the relations of the Church to the Emperor through Florinus would have been favourable for the presentation of the Apology.

Let us then say, in recapitulation, that we have found it difficult to assign the Apology to any other period than the early years of the reign of Antoninus Pius; and it is at least conceivable that it may have been presented to the Emperor, along with other Christian writings, during an unrecorded visit of his to his ancient seat of government in Smyrna.

[1] *Mart. Polyc.* 20.

[2] Euseb. *H. E.* v. 26.

There are a few later references to Aristides to which we have drawn no attention hitherto, because it seemed to be impossible to extract any trustworthy data from them: they are as follows:

(1) A passage in a letter of Jerome to Magnus, "Aristides philosophus, vir eloquentissimus, eidem principi (Hadriano) Apologeticum pro Christianis obtulit, contextum philosophorum sententiis, quem imitatus postea Justinus, et ipse philosophus." This is simply a réchauffé of the Eusebian data, with reflections thereupon. Justin being a philosopher, his Apology naturally imitates the philosophical treatise which has preceded his own.

(2) Martyrologium Vetus Romanum[1] ad v. Nonas Octobris. "Athenis Dionysii Areopagitae sub Hadriano diversis tormentis passi, ut Aristides testis est in opere quod de Christiana religione composuit; hoc opus apud Athenienses inter antiquorum memorias clarissimum tenetur." Aristides himself is commemorated on ii. Kal. Septr. and it is said that in his treatise he maintained "quod Christus Jesus solus esset Deus."

It would be very interesting to determine how the Martyrologies arrived at these statements. Our Syriac Apology certainly contains no trace of an allusion to Dionysius the Areopagite; on the other hand it fairly enough teaches the Divinity of Christ. We would dismiss the statements at once as archæological fictions if it had not been that evidence has been produced for the existence of a Latin version of Aristides. Harnack's attention was drawn by the pastor Kawerau to the following letter of Witzel to Beatus Rhenanus, dated Bartholomew's day 1534. "Dedisti nobis Eusebium, praeterea Tertullianum. Restat ut pari nitore des Justinum Martyrem, Papiam et Ignatium graece excusum. Amabo, per Bibliothecas oberrare, venaturus si quid scripsit Quadratus, si praeter epistolam alia Polycarpus, si nonnihil praeter Apologeticon Aristides. Despice, si quae supersunt Cornelii et tanta bonorum librorum panolethria. Plures sunt Dionysii scriptores, sed omnes praeter unum Areopagitem desyderamus, qui utinam sua quoque in lingua extaret. Utinam exorirentur Stromata Clementis, breviter quicquid est *κρόνϊον*. Tineae pascuntur libris, quibus

[1] Migne, *Patr. Lat.* CXXIII.

homines pasci debebamus &c." I have given the extract from Harnack's copy[1], not having access to the original letter.

It seems to me that Witzel's language almost implies that the Apology was already in print in Latin. Is it conceivable that some portion of the Apology may have found its way into print before the year 1534 and remained unnoticed in later times?

But even if it existed in manuscript, we must leave it an open question whether it may not have contained some matter which is wanting in the Syriac; nevertheless it is *à priori* extremely improbable that the story about the martyrdom of Dionysius the Areopagite can belong here.

Celsus and Aristides.

We have alluded above to a possible connexion between the True Word of Celsus and the Apology of Aristides, and it may be worth while to follow the matter up a little closer for the following reasons:

1. Celsus is undoubtedly very nearly contemporary with Aristides; although it is difficult to determine his date exactly (and even Origen was doubtful as to his identity), we may probably say with a good assurance of safety that he was at the zenith of his influence and fame under the reign of Antoninus Pius.

2. It is peculiarly difficult to determine what Christian books had come into the hands of Celsus, whether gospels or other literature. We know however for certain that he had read the dialogue between Jason and Papiscus, a work of Aristo of Pella, written not long after the close of the Jewish war under Hadrian, and so at a period very near to the one in which we are interested. Now if he were reading contemporary Christian literature he could hardly miss Aristides.

3. And since we find more and closer parallels between the fragments preserved by Origen from the great work of Celsus and our Apology than between most of the other books of the century, it is at least a fair question whether Aristides was not one of the persons to whom Celsus undertook to reply.

[1] *Die Griechischen Apologeten*, p. 107 note. I cannot find it in *Briefwechsel des Beatus Rhenanus* by Horawitz and Hartfelder, Leipzig, 1886. I understand, however, from Prof. Kawerau, that it may be found in *Epistolarum G. Wicelii libri tres*, Lipsiae, 1537.

One of the leading beliefs in Aristides is that God made all things *for the sake of man.* This doctrine he repeats in various forms, shewing that the separate elements, the earth, the air, the fire, and the water together with the sun, moon and stars, are his ministers. Now Celsus seems to have been particularly opposed to this doctrine and to have discussed it at length: it was one of the points of contact between the Stoic philosophy and the Jewish and Christian faiths, and Celsus was, no doubt, well prepared to be diffuse on the subject by many previous philosophical encounters.

He draws ridiculous pictures of the philosophy of the frogs in the swamp, of the ants in their ant-hill, and of bevies of bats, discussing the to them obvious proposition that the world has been made solely for their benefit. Accordingly Origen remarks, *παραπλησίους ἡμᾶς ποιεῖ σκώληξι φάσκουσιν ὅτι Θεός ἐστιν, εἶτα μετ' ἐκεῖνον ἡμεῖς ὑπ' αὐτοῦ γεγονότες πάντῃ, ὅμοιοι τῷ Θεῷ· καὶ ἡμῖν πάντα ὑποβέβληται, γῆ καὶ ὕδωρ καὶ ἀὴρ καὶ ἄστρα, καὶ ἡμῶν ἕνεκα πάντα καὶ ἡμῖν δουλεύειν τέτακται*[1]. In which sentence he has pretty well covered the argument from Providence as stated by Aristides. Were the elements and the stars, says he, made for the self-congratulation and self-exaltation of the bat, the frog, or—the man?

But he carries out the argument in detail: a providence over man is as reasonable as a providence over beasts and vegetables, which can be proved from the same data. *Διὰ πολλῶν δ' ἑξῆς ἐγκαλεῖ ἡμῖν ὡς τῷ ἀνθρώπῳ φάσκουσι πάντα πεποιηκέναι τὸν Θεόν, καὶ βούλεται ἐκ τῆς περὶ τῶν ζώων ἱστορίας καὶ τῆς ἐμφαινομένης αὐτοῖς ἀγχινοίας δεικνύναι, οὐδὲν μᾶλλον ἀνθρώπων ἢ τῶν ἀλόγων ζώων ἕνεκεν γεγονέναι τὰ πάντα*[2]. Indeed, according to Celsus, Providence is more apparent in the case of ants and bees and the like, which obtain their food without labour or with much less labour than happens in the case of man. He will not hear of such a statement as that the sun and stars serve man, much less what Aristides affirms, that the sun was *created* to serve the multiplicity of human need. Do not, says he, quote me verses from Euripides about sunshine and shade serving man; how do they serve him any more than the ants or the flies, which sleep

[1] Origen c. *Celsum*, lib. IV. 23. [2] lib. IV. 74.

and wake much as we do? εἰ δὲ καὶ τό, "Ἥλιος μὲν νύξ τε δουλεύει βροτοῖς," τί μᾶλλον ἡμῖν ἢ τοῖς μύρμηξι καὶ ταῖς μυίαις[1];

Now of course we do not mean to suggest that Aristides invented the argument from Providence or that Celsus was the first to heap easy scorn upon it. The argument and the reply are commonplaces. Celsus's question as to whether the world was created for the sake of vegetables will be found discussed in Cicero, *de Natura Deorum* II. 133. "Cuiusnam causa tantarum rerum molitio sit? Arborumne et herbarum? quae quamquam sine sensu sunt, tamen a natura sustinentur. At id quidem absurdum est. An bestiarum? Nihilo probabilius, deos mutorum et nihil intelligentium causa tantum laborasse....Ita fit credibile deorum et hominum causa factum esse mundum, quaeque in eo sint omnia."

It is easy to see how both the Jewish and Christian teachers, starting from the same text, the first verse in the book of Genesis, and formulating the same statement of faith, that the Almighty was 'Maker of Heaven and Earth,' found themselves fighting in the ranks with the Stoics against the Epicureans, and so exposed from time to time to the infinite raillery which seemed to the latter school to be proper to the situation. As we have said, Aristides does not stand alone in the statement. Justin Martyr takes the same ground and implies that it is a part of the regular Christian teaching. "We are taught," says he, "that God in His goodness created all things in the beginning from formless matter, for the sake of man[2];" and the unknown writer of the Epistle to Diognetus affirms that "God loved men, *for whom He made the world*, to whom He subjected all things that are in the earth[3]."

It is however worthy of notice that in Aristides the argument is repeated over and over, and that Celsus answers it, as Origen thought, at unnecessary length. It is not therefore inconceivable that Aristides may have drawn the Epicurean fire upon himself (and in this matter we may certainly count Celsus with the Epicureans) by the stress which he laid on the point in his Apology.

Let us pass on to another point upon which Aristides is

[1] lib. IV. 77.
[2] Justin *Apol.* I. c. 10.
[3] *Ep. ad Diogn.* 10.

somewhat original, viz. the doctrine of the races of the world and of their origin.

Aristides divides the world into four races, the Barbarian, the Greek, the Jew, the Christian. The last two races are curiously described; the Jews derive their origin from Abraham, Isaac and Jacob: they went down from Syria into Egypt; they came back from Egypt into Syria. As for the Christians, the new race, they derive their origin from Jesus the Messiah, and He is called the Son of God Most High.

Now in the first book against Celsus, Origen remarks as follows: "Celsus promises that he will speak on the subject of the Jews later on, and he begins his discourse concerning our Saviour, as being the leader of our generation in so far as we are Christians[1], and he goes on to say that he was the leader of this teaching, a few years ago, being regarded by the Christians as the Son of God."

Now it is worthy of note that if Celsus is handling any written document, that document proceeded from the discussion of the Jews to the Christians, affirmed Christ to be the head of the new race, and declared that His followers regarded Him as the Son of God. The agreement at this point with Aristides is certainly striking.

When moreover we come to the discussion of the Jews, Celsus breaks out that the 'Jews were mere Egyptian runaways, and that this darling people of God had never done anything worth remembering[2],' just as if he had passed over the names of the Patriarchs and fastened on the admission that the Jews had come out of Egypt. Accordingly Origen replies that it is universally agreed that the Jews reckon their genealogy from Abraham, Isaac and Jacob; *σαφὲς δὴ ὅτι καὶ γενεαλογοῦνται Ἰουδαῖοι ἀπὸ τῶν τριῶν πατέρων τοῦ Ἀβραὰμ καὶ τοῦ Ἰσαὰκ καὶ τοῦ Ἰακώβ.*

When Aristides deals with the beliefs of the Jews he expresses the remarkable opinion that the Jewish ritual is rather an adoration of angels than a worship of God. The expression is the more remarkable, because Aristides affects to reason throughout as the

[1] Orig. c. *Cels.* I. 26 *ὡς γενομένου ἡγεμόνος τῇ καθὸ Χριστιανοί ἐσμεν γενέσει ἡμῶν.*

[2] Orig. c. *Cels.* IV. 32.

philosopher rather than the Christian, and he forgets himself and introduces the angels without even an explanation to the emperor, as to what beings are intended. What shall we say then when we find Celsus affirming that the Jews worship angels[1]? λέγων αὐτοὺς σέβειν ἀγγέλους καὶ γοητείᾳ προσκεῖσθαι ἧς ὁ Μωϋσῆς αὐτοῖς γέγονεν ἐξηγητής. And Origen is so puzzled as to ask 'where in the world did Celsus find in the Mosaic writings instruction in the worship of angels?' It is certainly curious that we find the missing link supplied by the Apology of Aristides.

No doubt further analogies might be traced; for example, Celsus is especially irate with the Christians for their ridicule of Egyptian superstitions[2], they see nothing except ephemeral animals, instead of grasping eternal ideas. Now there is no doubt that it is a very common subject of Christian merriment, but perhaps no one of the early Christian writers has laughed so much in detail about it as Aristides. We will not however press the matter further: there are always numerous points of contact and necessary collisions between the attack and the defence of given religions: suffice it to say that we have shewn it to be by no means an inconceivable proposition that Celsus had read the Apology of Aristides before he penned his Ἀληθὴς λόγος.

The Symbol of the Faith in the time of Aristides.

Aristides the Philosopher is a Christian who has preserved the philosophic manner, and probably the philosophic dress, with a view to future service in the gospel. It seems to have been the practice of not a few of the famous second-century Christians to attract an audience in this way. Justin certainly did so, and almost as surely Tatian; and if these why not Aristides? But as we have already said, the professedly dispassionate presentation of the Christian case, the endeavour to talk reasonably on all sides successively, soon breaks down; the man throws off his disguise and gives the note of challenge: Christianus sum; nihil Christianum alienum a me puto. He talks of angels as though all men knew them, dashes through the dogmatic statements of the Church as though they were perfectly familiar, and without a

[1] Orig. *c. Cels.* I. 26.

[2] Orig. *c. Cels.* III. 19.

word of preliminary explanation of terms, makes a peroration of the impending judgment-day. And so the philosopher with an imperial audience turns out to be another illustration of the Christian city that is set on a hill and cannot be hid.

It is especially interesting to observe that in the time of Aristides the Church already had a Symbol of the Faith: and we may reconstruct a good many of its sentences. Of course in such matters we proceed from the things that are practically certain to those which are less demonstrable; we should not start by saying that the words "Maker of heaven and earth" were proof of the existence of an approximately fixed symbol. But if we can establish other sentences with good confidence, there is no reason to omit these words from the reconstructed formula.

The certain passage from which we proceed is in the words:

"He was pierced (crucified) by the Jews;
"He died and was buried;"

"and they say that

after three days He rose,
and ascended into Heaven."

It may be taken for granted that these words represent a part of the Symbolum Fidei as known to Aristides.

What else may we say was contained in his creed? We may add words which must have stood respectively at the beginning and ending of the Creed: viz. that God was the Maker of Heaven and Earth; and that Jesus Christ was to come to judge the world.

Whether we can go further is a more difficult question: but there is at least a strong suspicion that the creed contained the clause "He was born of the Virgin Mary;" for in Aristides' statement the language about the 'Hebrew virgin' precedes the account of the Crucifixion; moreover, here also, we find Aristides is most pronounced in the enunciation of the doctrine, and Celsus is emphatically scornful in the rejection of it. Accordingly Celsus brings forward the story of the infidelity of Mary, affirming that the father of Jesus was in reality a soldier whose name was Panthera[1]. The same story appears in the Talmud under the name Pandera, which is a transliteration of the foregoing.

[1] Orig. *c. Cels.* I. 32.

Indeed it has been generally held that the legend was invented by the Jews, through the difficulty of accounting for our Lord's birth; apparently, therefore, the Jews were in search of a more tenable hypothesis than the paternity of Joseph; and it is not unreasonable to refer to an early Jewish scandal the story which we find in the Talmud and in Celsus.

But if the story be Jewish in origin, it was certainly Greek in manufacture. Some persons have tried to explain the Greek name Panthera by regarding it as a symbol of violent and unrestrained lust. They are, however, mistaken: the name is simply a Greek anagram on the word 'Parthenos,' by which the Blessed Virgin was commonly known. Those who are familiar with the literary tricks of that time, its anagrams, acrostics, isopsephics, and the like, will have not the least difficulty in seeing that this is the true solution. The inventor has only changed the order of the letters and slightly altered the ending of the word. Everything that we know of the dogmatics of the early part of the second century agrees with the belief that at that period the Virginity of Mary was a part of the formulated Christian belief. Nor need we hesitate, in view of the antiquity of the Panthera-fable, to give the doctrine a place in the creed of Aristides.

We restore the fragments of Aristides' creed, then, as follows:

We believe in one God, Almighty
Maker of Heaven and Earth:
And in Jesus Christ His Son
* * * * *
Born of the Virgin Mary:
* * * * *
He was pierced by the Jews:
He died and was buried:
The third day He rose again:
He ascended into Heaven:
* * * * *
He is about to come to judge.
* * * * *

The Armenian Fragment of the Apology.

We give, later on, the Latin translation of the Armenian fragment, as published by the Venetian editors. The passage has also been translated into German by von Himpel[1], and this translation will be found in Harnack's *Griechische Apologeten*, pp. 110—112. Von Himpel rightly affirms the Armenian text to have been made from the Greek: it will be observed, however, that the Armenian text has the same lacuna as the Syriac in the discourse on the four elements and the powers to which they are respectively subject. This lacuna would seem to be an early feature of the Greek text.

There are one or two points in which we may get some authority from the Armenian for the original text. For instance in c. ii. where the Syriac reads that the origin of the Greeks is to be traced through "Danaus the Egyptian, and through Kadmus, and through Dionysus." Here the Armenian reads "Danaus the Egyptian and Kadmus the Sidonian and Dionysus the Theban," and I am disposed to believe the words added in the Armenian belong there: for instance, we may compare Tatian's language[2], "Dionysus is absolute sovereign over the Thebans." In a similar manner something seems to have dropped in the Syriac after the statement that in God there is no distinction of male or female; for the Armenian text adds the reason "quia cupiditatibus agitatur qui huic est distinctioni obnoxius." Again in the opening sentences of the Apology the Armenian text has the words, "Eum autem qui rector atque creator est omnium, investigare perdifficile est[3]." We recognize at once in these words the ring of the characteristic Christian quotation from the *Timaeus*, which is usually employed to shew the superior illuminating power of Christian grace over philosophic research, but seems here to be taken in the Platonic sense. The Armenian is perhaps a little nearer to the Platonic language than the Syriac; both versions however will claim the passage from the *Timaeus* as a parallel.

[1] *Tüb. Theol. Quartalschrift*, 1877, II. p. 289, f. 1880, I. p. 109—127.

[2] *Cohortatio*, c. VIII.

[3] Plato, *Timaeus*, 28 C, *τὸν μὲν οὖν ποιητὴν καὶ πατέρα τοῦδε τοῦ παντὸς εὑρεῖν τε ἔργον καὶ εὑρόντα εἰς πάντας ἀδύνατον λέγειν.*

Allowing then for the occasional preservation of a passage in greater purity by the Armenian fragment, we shall find that the Armenian translator has often made changes, and added glosses, and epitomized sentences. For example, in the summary of the Christian Faith, he describes the Son as the Logos, His mother as the Theotokos. When the disciples are sent forth, in order that a certain *οἰκονομία* may be fulfilled, the Armenian translator calls it a dispensation of illuminating truth; the preaching too is with 'signs following,' 'comitantibus prodigiis,' which seems to come from Mark xvi. 20 and would be, if genuine, one of the earliest illustrations of that text. It will be seen how large an element of paraphrase is found in the Armenian text.

The Armenian Fragment

(from the Venice edition).

IMPERATORI CÆSARI HADRIANO,

ARISTIDES,

PHILOSOPHUS ATHENIENSIS.

Ego, O Rex, Dei providentia creatus, hunc mundum ingressus sum, et caelis, terra ac mari, sole, luna et stellis, caeterisque omnibus creaturis conspectis, huius mundi constitutionem admirans miratus sum, atque conscius factus sum mihi, quoniam omnia quae sunt in mundo necessitate ac vi diriguntur, omnium creatorem et rectorem esse Deum: quia iis omnibus quae reguntur atque moventur, fortior est creator et rector.

Eum autem, qui rector atque creator est omnium, investigare perdifficile atque in immensum pertinens mihi videtur: penitus vero eum et certa ratione describere, quum inexplicabilis et ineffabilis sit, impossibile et sine ulla prorsus utilitate. Deus enim naturam habet infinitam, imperscrutabilem et creaturis omnibus incomprehensibilem. Hoc unum scire necesse est, qui creaturas universas Providentia sua gubernat, ipsum esse Dominum Deum et creatorem omnium: quia visibilia omnia creavit bonitate sua, eaque humano generi donavit. Quapropter Illum solum, utpote unum Deum, nos adorare et glorificare oportet: unumquemque autem nostrum proximum suum sicut semetipsum diligere.

Verumtamen de Deo saltem sciendum est, Eum ab alio factum non fuisse, neque semetipsum fecisse, atque, a nullo circumscriptum, omnia comprehendere. Ex se ipsomet est[1]. Ipse sapientia immortalis, principio et fine carens, immortalis atque aeternus, perfectus, nulli necessitati obnoxius, et necessitatibus omnium satisfaciens, nullo indigens et indigentiis omnium ipse magnificus opitulator.

Ipse est principio carens, quia, qui habet principium, habet et finem. Ipse sine nomine, quod quicumque nomine appellatur, creatus est factusque ab alio. Ei neque colores sunt neque forma: quod, quicumque his praeditus est, mensurabilis est, limitibusque cogitur. Eius naturae nulla inest maris et feminae distinctio, quia cupiditatibus agitatur qui huic est distinctioni obnoxius. Ipse sub caelis incomprehensibilis est, quia caelos excedit: nec caeli caelorum Illo maiores sunt, quia caeli caelorum et creaturae omnes quae sub caelis sunt, ab Illo comprehenduntur.

Ipsi nemo contrarius neque adversarius: quod si quis Ei contrarius et adversarius esse posset, eidem compar fieri videretur.

Ipse immobilis est atque praeter quemcumque terminum et circuitum: quia ubi et unde moveri possit locus deest. Ipse neque mensura comprehendi, neque circumdari potest, quia Ipse omnia replet, atque est ultra omnes visibiles et invisibiles creaturas. Ipse neque ira, neque indignatione movetur, quia nulla caecitate afficitur, quum omnino et absolute sit intellectualis. Propterea hisce omnibus miraculis variis omnibusque beneficiis Ipse omnia creavit. Sacrificiis, oblationibus et hostiis Ipse non indiget, neque, ulla in re, visibilibus creaturis opus habet; quia omnia replet, et omnium egestatibus satisfacit, Ipse numquam indigens ac semper gloriosus.

De Deo sapienter loqui ab ipso Deo mihi datum est, et pro meis viribus locutus sum, quin tamen altitudinem imperscrutabilis magnitudinis Ejus comprehendere possem. Sola fide vero Illum glorificans adoro.

Nunc igitur ad genus humanum veniamus et quinam praefatas veritates secuti fuerint videbimus, et quinam ab eis erraverint. Compertum est nobis, o Rex, quatuor esse humani generis stirpes, quae sunt Barbarorum, Graecorum, Hebraeorum atque Christianorum. Ethnici et Barbari genus suum ducunt a Belo, Crono et

[1] Sensus dubius: armeniaca verba idem sonant ac graeca *αὐτογενὲς εἶδος*.

Hiera, aliisque suis Divis pluribus. Graeci vero a Jove, qui Zeus vel Jupiter dicitur, originem trahunt, per Helenum, Xuthum, aliosque eorum descendentes, nempe Helladem, Inacum, Phoroneum, ac demum Danaum Aegyptium, Cadmum Sidonium, ac Dionysium Thebanum. Hebraei autem genus suum ducunt ex Abrahamo, Isaaco, Jacobo, et duodecim Jacobi filiis, qui e Syria in Aegyptum se receperunt, et a legislatore suo Hebraei nuncupati fuerunt, inde vero terram promissionis ingressi, Judaei sunt appellati. Christianorum tandem genus a Domino Jesu Christo oritur.

Ipse Dei altissimi est Filius, et una cum Spiritu Sancto revelatus est nobis: de caelis descendit ex Hebraea Virgine natus, ex Virgine carnem assumpsit, assumptaque humana natura, semetipsum Dei filium revelavit. Qui Evangelio suo vivificante mundum universum, consolatoria sua bonitate, sibi captivum fecit.

Ipse est Verbum, qui ex progenie Hebraica, secundum carnem, ex Maria virgine Deipara natus est. Ipse est qui Apostolos duodecim inter suos discipulos elegit, ut mundum universum dispensatione illuminantis Veritatis suae institueret. Ipse ab Hebraeis crucifixus est: a mortuis resurrexit et ad caelos ascendit: in mundum universum discipulos suos mittens, qui divino et admirabili lumine suo, comitantibus prodigiis, omnes gentes sapientiam docerent. Quorum praedicatio in hunc usque diem germinat atque fructificat, orbem universum vocans ad lucem.

Quatuor ergo nationes, O Rex, ostendi tibi: Barbaros, Graecos, Hebraeos atque Christianos.

* * * * * * * * * *

Divinitati spiritualis natura propria est, Angelis ignea, daemoniis aquosa, generique humano terrestris.

* * * * * * * * * *

We have now reprinted all that is known of the Armenian translation of the Apology; it is out of our limit and beyond our measure to think of reprinting the actual Armenian text. For the purpose of comparison we add, however, another copy of the same Armenian fragment, taken from a MS. at Edschmiazin, and translated into English by Mr F. C. Conybeare, of Oxford, for whose kindly aid we are very grateful. According to the information which he has supplied, the MS. at Edschmiazin was written on paper, and is much worn by age. The date was certainly not later than the eleventh century. The fragment from the Apology which it contains was followed by the fragment from the Homily on the Penitent Thief. Here and there the text was illegible, and in these cases the missing words have been supplied from the Venice text, as reprinted by Pitra. The two texts in question are moreover in very close agreement, except for the occasional addition of a word or two by the Edschmiazin MS. The rendering is designedly a literal one.

The Armenian Fragment

(*from the Edschmiazin MS.*).

TO THE AUTOCRATIC CAESAR ADRIANOS FROM ARISTIDES, ATHENIAN PHILOSOPHER.

I, O Ruler, who was by the providence of God created and fashioned man in the world, and who have beheld the heaven and the earth and the sea, the sun and the moon and the stars and all creatures, wondered and was amazed at the eternal[1] order thereof. I also by reflection learned that the world and all that is therein is by necessity and force guided and moved and of the whole God is controuler and orderer: for that which controuls is more powerful than that which is controuled and moved. To enquire about Him who is guardian and controuls all things seems to me to quite exceed the comprehension and to be most difficult, and to speak accurately concerning Him is beyond compass of thought and of speech, and bringeth no advantage; for His nature is infinite and unsearchable, and imperceptible,[2] and inaccessible to all creatures. We can only know that He who governs by His providence all created things, He is Lord and God and creator of all, who ordered all things visible in His beneficence, and graciously bestowed them on the race of man. Now it is meet that we serve and glorify Him alone as God, and love one another as ourselves. But this much alone can we know concerning God,

[1] Here there is a copyist's error in the Edschmiazin text.

[2] Here the Edschmiazin text adds a word which means 'not to be observed or looked at.'

that He was not generated from any source, and did not Himself make Himself, and is not contained by aught, but Himself contains all. Αὐτογενὲς εἶδος[1] and wisdom immortal, without beginning or end, not passing away and undying, He is complete and wanteth nothing, while He fulfilleth all wants. In Himself He wanteth nought, but gives to and fulfils the needs of all. In Himself He is without beginning, for He is beginning of everything whatever, and is perfect. In Himself He is nameless, for whatever is named is fashioned out of something else[2] and created. Colour and form of Him there is not, for that falls under measure and limit, unto whatsoever colour and form belong. Male and female in that nature there is not, for that is subject to particular passions, in whatsoever that distinction exists. Within the heavens He is not contained, for He is beyond[3] the heavens; neither are the heavens greater than He, for the heavens and all creation are contained in Him. Counter to Him and opposed there is no one: if any one be found counter to Him, it appears that that one becometh associate with Him. He is unmoved and unmeasured and ineffable; for there is no place whence or with which He could move; and He is not, by being measured, contained or environed on any side, for it is Himself that filleth all, and He transcends all things visible and invisible. Wrath and anger there is not in Him, for there is not in Him blindness, but He is wholly and entirely rational, and on that account He established creation with divers wonders and entire beneficence. Need hath He none of victims and oblations and sacrifices, and of all that is in the visible creation He wanteth nought. For He fulfilleth the wants of all and completeth them, and being in need of nothing He is glorified unto all time.

Now by the grace of God it was given me to speak wisely concerning Him. So far as I have received the faculty I will speak, yet not according to the measure of the inscrutability of His greatness shall I be able to do so, but by faith alone do I glorify and adore Him.

Let us next come to the race of man, and see who are capable

[1] αὐτογενὲς (or αὐτογέννητον) εἶδος is the Greek that answers to the Armenian texts. 'Ex se ipsomet est' does not give the sense. I give the Greek, for I really hardly know how to render it in English.

[2] Or "by another."

[3] ἐπέκεινα.

of receiving the truth of these sayings, and who are gone astray. It is manifest[1], O Ruler, for there are four tribes[2] of the human race. There are barbarians, and some are Greeks and others Hebrews, and there are who are Christians. But the heathens and barbarians count their descent from Baal, and from Cronos, and from Hera, and from many others of their gods. But the Greeks say Zeus (who is Dios) is their founder[3], and reckon their descent from Helenos and Xuthos, and one after another from Hellas, Inachos and Phoroneus, and also finally from Danaus the Egyptian, and from Cadmus the Sidonian, and Dionysius the Theban.

But the Jews reckon their race from Abraham, and Abraham's son they say was Isaac, and from Isaac Jacob, and from Jacob the twelve who migrated from Assyria into Egypt and were there named the tribes of the Hebrews by their lawgiver, and having come into the land of recompence, were named......[4] the tribes of the Jews.

But the Christians reckon their race from the Lord Jesus Christ. He is Himself Son of God on high, who was manifested of the Holy Spirit, came down from heaven, and being born of a Hebrew virgin took on His flesh from the virgin, and was manifested in the nature of humanity the Son of God: who sought to win the entire world to His eternal goodness by His life-giving preaching[5]. He it is who was according to the flesh born of the race of the Hebrews, by the God-bearing[6] virgin Miriam. He chose the twelve disciples, and He by his illuminating truth, dispensing

[1] So it stands in the Venice text: but in the Edschmiazin copy, for 'manifest' there is a word which means 'the name' followed by a lacuna of a few letters, as if the scribe had intended to read 'I will recount the names, O Ruler,' or something of that kind.

[2] The word answers to the Greek φυλαί or δῆμοι. In the same sense at the end of the fragment another word is used, answering rather to γένη.

[3] These three words are added to make sense, the whole passage being grammatically much confused.

[4] Here the Edschmiazin MS. was unreadable from age. The printed text has no lacuna and gives no hint of the word whatever it was which was read in the Edschmiazin text.

[5] εὐαγγέλιον.

[6] The word Θεοτόκος is implied.

it[1] taught, all the world, and was nailed on the cross by the Jews. Who rose from the dead and ascended into heaven, and sent forth His disciples into the whole world[2], and taught all with divinely miraculous and profoundly wise wonders. Their preaching until this day blossoms and bears fruit, and summons all the world to receive the light.

These are the four tribes, whom we set before thee, O Ruler, Barbarians, Greeks, Jews and Christians. But to the Deity is appointed the spiritual, and to angels the fiery, and to devils the watery, and to the race of men the earth.

* * * * * * * * *

An additional Armenian Fragment of Aristides.

Over and above the fragments of the lost Apology of Aristides, and the homily *de Latrone*, there is a scrap printed by Pitra in his *Spicilegium Solesmense* which professes to come from an epistle of Aristides to all Philosophers. It is, as far as we can judge, in the form in which we have it presented to us, a theological product of the time of the Monophysite controversy. But we must bear in mind what we have learned from the Armenian fragment of the Apology, that an Armenian translation is made up out of the matter of the original writer *plus* the terms and definitions of the translator, as for instance we see to have happened in the ascription of the term Θεοτόκος to the Blessed Virgin. And the question is whether under the amplified folds of the theology of this fragment printed by Pitra there may be hidden the more scanty terms of a theologian of the second century, and if so, whether the writer be our Aristides, and the work quoted be the Apology or some other work. In order to test this point, we will give a rendering of the fragment into Greek, for which again I am indebted to the kindness of Mr Conybeare.

[1] Οἰκονομικὸς is here rendered. Perhaps it should be taken as an epithet of 'truth,' for in the original it precedes the word 'illuminating.'

[2] Οἰκουμένην.

Armenian Fragment.

(*Frag.* iii. *of Pitra.*)

FROM AN EPISTLE OF ARISTIDES TO ALL PHILOSOPHERS.

Πάντ' ἔπαθε παθήματα ἀληθινῷ σὺν αὐτοῦ σώματι, ὃ θελήματι Κυρίου καὶ τοῦ ἁγίου Πνεύματος δεξάμενος, ἥνωσε τὴν σάρκα[1] *ἑαυτῷ*[2] *τὴν παρὰ*[3] *παρθένου Ἑβραϊκῆς τῆς ἁγίας Μαριὰμ ἀρρητῷ καὶ ἀτόμῳ ἑνότητι.*

Now with reference to the foregoing passage, we may say at once that the concluding terms are not second-century language at all. On the other hand, the reference to the "Hebrew virgin" is precisely the language of the Apology. Further, the opening words of the fragment, with their allusion to a real passion of a real body, are certainly anti-Docetic, and therefore may be taken as second-century theology. We may compare with them the sentiments of the Ignatian epistles, as for example the letter to the Smyrnaeans (c. ii.), where we read:—

ταῦτα γὰρ πάντα ἔπαθεν δι' ἡμᾶς· καὶ ἀληθῶς ἔπαθεν, ὡς καὶ ἀληθῶς ἀνέστησεν ἑαυτόν· οὐχ ὥσπερ ἄπιστοί τινες λέγουσιν τὸ δοκεῖν αὐτὸν πεπονθέναι.

It does not, therefore, seem as if these words in the opening of the fragment were a translator's invention or addition. They have a second-century ring about them. If so, then the extract is either a translation of a paragraph of the Apology, or of some other tract by the same writer, and probably the latter. We have, however, no means of discriminating further the original form of the sentence from the later accretions. It is, however, by no means impossible that the heading may be correct; that Aristides may have written an epistle or address to Philosophers on the subject of the Christian religion in general, or of the Incarnation in particular.

1 The same word is used by the translator to render *σῶμα* and *σάρξ*.

2 More exactly *ἑαυτοῦ*: an additional word being necessary in the Armenian in order to give the sense 'conjunxit sibi': but the sense seems to require *ἑαυτῷ*.

3 Or *ἐκ*.

THE APOLOGY OF ARISTIDES, TRANSLATED FROM THE SYRIAC.

Again, the apology which Aristides the philosopher made ܐ
before Hadrian the king concerning the worship of God.

[To the Emperor] Caesar Titus Hadrianus Antoninus Augustus Pius, from Marcianus Aristides, a philosopher of Athens.

I. I, O king, by the grace of God came into this world; and having contemplated the heavens and the earth and the seas, and beheld the sun and the rest of the orderly creation, I was amazed at the arrangement of the world; and I comprehended that the world and all that is therein are moved by the impulse of another, and I understood that he that moveth them is God, who is hidden in them and concealed from them: and this is well known, that that which moveth is more powerful than that which is moved. And that I should investigate concerning this Mover of all, as to how He exists—for this is evident to me, for He is incomprehensible in His nature—and that I should dispute concerning the stedfastness of His government, so as to comprehend it fully, is not profitable for me; for no one is able perfectly to comprehend it. But I say concerning the Mover of the world,
that He is God of all, who made all for the sake of man; and it ܒ
is evident to me that this is expedient, that one should fear God, and not grieve man.

Now I say that God is not begotten, not made; a constant nature, without beginning and without end; immortal, complete, and incomprehensible: and in saying that He is complete, I mean this; that there is no deficiency in Him, and He stands in need of nought, but everything stands in need of Him: and in saying that He is without beginning, I mean this; that everything which has a beginning has also an end; and that which has an end is dissoluble. He has no name; for everything that has a name is associated with the created; He has no likeness, nor composition of members; for he who possesses this is associated with things fashioned. He is not male, nor is He female: the heavens do not contain Him; but the heavens and all things visible and invisible are contained in Him. Adversary He has none; for there is none that is more powerful than He; anger and wrath He possesses not, for there is nothing that can stand against Him. Error and forgetfulness are not in His nature, for He is altogether wisdom and understanding, and in Him consists all that consists. He asks no sacrifice and no libation, nor any of the things that are visible; He asks not anything from anyone; but all ask from Him.

II. Since then it has been spoken to you by us concerning God, as far as our mind was capable of discoursing concerning Him, let us now come to the race of men, in order that we may know which of them hold any part of that truth which we have spoken concerning Him, and which of them are in error therefrom.

This is plain to you, O king, that there are four races of men in this world; Barbarians and Greeks, Jews and Christians.

Now the Barbarians reckon the head of the race of their religion from Kronos and from Rhea and the rest of their gods: but the Greeks from Helenus, who is said to be from Zeus; and from Helenus was born Aeolus and Xythus, and the rest of the family from Inachus and Phoroneus, and last of all from Danaus the Egyptian and from Kadmus and from Dionysus.

Moreover the Jews reckon the head of their race from Abraham, who begat Isaac, from whom was born Jacob, who begat twelve sons who removed from Syria and settled in Egypt, and there were called the race of the Hebrews by their law-giver: but at last they were named Jews.

The Christians, then, reckon the beginning of their religion from Jesus Christ, who is named the Son of God most High; and it is said that God came down from heaven, and from a Hebrew virgin took and clad Himself with flesh, and in a daughter of man there dwelt the Son of God. This is taught from that Gospel which a little while ago was spoken among them as being preached; wherein if ye also will read, ye will comprehend the power that is upon it. This Jesus, then, was born of the tribe of the Hebrews; and He had twelve disciples, in order that a certain dispensation of His might be fulfilled. He was pierced by the Jews; and He died and was buried; and they say that after three days He rose and ascended to heaven; and then these twelve disciples went forth into the known parts of the world, and taught concerning His greatness with all humility and sobriety; and on this account those also who to-day believe in this preaching are called Christians, who are well known. There are then four races of mankind, as I said before, Barbarians and Greeks, Jews and Christians.

To God then ministers wind, and to angels fire; but to demons water, and to men earth.

III. Let us then begin with the Barbarians, and by degrees we will proceed to the rest of the peoples, in order that we may understand which of them hold the truth concerning God, and which of them error.

The Barbarians then, inasmuch as they did not comprehend God, erred with the elements; and they began to serve created things instead of the Creator of them[1], and on this account they made likenesses and they enclosed them in temples; and lo! they worship them and guard them with great precaution, that their gods may not be stolen by robbers; and the Barbarians have not understood that whatsoever watches must be greater than that which is watched; and that whatsoever creates must be greater than that whatever is created: if so be then that their gods are too weak for their own salvation, how will they furnish salvation to mankind? The Barbarians then have erred with a great error in worshipping dead images which profit them not. And it comes to me to wonder also, O king, at their philosophers, how they too have erred and have named gods those likenesses which have been made in honour of the elements; and the wise men have not understood that these very elements are corruptible and dissoluble; for if a little part of the element be dissolved or corrupted, all of it is dissolved and corrupted. If then these elements are dissolved and corrupted, and compelled to be subject to another harder than themselves, and are not in their nature gods, how can they call gods those likenesses which are made in their honour? Great then is the error which their philosophers have brought upon their followers.

[1] Rom. i. 25.

IV. Let us turn then, O king, to the elements themselves, in order that we may shew concerning them that they are not gods, but a creation, corruptible and changeable, which is in the likeness of man[1]. But God is incorruptible and unchangeable and invisible, while seeing, turning and changing all things.

Those therefore who think concerning earth that it is God have already erred, since it is digged and planted and delved; and since it receives the defilement of the excrement of men and of beasts and of cattle: and since sometimes it becomes what is useless; for if it be burned it becomes dead, for from baked clay there springs nothing: and again, if water be collected on it, it becomes corrupted along with its fruits: and lo! it is trodden on by men and beasts, and it receives the impurity of the blood of the slain; and it is digged and filled with the dead and becomes a repository for bodies: none of which things can that holy and venerable and blessed and incorruptible nature receive. And from this we have perceived that the earth is not God but a creature of God.

V. And in like manner again have those erred who have thought concerning water that it is God. For water was created for the use of man and in many ways it is made subject to him. For it is changed, and receives defilement, and is corrupted, and loses its own nature when cooked with many things, and receives colours which are not its own; being moreover hardened by the cold and mixed and mingled with the excrement of men and beasts and with the blood of the slain: and it is compelled by workmen, by means of the compulsion of channels, to flow and be conducted against its own will, and to come into gardens and other places, so as to cleanse and carry out all the filth of men, and wash away all defilement, and supply man's need of itself. Wherefore it is impossible that water should be God, but it is a work of God and a part of the world.

So too those have erred not a little who thought concerning fire that it is God: for it too was created for the need of men: and in many ways it is made subject to them, in the service of food and in the preparation of ornaments and the other things of

[1] Rom. i. 23.

which your majesty is aware: whilst in many ways it is extinguished and destroyed.

And again those who have thought concerning the blast of winds that it is God, these also have erred: and this is evident to us, that these winds are subject to another, since sometimes their blast is increased and sometimes it is diminished and ceases, according to the commandment of Him who subjects them. Since for the sake of man they were created by God, in order that they might fulfil the needs of trees and fruits and seeds, and that they might transport ships upon the sea; those ships which bring to men their necessary things, from a place where they are found to a place where they are not found; and furnish the different parts of the world. Since then this wind is sometimes increased and sometimes diminished, there is one place in which it does good and another where it does harm, according to the nod of Him who rules it: and even men are able by means of well-known instruments to catch and coerce it that it may fulfil for them the necessities which they demand of it: and over itself it has no power at all; wherefore it is not possible that winds should be called gods, but a work of God.

VI. So too those have erred who have thought concerning the sun that he is God. For lo! we see him, that by the necessity of another he is moved and turned and runs his course; and he proceeds from degree to degree, rising and setting every day, in order that he may warm the shoots of plants and shrubs, and may bring forth in the air which is mingled with him every herb which is on the earth. And in calculation the sun has a part with the rest of the stars in his course, and although he is one in his nature, he is mixed with many parts, according to the advantage of the needs of men: and that not according to his own will, but according to the will of Him that ruleth him. Wherefore it is not possible that the sun should be God, but a work of God; and in like manner also the moon and stars.

VII. But those who have thought concerning men of old, that some of them are gods, these have greatly erred: as thou, even thou, O king, art aware, that man consists of the four elements and of soul and spirit, and therefore is he even called World, and apart from any one of these parts he does not exist. He has beginning and end, and he is born and also suffers corruption. But God, as I have said, has none of this in His nature, but He is unmade and incorruptible. On this account, then, it is impossible that we should represent him as God who is man by nature, one to whom sometimes, when he looketh for joy, grief happens; and for laughter, and weeping befals him; one that is passionate and jealous, envious and regretful, along with the rest of the other defects: and in many ways more corrupted than the elements or even than the beasts.

And thence, O king, it is right for us to understand the error of the Barbarians, that, whereas they have not investigated concerning the true God, they have fallen away from the truth and have gone after the desire of their own mind, in serving elements subject to dissolution, and dead images: and on account of their error they do not perceive who is the true God.

VIII. Let us return now to the Greeks in order that we may know what opinion they have concerning the true God.

The Greeks then because they are wiser than the Barbarians have erred even more than the Barbarians, in that they have introduced many gods that are made; and some of them they have represented as male and some of them as female; and in such a way that some of their gods were found to be adulterers and murderers, and jealous and envious, and angry and passionate, and murderers of fathers, and thieves and plunderers. And they say that some of them were lame and maimed; and some of them wizards, and some of them utterly mad; and some of them played on harps; and some of them wandered on mountains: and some of them died outright; and some were struck by lightning, and some were made subject to men, and some went off in flight, and some were stolen by men; and lo! some of them were wept and bewailed by men; and some, they say, went down to Hades; and some were sorely wounded, and some were changed into the likeness of beasts in order that they might commit adultery with the race of mortal women; and some of them have been reviled for sleeping with males: and some of them, they say, were in wedlock with their mothers and sisters and daughters; and they say of their gods that they committed adultery with the daughters of men, and from them was born a certain race which was also mortal. And of some of their goddesses they say that they contended about beauty and came for judgment before men. The Greeks, then, O king, have brought forward what is wicked, ridiculous and foolish concerning their gods and themselves; in that they called such like persons gods, who are no gods: and hence men have taken occasion to commit adultery and fornication, and to plunder and do everything that is wicked and hateful and abominable. For if those who are called their gods have done all those things that are written above, how much more shall men do them who believe in those who have done these things! and from the wickedness of this error, lo! there have happened to men frequent wars and mighty famines, and bitter captivity and deprivation of all things: and lo! they endure them, and all these things befal them from this cause alone: and when they endure them they do not perceive in their conscience that because of their error these things happen to them.

IX. Now let us come to the history of these their gods in order that we may prove accurately concerning all those things which we have said above.

Before everything else the Greeks introduce as a god Kronos, which is interpreted Chiun; and the worshippers of this deity sacrifice to him their children: and some of them they burn while yet living. Concerning him they say that he took him Rhea to wife; and from her he begat many sons; from whom he begat also Dios, who is called Zeus; and at the last he went mad and, for fear of an oracle which was told him, began to eat his children. And from him Zeus was stolen away, and he did not perceive it: and at the last Zeus bound him and cut off his genitals and cast them in the sea: whence, as they say in the fable, was born Aphrodite, who is called Astera: and he cast Kronos bound into darkness. Great then is the error and scorn which the Greeks have introduced concerning the head of their gods, in that they have said all these things about him, O king. It is not possible that God should be bound or amputated; otherwise it is a great misfortune.

And after Kronos they introduce another god, Zeus; and they say concerning this one, that he received the headship and became king of all the gods; and they say concerning him that he was changed into cattle and everything else, in order that he might commit adultery with mortal women, and might raise up to himself children from them. Since at one time they say he was changed into a bull on account of his passion for Europa and for Pasiphae; and again he was changed into the likeness of gold on account of his passion for Danae: and into a swan, through his passion for Leda; and into a man through his passion for Antiope; and into lightning on account of his passion for the Moon: so that from these he begat many children: for they say that from Antiope he begat Zethus and Amphion; and from the Moon, Dionysus; from Alkmena, Herakles; and from Leto, Apollo and Artemis; and from Danae, Perseus; and from Leda, Castor and Polydeuces and Helene; and from Mnemosyne he begat nine daughters, those whom he called the Muses; and from Europa, Minos and Rhadamanthus and Sarpedon. But last of all he was changed into the likeness of an eagle on account of his passion for Ganymede the shepherd.

Because of these stories, O king, much evil has befallen the race of men who are at this present day, since they imitate their gods, and commit adultery, and are defiled with their mothers and sisters, and in sleeping with males: and some of them have dared to kill even their fathers. For if he, who is said to be the head and king of their gods, has done these things, how much more shall his worshippers imitate him! And great is the madness which the Greeks have introduced into their history concerning him: for it is not possible that a god should commit adultery or fornication, or should approach to sleep with males, or that he should be a parricide; otherwise he is much worse than a destructive demon.

X. And again they introduce another god, Hephaestus; and they say of him that he is lame and wearing a cap on his head, and holding in his hand tongs and hammer; and working in brass in order that therefrom he may find his needed sustenance. Is then this god so much in need? Whereas it is impossible for a god to be needy or lame: otherwise he is very weak.

And again they introduce another god and call him Hermes; and they say that he is a thief, loving avarice and coveting gains, and a magician and maimed and an athlete and an interpreter of words: whereas it is impossible for a god to be a magician, or avaricious, or maimed, or coveting anything that is not his, or an athlete: and if it be found to be otherwise, he is of no use.

And after him they introduce another god, Asclepius; and they say that he is a physician and prepares medicines and bandages in order that he may satisfy his need of sustenance. Is then this god in need? And he at last was struck by lightning by Zeus, on account of Tyndareus the Lacedemonian; and so he died. If then Asclepius was a god, and when struck by lightning was unable to help himself, how is it that he was able to help others? Whereas it is an impossible thing that the divine nature should be in need, or that it should be struck by lightning.

And again they introduce another god and call him Ares, and they say that he is a warrior and jealous, and covets sheep and things which do not belong to him, and acquires possessions through his weapons; and of him they say that at last he committed adultery with Aphrodite and was bound by a tiny boy Eros, and by Hephaestus the husband of Aphrodite: whereas it is impossible that a god should be a warrior or a prisoner or an adulterer.

And again they say of Dionysus that he too is a god, who celebrates festivals by night and teaches drunkenness, and carries off women that do not belong to him: and at the last they say that he went mad and left his female attendants and fled to the wilderness; and in this madness of his he ate serpents; and at the last he was killed by Titan. If then Dionysus was a god, and when slain was not able to help himself; how is it that he was able to help others?

Herakles, too, they introduce, and they say of him that he is a god, a hater of things hateful, a tyrant and a warrior, and a slayer of the wicked: and of him they say that at the last he went mad and slew his children and cast himself into the fire and died. If therefore Herakles be a god and in all these evils was unable to stand up for himself, how was it that others were asking help from him? Whereas it is impossible that a god should be mad or drunken or a slayer of his children, or destroyed by fire.

XI. And after him they introduce another god and call him Apollo: and they say of him that he is jealous and changeable; and sometimes he holds a bow and a quiver, and sometimes a lyre and a plectrum; and he gives oracles to men, in order that he may receive a reward from them. Is then this god in need of reward? Whereas it is disgraceful that all these things should be found in a god.

And after him they introduce Artemis a goddess, the sister of Apollo; and they say that she was a huntress; and she carried a bow and arrows, and went about on mountains leading dogs, either to hunt the deer or the wild boars. Whereas it is disgraceful that a maid should go about by herself on mountains and follow the chase of beasts. And therefore it is not possible that Artemis should be a goddess.

Again they say of Aphrodite that she forsooth is a goddess; and sometimes forsooth she dwells with their gods, and sometimes she commits adultery with men; and sometimes she has Ares for her lover and sometimes Adonis, who is Tammuz: and sometimes forsooth Aphrodite is wailing and weeping for the death of Tammuz: and they say that she went down to Hades in order that she might ransom Adonis from Persephone, who was the daughter of Hades. If then Aphrodite be a goddess and was unable to help her lover in his death, how is she able to help others? And this is a thing impossible to be listened to, that the divine nature should come to weeping and wailing and adultery.

And again they say of Tammuz that he is a god; and he is forsooth a hunter and an adulterer; and they say that he was killed by a blow from a wild boar, and was not able to help himself. And if he was not able to help himself, how is he able to take care of the human race? And this is impossible, that a god should be an adulterer or a hunter or that he should have died by violence.

And again they say of Rhea that she forsooth is the mother of their gods; and they say of her that she had at one time a lover Atys, and she was rejoicing in corruptible men; and at the last she established lamentations, and was bewailing her lover Atys. If then the mother of their gods was not able to help her lover and rescue him from death, how is it possible that she should help others? It is disgraceful then that a goddess should lament and weep, and that she should have joy over corruptible beings.

Again they bring forward Kore; and they say that she was a goddess and that she was carried off by Pluto and was not able to help herself. If then she is a goddess and was not able to help herself, how is she able to help others? For a goddess who is carried off is extremely weak.

All these things, then, O king, the Greeks have introduced forward about their gods, and have invented and said concerning them: whence all men have taken occasion to do all wicked and impure things: and thereby the whole earth has been corrupted.

XII. Now the Egyptians, because they are more evil and ignorant than all peoples upon the earth, have erred more than all men. For the worship of the Barbarians and the Greeks did not suffice them, but they introduced also the nature of beasts, and said concerning it that they were gods: and also of the creeping things which are found on the dry land and in the waters, and of the plants and herbs they have said that some of them are gods, and they have become corrupt in all madness and impurity more than all peoples that are upon the earth. For of old time they worshipped Isis; and they say that she forsooth is a goddess, who had forsooth a husband Osiris, her brother; but when forsooth Osiris was killed by his brother Typhon, Isis fled with her son Horus to Byblos in Syria and was there for a certain time until that her son was grown: and he contended with his uncle Typhon and killed him, and thereupon Isis returned and went about with her son Horus, and was seeking for the body of Osiris her lord, and bitterly bewailing his death. If therefore Isis be a goddess, and was not able to help Osiris her brother and lord, how is it possible that she should help others? Whereas it is impossible that the divine nature should be afraid and flee, or weep and wail. Otherwise it is a great misfortune.

But of Osiris they say that he is a god, a beneficent one; and he was killed by Typhon and could not help himself; and it is evident that this cannot be said of Deity.

And again they say of Typhon, his brother, that he is a god, a fratricide, and slain by his brother's son and wife since he was unable to help himself. And how can one who does not help himself be a god?

Now because the Egyptians are more ignorant than the rest of the peoples, these and the like gods did not suffice them, but they also put the name of gods on the beasts which are merely soulless. For some men among them worship the sheep, and others the calf; and some of them the pig, and others the shad-fish; and some of them the crocodile, and the hawk, and the cormorant, and the kite, and the vulture, and the eagle, and the crow; some of them worship the cat, and others the fish Shibbuta; some of them the dog, and some of them the serpent, and some the asp, and others the lion, and others garlic, and onions, and thorns, and others the leopard, and the like.

And the poor wretches do not perceive with regard to all these things that they are nought; while every day they look upon their gods, who are eaten and destroyed by men, yea even by their own fellows; and some of them being burned, and some of them dying and putrifying and becoming refuse; and they do not understand that they are destroyed in many ways.

And accordingly the Egyptians have not understood that the like of these are not gods, since their salvation is not within their own power; and if they are too weak for their own salvation, then as regards the salvation of their worshippers pray whence will they have the power to help them?

XIII. The Egyptians then have erred with a great error, above all peoples that are upon the face of the earth. But it is a matter of wonder, O king, concerning the Greeks, whereas they excel all the rest of the peoples in their manners and in their reason, how thus they have gone astray after dead idols and senseless images: while they see their gods sawn and polished by their makers, and curtailed and cut and burnt and shaped and transformed into every shape by them. And when they are grown old and fail by the length of time, and are melted and broken in pieces, how is it that they do not understand concerning them that they are not gods? And those who have not ability for their own preservation, how will they be able to take care of men? But even the poets and philosophers among them being in error have introduced concerning them that they are gods, things like these which are made for the honour of God Almighty; and being in error they seek to make them like to God as to whom no man has ever seen to whom He is like; nor is

he able to see Him[1]; and together with these things they introduce concerning Deity as if it were that deficiency were found
with it; in that they say that He accepts sacrifice and asks for
burnt-offering and libation and murders of men and temples. But
God is not needy, and none of these things is sought for by Him:
and it is clear that men are in error in those things that they
imagine. But their poets and philosophers introduce and say, ܒܐ
that the nature of all their gods is one; but they have not understood of God our Lord, that while He is one, He is yet in all. They,
then, are in error; for if, while the body of man is many in its
parts, no member is afraid of its fellow, but whilst it is a com-
posite body, all is on an equality with all: so also God who is one
in His nature has a single essence proper to Him, and He is
equal in His nature and His essence, nor is He afraid of Himself.
If therefore the nature of the gods is one, it is not proper that
a god should persecute a god, nor kill nor do him that which is
evil.

If then gods were persecuted and transfixed by gods, and some
of them were carried off and some were struck by lightning; it is
clear that the nature of their gods is not one, and hence it is clear,
O king, that that is an error which they speculate about the
nature of their gods, and that they reduce them to one nature.
If then it is proper that we should admire a god who is visible
and does not see, how much more is this worthy of admiration
that a man should believe in a nature which is invisible and
all-seeing! and if again it is right that a man should investigate
the works of an artificer, how much more is it right that he
should praise the Maker of the artificer! For behold! while the
Greeks have established laws, they have not understood that by
their laws they were condemning their gods; for if their laws are ܒܒ
just, their gods are unjust, who have committed transgression in
killing one another and practising sorcery, committing adultery,
plundering, stealing and sleeping with males, along with the rest
of their other doings. But if their gods excellently and as they
describe have done all these things, then the laws of the Greeks
are unjust; and they are not laid down according to the will of
the gods; and in this the whole world has erred.

[1] 1 Tim. vi. 16.

For as for the histories of their gods, some of them are myths, some of them physical, and some hymns and songs: the hymns and songs, then, are empty words and sound; and as to the physical, if they were done as they say, then they are not gods, since they have done these things and suffered and endured these things: and these myths are flimsy words, altogether devoid of force.

XIV. Let us come now, O king, also to the history of the Jews and let us see what sort of opinion they have concerning God. The Jews then say that God is one, Creator of all and almighty: and that it is not proper for us that anything else should be worshipped, but this God only: and in this they appear to be much nearer to the truth than all the peoples, in that they worship God more exceedingly and not His works; and they imitate God by reason of the love which they have for man; for they have compassion on the poor and ransom the captive and bury the dead, and do things of a similar nature to these: things which are acceptable to God and are well-pleasing also to men, things which they have received from their fathers of old. Nevertheless they too have gone astray from accurate knowledge, and they suppose in their minds that they are serving God, but in the methods of their actions their service is to angels and not to God, in that they observe sabbaths and new moons and the passover and the great fast, and the fast, and circumcision, and cleanness of meats: which things not even thus have they perfectly observed.

XV. Now the Christians, O king, by going about and seeking have found the truth, and as we have comprehended from their writings they are nearer to the truth and to exact knowledge than the rest of the peoples. For they know and believe in God, the Maker of heaven and earth, in whom are all things and from whom are all things: He who has no other god as His fellow: from whom they have received those commandments which they have engraved on their minds, which they keep in the hope and expectation of the world to come; so that on this account they do not commit adultery nor fornication, they do not bear false witness, they do not deny a deposit, nor covet what is not theirs: they honour father and mother; they do good to those who are their neighbours, and when they are judges they judge uprightly; and they do not worship idols in the form of man; and whatever they do not wish that others should do to them, they do not practise towards any one[1], and they do not eat of the meats of idol sacrifices, for they are undefiled: and those who grieve them they comfort, and ܒܢ make them their friends; and they do good to their enemies: and their wives, O king, are pure as virgins, and their daughters modest: and their men abstain from all unlawful wedlock and from all impurity, in the hope of the recompense that is to come in another world: but as for their servants or handmaids, or their children if any of them have any, they persuade them to become Christians for the love that they have towards them; and when they have become so, they call them without distinction brethren: they do not worship strange gods: and they walk in all humility and kindness, and falsehood is not found among them, and they love one another: and from the widows they do not turn away their countenance: and they rescue the orphan from him who does him violence: and he who has gives to him who has not, without grudging; and when they see the stranger they bring him to their dwellings, and rejoice over him as over a true brother; for they do not call brothers those who are after the flesh, but those who are in the spirit and in God: but when one of their poor passes away from the world, and any of them sees him, then he provides for his burial according to his ability; and if they hear that any of their number is imprisoned or oppressed for the name of their Messiah, all of them provide for his needs, and if it is possible that he may be delivered, they deliver him.

And if there is among them a man that is poor or needy, and they have not an abundance of necessaries, they fast two or three days that they may supply the needy with their necessary food. And they observe scrupulously the commandments of their Messiah: they live honestly and soberly, as the Lord their God ܒܡ commanded them: every morning and at all hours on account of the goodnesses of God toward them they praise and laud Him: and over their food and over their drink they render Him thanks. And if any righteous person of their number passes away from the world they rejoice and give thanks to God, and they follow his body, as if he were moving from one place to another: and when a child is born to any one of them, they praise God, and if again

[1] Cf. *Teaching of the Twelve Apostles*, cc. 1—4.

it chance to die in its infancy, they praise God mightily, as for one who has passed through the world without sins. And if again they see that one of their number has died in his iniquity or in his sins, over this one they weep bitterly and sigh, as over one who is about to go to punishment: such is the ordinance of the law of the Christians, O king, and such their conduct.

XVI. As men who know God, they ask from Him petitions which are proper for Him to give and for them to receive: and thus they accomplish the course of their lives. And because they acknowledge the goodnesses of God towards them, lo! on account of them there flows forth the beauty that is in the world. And truly they are of the number of those that have found the truth by going about and seeking it, and as far as we have comprehended, we have understood that they only are near to the knowledge of the truth.

But the good deeds which they do, they do not proclaim in the ears of the multitude, and they take care that no one shall perceive them, and hide their gift, as he who has found a treasure and hides it[1]. And they labour to become righteous as those that expect to see their Messiah and receive from Him the promises made to them with great glory.

But their sayings and their ordinances, O king, and the glory of their service, and the expectation of their recompense of reward, according to the doing of each one of them, which they expect in another world, thou art able to know from their writings. It sufficeth for us that we have briefly made known to your majesty concerning the conversation and the truth of the Christians. For truly great and wonderful is their teaching to him that is willing to examine and understand it. And truly this people is a new people, and there is something divine mingled with it. Take now their writings and read in them, and lo! ye will find that not of myself have I brought these things forward nor as their advocate have I said them, but as I have read in their writings, these things I firmly believe, and those things also that are to come. And therefore I was constrained to set forth the truth to them that take pleasure therein and seek after the world to come.

And I have no doubt that the world stands by reason of

[1] Matt. xiii. 44.

the intercession of Christians. But the rest of the peoples are deceived and deceivers, rolling themselves before the elements of the world, according as the sight of their understanding is unwilling to pass by them; and they grope as if in the dark, because they are unwilling to know the truth, and like drunken men they stagger and thrust one another and fall down.

XVII. Thus far, O king, it is I that have spoken. For as to what remains, as was said above, there are found in their other writings words which are difficult to speak, or that one should repeat them; things which are not only said, but actually done.

The Greeks, then, O king, because they practise foul things in sleeping with males, and with mother and sister and daughter, turn the ridicule of their foulness upon the Christians; but the Christians are honest and pious, and the truth is set before their eyes, and they are long-suffering; and therefore while they know their error and are buffeted by them, they endure and suffer them: and more exceedingly do they pity them as men who are destitute of knowledge: and in their behalf they offer up prayers that they may turn from their error. And when it chances that one of them turns, he is ashamed before the Christians of the deeds that are done by him: and he confesses to God, saying, In ignorance I did these things: and he cleanses his heart, and his sins are forgiven him, because he did them in ignorance in former time, when he was blaspheming and reviling the true knowledge of the Christians. And truly blessed is the race of the Christians, more than all men that are upon the face of the earth.

Let the tongues of those now be silenced who talk vanity, and who oppress the Christians, and let them now speak the truth. For it is better that they should worship the true God rather than that they should worship a sound without intelligence; and truly divine is that which is spoken by the mouth of the Christians, and their teaching is the gateway of light. Let all those then approach thereunto who do not know God, and let them receive incorruptible words, those which are so always and from eternity: let them, therefore, anticipate the dread judgment which is to come by Jesus the Messiah upon the whole race of men.

The Apology of Aristides the Philosopher is ended.

NOTES ON THE SYRIAC VERSION.

p. 35, l. 4 (ܐ 3). We have given in the introductory remarks the reasons for believing that the words ܣܓܝܕܐ and ܡܪ̈ܚܡܢܐ are a part of the name of the emperor addressed. Both of these words, however, might have been used generally, as royal adjectives. For example, in the recently published *Acta Mar Kardaghi* of Abbeloos p. 87 they occur as titles of the king of Persia:

ܘܠܐ ܢܥܒܕ ܠܒܘܪܟܐ ܕܥܠ ܣܓܝܕܐ ܡܠܟ ܡ̈ܠܟܐ.

which Abbeloos renders by "contra adorabilem regem regum."

ܡܠܟ ܡ̈ܠܟܐ ܡܪ̈ܚܡܢܐ ܦܩܕ. (rex regum clemens jussit).

[The plural points in these two titles, though obviously wrong, have been retained in our text, in accordance with the principle of reproducing the punctuation of the MS. exactly as it stands. In the first sentence the MS. has a slight stop after ܐܠܗܐ, while there is no stop after ܐܚܝܕ ܟܠ. 'Almighty' can only be retained as an epithet of the Deity: but possibly there has been some confusion of the original, which may have run: περὶ θεοσεβείας· αὐτοκράτορι, κ.τ.λ.]

l. 7 (ܐ 7). The demonstration of Divine Providence from the contemplation of the heavenly bodies is common to all forms of Theistic teaching: consequently it occurs freely in Christian Apologetics. We may compare the following passages:

Melito, *Oration to Antoninus Caesar* (Cureton, *Spic. Syr.* p. 46). "He hath set before thee the heavens, and He has placed in them the stars. He hath set before thee the sun and the moon, and they every day fulfil their course therein...He hath set before thee the clouds which by ordinance bring water from above and satisfy the earth: that from these things thou mightest understand, that He who moveth these is greater than they all,

[ܕܡ̇ܢ ܕܗܠܝܢ ܡܫܢܐ ܡܢ ܟܠܗܘܢ ܝܬܝܪ ܗܘ.]

and that thou mightest accept the goodness of Him who hath given to thee a mind by which thou mayest distinguish these things."

Origen, *De Principiis*, II. 1. 5. "But that we may believe on the authority of Holy Scripture, that such is the case, hear how in the books of Maccabees, where the mother of the seven martyrs exhorts her son to endure torture, this truth is confirmed: for she says, 'I ask of thee, my son, to look at the heaven and earth, and at all things which are in them, and beholding them, to know that God made all these things when they did not exist.'" [2 Macc. vii. 28.]

Id. IV. 1. 7. "The artistic plan of a providential Ruler is not so evident in matters belonging to the earth, as in the case of the sun, moon and stars."

l. 11 (ܐ 11). Cf. Melito, *Oration* p. 50. "He made the lights that His works might behold one another, and *He concealeth Himself* in His might *from all His works.*"

[l. 11 (ܐ 13). ܘܕܐܬܒܩܝܢ. If this reading be correct, the Ethpa. seems to be here used in the sense of 'sibi investigare,' of which only one example is cited in the *Thes. Syr.*, viz. from the unpublished Hexaem. of Bar Cephas. The context however of the quotation shews that there at least such a meaning is inadmissible. The words (kindly supplied by Dr Zotenberg) are: ܐܠܐ ܚܢܢ ܢܒܠܐ ܒܪܘܝܐ ܕܠܗܘܢ ܠܐ ܡܨܝܢ ܗܘܐ ܠܗܘܢ. ܐܪܥܐ ܘܫܡܝܐ ܠܐ ܡܨܝܢ ܥܒܕܝܢ ܗܘܘ ܡܢ ܗܝ ܕܠܒܘܬܐ ܐܡܟܢܐܝܬ ܢܣܒܝܢ ܗܘܘ ܘܡܬܒܩܝܢ ܐܝܟ ܕܠܒܘܬܐ ܕܠܗܘܢ. ܘܐܐܪ ܘܢܘܪܐ ܠܐ ܦܪܫܝܢ ܗܘܘ ܡܢ ܗܝ ܕܠܒܡ ܘܥܠܝܡ ܠܟܠ ܐܝܟ ܕܠܒܘܬܐ ܕܠܗܘܢ.

ll. 14, 15 (ܐ 14, 15). A comparison with the Armenian suggests that something has fallen out here. The Syriac cannot be translated as it stands. The Greek unfortunately fails us at this point.]

l. 19 (ܐ 19). The early Christian teachers emphasised strongly this belief that the world was made for the sake of man: consequently we must not assume, if we find the same statement in Justin Martyr, that the idea was borrowed from Aristides, for it is a part of the regular second-century teaching. The following parallels may be quoted:

Justin, *Apol.* I. 10. καὶ πάντα τὴν ἀρχὴν ἀγαθὸν ὄντα δημιουργῆσαι αὐτὸν ἐξ ἀμόρφου ὕλης δι' ἀνθρώπους δεδιδάγμεθα.

Dial. 41. ἵνα ἅμα τε εὐχαριστῶμεν τῷ θεῷ ὑπέρ τε τοῦ τὸν κόσμον ἐκτικέναι σὺν πᾶσι τοῖς ἐν αὐτῷ διὰ τὸν ἄνθρωπον.

Ps. Justin, *Ep. ad Diogn.* 10. ὁ γὰρ θεὸς τοὺς ἀνθρώπους ἠγάπησε, δι' οὓς ἐποίησε τὸν κόσμον, οἷς ὑπέταξε πάντα, κτέ.

l. 23 (ܒ 5). Cf. Philo, *Fragments*, p. 70: ἐν θεῷ μόνον τὸ τέλειον καὶ ἀνενδεές, ἐν δὲ ἀνθρώπῳ τὸ ἐπιδεὲς καὶ ἀτελές.

Id. *de Fortitudine* § 3. Ὁ σπουδαῖος ὀλιγοδεής, ἀθανάτου καὶ θνητῆς φύσεως μεθόριος.

Acta Mar Kardaghi (ed. Abbeloos, p. 30):

ܩܕܝܡ ܐܝܬܝܘܬ ܕܗܝ̈ܘܠܐ ܐܝܟܢ. ܘܐܝܟ ܗܝ̈ܘܠܐ
ܐܝܟܢ: ܐܦ ܐܠܗܘܬܐ ܐܝܟܢ.

l. 28 (ܒ 8). The same philosophical opinion will be found almost in the same words in Eustathius *contra Arianos* quoted in John of Damascus, *Parallels* p. 314,

πᾶν τὴν ἀρχὴν ἔχον, καὶ τέλος ἐπιδέχεται· τὸ δὲ τέλος ἐπιδεχόμενον, φθορᾶς ἐστὶ δεκτικόν.

l. 30 (ܒ 10). We may compare the following passages from Justin and from the Epistle to Diognetus, in view of Jerome's statement that Justin imitated Aristides, and the modern theory of Doulcet as to the authorship of the anonymous epistle to Diognetus.

Justin, *Apol.* I. 9. οὐ γὰρ τοιαύτην ἡγούμεθα τὸν θεὸν ἔχειν τὴν μορφήν, ἥν φασί τινες εἰς τιμὴν μεμιμῆσθαι.

Justin, *Apol.* II. 6. ὄνομα δὲ τῷ πάντων πατρὶ θετόν, ἀγεννήτῳ ὄντι, οὐκ ἔστιν· ᾧ γὰρ ἂν καὶ ὄνομά τι προσαγορεύηται, πρεσβύτερον ἔχει τὸν θέμενον τὸ ὄνομα.

Justin, *Dial.* 4. φησὶ γὰρ Πλάτων, ἦν δ' ἐγώ, αὐτὸ τοιοῦτον εἶναι τὸ τοῦ νοῦ ὄμμα καὶ πρὸς τοῦτο ἡμῖν δεδόσθαι, ὡς δύνασθαι καθορᾶν αὐτὸ ἐκεῖνο τὸ ὂν εἰλικρινεῖ αὐτῷ ἐκείνῳ, ὃ τῶν νοητῶν ἁπάντων ἐστὶν αἴτιον, οὐ χρῶμα ἔχον, οὐ σχῆμα, οὐ μέγεθος, οὐδὲ οὐδὲν ὧν ὀφθαλμὸς βλέπει.

Justin, *Apol.* I. 10. ἀλλ' οὐδὲ δέεσθαι τῆς παρ' ἀνθρώπων ὑλικῆς προσφορᾶς προσειλήφαμεν τὸν θεόν, αὐτὸν παρέχοντα πάντα ὁρῶντες.

Ep. ad Diogn. 3. ὁ γὰρ ποιήσας τὸν οὐρανὸν καὶ τὴν γῆν καὶ πάντα τὰ ἐν αὐτοῖς, καὶ πᾶσιν ἡμῖν χορηγῶν ὧν προσδεόμεθα, οὐδενὸς ἂν αὐτὸς προσδέοιτο τούτων ὧν τοῖς οἰομένοις διδόναι παρέχει αὐτός.

[p. 36, l. 13 (ܠ 2). ἴδωμεν Gr. (p. 100, l. 16) Arm., εἴδωμεν Syr. A comparison between the Gr. and Syr. shews a like variation in ܕ 18 (Gr. p. 101, l. 3) and ܠ 18 (Gr. p. 104, l. 1).

l. 18 (ܠ 8). 'The head of the race of their religion.' This seems to be a conflation of the two phrases which occur lower down: 'the head of their race,' and 'the beginning of their religion.' It should be simply 'the head of their race,' as we see from the Greek.]

l. 23 (ܠ 13). The Armenian has 'Kadmus the Sidonian and Dionysus the Theban.' Cf. Herod. II. 91 τὸν γὰρ Δαναὸν καὶ τὸν Λυγκέα ἐόντας Χεμμίτας ἐκπλῶσαι ἐς τὴν Ἑλλάδα, and II. 49 παρὰ Κάδμου τε τοῦ Τυρίου καὶ τῶν σὺν αὐτῷ ἐκ Φοινίκης. But Kadmus is a Sidonian in Eur. *Bacch.* 171 and Ovid, *Met.* IV. 571.

[l. 27 (ܠ 17). The statement that the people received the name of 'Hebrews' from Moses is peculiar to the Syr. and Arm. translations.]

l. 29 (ܠ 20). The writer not only deduces the name of the Christians from the title of their founder, but he is also ready, like Justin and other fathers, to compare the name with the Greek word χρηστός, as we shall see in the closing chapter. The following parallels may be noted in Justin.

Justin, *Apol.* I. 12. Ἰησοῦς Χριστός, ἀφ' οὗ καὶ τὸ χριστιανοὶ ἐπονομάζεσθαι ἐσχήκαμεν.

Dial. 63. τῇ ἐκκλησίᾳ τῇ ἐξ ὀνόματος αὐτοῦ γενομένῃ καὶ μετασχούσῃ τοῦ ὀνόματος αὐτοῦ, χριστιανοὶ γὰρ πάντες καλούμεθα.

Ibid. 138. ὁ γὰρ χριστός, πρωτότοκος πάσης κτίσεως ὤν, καὶ ἀρχὴ πάλιν ἄλλου γένους γέγονεν, τοῦ ἀναγεννηθέντος ὑπ' αὐτοῦ δι' ὕδατος καὶ πίστεως καὶ ξύλου, τοῦ τὸ μυστήριον τοῦ σταυροῦ ἔχοντος, ὃν τρόπον καὶ ὁ Νῶε κτέ.

l. 32 (ܠ 23). With the closing words of this sentence we may compare the Syriac *Acts of John* (ed. Wright), p. 37,

ܘܟܕ ܓܐܪ ܓܒܠܐ ܒܟܪ̈ܣܬܐ ܥܡ ܐܒܘܗܝ ܗܘܐ.

where we should correct the text so as to read "and when formed as a child in the womb He was with His Father."

l. 34 (ܕ 1). The Gospel is clearly a written one, and not the general message (εὐαγγέλιον). In c. xvi. we again find Aristides offering the Emperor the Christian Scriptures.

[l. 38 (ܕ 5). The Greek text has καὶ τελέσας τὴν θαυμαστὴν αὐτοῦ οἰκονομίαν. Cf. Justin, *Dial.* 103, and Otto's note on that passage, where the use of οἰκονομία is illustrated. In the Syriac ܡܕܡ is unsatisfactory. It can hardly be intended to represent (οἰκονομίαν) τινά. Possibly it is a corruption of some word which corresponded to θαυμαστήν.]

p. 37, l. 1 (ܕ 6). Another instance of the formula 'He was crucified by the Jews,' beyond those to which we have already drawn attention, may be found in a fragment of Melito preserved by Anastasius Sinaita;

Ὁ θεὸς πέπονθεν ὑπὸ δεξιᾶς Ἰσραηλίτιδος,

for which the Syriac rendering is given by Cureton, *Spic. Syr.* ܡܛ, ܕ.

ܐܠܗܐ· ܡܩܛܠ. ܡܠܟܐ ܕܐܝܣܪܐܝܠ ܢܟܣܘ ܡܢ ܝܡܝܢܐ
ܐܝܣܪܝܠܝܬܐ.

In later times we may expect to find similar language, though the expression itself disappears from the Creed. In *Acta Mar Kardaghi* p. 37 we have the following (loquitur Satanas),

ܠܡܫܝܚܐ ܕܓܠܬ ܒܗ ܘܡܫܡܫܬܢ ܘܐܪܕܬ
ܒܬܪ ܗܘ ܠܝܠ ܣܘܪ̈ܬܐ ܠܬܠܡܝܕܘܗܝ ܕܝܫܘܥ:
ܗܘ ܕܙܩܦܘ ܣܢ̈ܐܝ ܝܗܘ̈ܕܝܐ ܒܐܘܪܫܠܡ...

and again in p. 74

ܘܐܘܪܕܬ ܒܡܫܝܚܐ ܐܢܫ ܗܘ ܕܙܩܦܘܗܝ ܝܗܘ̈ܕܝܐ

The idea of the Jews being the special agents of Satan in the Crucifixion comes out also in an unpublished Ἀντιλογία between the Devil and Christ, which is preserved in a MS. at Jerusalem (Cod. 66, S. Sep.), where we read

Καὶ ὁ διάβολος λέγει· Πορεύσομαι πρὸς Ἄνναν καὶ Καϊάφαν τοὺς ἀρχιερεῖς τοὺς ἐμοὺς Ἰουδαίους· καὶ ποιήσω αὐτοὺς ἵνα σὲ σταυρώσωσι.

[Compare also the Letter of Pilate in the Acts of Peter and Paul § 42 (Tisch. *Acta Apocr.*, Lips. 1851, p. 17): οἱ δὲ ἐσταύρωσαν αὐτόν, καὶ ταφέντος αὐτοῦ φύλακας κατέστησαν ἐπ' αὐτόν.]

l. 20 (ܠ 25). The injunction to have a care that your gods be not stolen is not uncommon with the early Christians, and it is not improbable that they were able to refer to special and notable cases of violation of temples and mutilation of images. We may refer, at all events, to the following parallels:

Justin, *Apol.* I. 9. καὶ τῶν ἱερῶν ἔνθα ἀνατίθενται φύλακας τοιούτους καθιστάναι, μὴ συνορῶντας ἀθέμιτον καὶ τὸ νοεῖν ἢ λέγειν ἀνθρώπους θεῶν εἶναι φύλακας.

Ep. ad Diogn. 2. τοὺς μὲν λιθίνους καὶ ὀστρακίνους σέβοντες ἀφυλάκτους, τοὺς δὲ ἀργυροῦς καὶ χρυσοῦς ἐγκλείοντες ταῖς νυξὶ καὶ ταῖς ἡμέραις φύλακας παρακαθιστάντες ἵνα μὴ κλαπῶσιν.

l. 26 (ܡ 5). Compare c. VII. From the "Teaching of the Apostles" (c. VI. 3) onwards, idolatry is known as a 'worship of dead gods': e.g. Melito, *Oration* p. 43, "But I affirm that also the Sibyl has said respecting them, that it is the images of kings, who are dead, they worship."

p. 38, l. 1 (ܡ 19). The writer now proceeds to discuss the views of those who either sought the First Principle in one of the elements or imagined it to be located in one of the heavenly bodies. And it is common for the early Christian writers to demolish the philosophic schools in detail according as they found them referring the origin of all things to water, as Thales; or air, as Anaximenes; or fire, as Heraclitus; or earth, as Pherecydes and Xenophanes. We may compare Plutarch *De placitis philosophorum* I. 3, and then notice how the Christian apologists deal with the matter. The writer of the Epistle to Diognetus thinks that, if a god is to be found amongst the elements, one element or created thing is as good as another:

Ep. ad Diogn. 8. οἱ μὲν πῦρ ἔφασαν εἶναι τὸν θεόν (οὗ μέλλουσι χωρήσειν αὐτοί, τοῦτο καλοῦσι θεόν)· οἱ δὲ ὕδωρ· οἱ δ' ἄλλο τι τῶν στοιχείων τῶν ἐκτισμένων ὑπὸ θεοῦ· καίτοιγε, εἴ τις τούτων τῶν λόγων ἀπόδεκτός ἐστι, δύναιτ' ἂν καὶ τῶν λοιπῶν κτισμάτων ἓν ἕκαστον ὁμοίως ἀποφαίνεσθαι θεόν.

Melito deals even more shortly with the matter, and in a rude commonsense manner says that we may call a creature God without making it to be divine:

Oration, p. 42. "And if, therefore, a man...say that there is another God, it is found from his own words that he calleth some created thing God. For if a man call fire God, it is not God, because it is fire; and if a man call the waters God, they are not God, because they are waters; and if this earth which we tread upon, and if those heavens which are seen by us, and if the sun, or the moon, or one of those stars which run their course by ordinance and rest not, nor proceed by their own will—and if a man call gold and silver gods: are not these things that we use as we please?"

It will be seen that their treatment of the subject was superficial, no other treatment being, in fact, necessary. Aristides, however, takes the matter more seriously and examines each case in detail by the light of his previously stated axioms concerning the divine nature.

[l. 1 (ܗ 19). ἔλθωμεν Gr., ἐπανέλθωμεν Syr. Comp. also ܠ 18 (Gr. p. 104, l. 1).

l. 36 (ܝ 10). ܦܘܪ̈ܣܐ. Probably for ܦܘܪ̊ܣܐ, examples of which are given under ܦܪܘܣ in the *Thes. Syr.*

p. 39, l. 1 (ܝ 11). ܡܠܟܘܬܟܘܢ. This phrase, 'your majesty,' does not in any way suggest that more than one person is addressed.

l. 11 (ܝ 20). A probable emendation is ܚܫܚܬܐ ܕܐܢܫܘܬܐ.

l. 27 (ܚ 13). ܦܠܓܘܬܐ ܐܝܬ ܠܗ:. This slight emendation brings the Syr. into more literal accordance with the Gk. The expression μερισμὸν ἔχοντα seems also to have suggested the next sentence in the Syriac, where it is combined with the preceding words εἰς χρῆσιν τῶν ἀνθρώπων.

l. 37 (ܠ 1). Similar language is applied to *the heaven* in a paragraph found only in the Gr. (p. 101, l. 30) καὶ ἐκ πολλῶν συνεστῶτα· διὸ καὶ κόσμος καλεῖται. Where the reference is to man, we should have expected μικρὸς κόσμος. See Suicer, *Thes.* II. 369 (1728). A treatise was written on this subject (ܡܐܡܪܐ ܥܠܡܐ ܙܥܘܪܐ) by Aḥudhemmeh († A.D. 575). See *Bibl. Or.* III. 1. 194.

p. 40, ll. 22 ff. (ܡ 2–12). In this classification of the gods of the Greeks the principal points in which the Syr. differs from the Gr. are: (1) ἀδελφοκτόνους (p. 104, l. 7) is not represented. It is absent also from the Pemb. Coll. MS. of the Greek. (2) After μαινομένους two clauses are inserted, the one taken from the description of Apollo (ܣ 21, 22), and the other from that of Artemis (ܦ 5). (3) An additional clause is inserted after καὶ φυγάδας γενομένους. (4) Two additional clauses, the one taken from the description of Aphrodite (ܦ 15), the other probably from that of Tammuz (ܦ 23), are inserted after the words καὶ κοπτομένους καὶ θρηνουμένους.

It may be remarked that the Greek participles just quoted are both rendered as passives ('wept and lamented by men') by the Syr. translator. The Latin version omits them: the translation of Billyus is: "nonnullos vulnera accepisse, ac lamenta edidisse."]

l. 25 (ܡ 7). He is referring to Apollo, Poseidon and Asklepios: cf. Tertullian, *Apol.* 14, Hic Apollinem Admeto regi pascendis pecoribus addicit, ille Neptuni structorias operas Laomedonti locat. Est et illis de lyricis (Pindarum dico) qui Aescolapium canit avaritiae merito, quia medicinam nocenter exercebat, fulmine iudicatum.

[l. 33 (ܝܗ 12). ܕܡܓܝܪܘܢ. The Pah. and Aph. of ܓܘܪ = moechari are not given in the Lexicons. The use of the former is however a marked feature in the language of our translator. It occurs again ܝܒ 9 with ܠ; ܝܓ 12, absol.; ܝܙ 20 and ܝܘ 11, with ܒ. Compare תגיר, Targ. Job xxxvi. 20. We have an instance of the Aph. in Mat. v. 32 (Cur.) ܗܘܐ ܡܓܝܪ ܠܗ̇ = ποιεῖ αὐτὴν μοιχευθῆναι.

p. 41, l. 20 (ܝܟ 14. Gr. p. 104, l. 22). The Syr. supports neither ὅπως nor ὁ πρῶτος.]

l. 21 (ܝܟ 15). The translator gives the Syriac name for Saturn, ܟ̇ܐܘܢ. In the *Classical Review* for June 1890, p. 259, Prof. Margoliouth reviewing Budge's *Pseudo-Callisthenes* remarks as follows, "On p. 9 after the name of each planet we are told what the Persian for it is: surely this implies that the book which the translator had before him was in Persian. I will quote one of these, because Mr Budge has by accident missed the truth. The name of *Saturn* is omitted from the list, but instead we read, *the colour* ܓܘܢ *of a black stone, and the horoscopus of helanī which is called in Persian Farnūg'*. Mr Budge would emend Farnūg', but it is a Persian word signifying Saturn...... Hence ܓܘܢ 'colour' must stand for a word signifying *Saturn;* and this will be the Persian کیوان which the translator has read گون 'colour'."

It would seem to be a more direct process simply to emend the Syriac ܓܘܢ into ܟ̇ܐܘܢ.

p. 42, l. 2 (ܝܒ 10). The amours of the gods are, as might have been expected, the staple of early Christian apologetics. A few references may be given in illustration of the scornful summary of Olympic history given by Aristides.

Justin, *Apol.* I. 21. πόσους γὰρ υἱοὺς φάσκουσι τοῦ Διὸς οἱ παρ' ὑμῖν τιμώμενοι συγγραφεῖς, ἐπίστασθε· Ἑρμῆν μέν, λόγον τὸν ἑρμηνευτικὸν καὶ πάντων διδάσκαλον, Ἀσκληπιὸν δέ, καὶ θεραπευτὴν γενόμενον, κεραυνωθέντα ἀνεληλυθέναι εἰς οὐρανόν, Διόνυσον δὲ διασπαραχθέντα, Ἡρακλέα δὲ φυγῇ πόνων ἑαυτὸν πυρὶ δόντα, τοὺς ἐκ Λήδας δὲ Διοσκούρους, καὶ τὸν ἐκ Δανάης Περσέα,...

Justin, *Apol.* I. 25. θεῷ δὲ τῷ ἀγεννήτῳ καὶ ἀπαθεῖ ἑαυτοὺς ἀνεθήκαμεν, ὃν οὔτε ἐπ' Ἀντιόπην καὶ τὰς ἄλλας ὁμοίως οὐδὲ ἐπὶ Γανυμήδην δι' οἶστρον ἐληλυθέναι πειθόμεθα.

Recog. Clement. x. 22. "Antiopen Nyctei versus in Satyrum corrupit: ex qua nascuntur Amphion et Zethus; Alcmenam, mutatus in virum eius Amphitryonem; ex qua nascitur Hercules: Aeginam Asopi, mutatus in aquilam, ex qua nascitur Aeacus. Sed et Ganymedem Dardani mutatus nihilominus in aquilam stuprat; Mantheam Phoci, mutatus in ursum; ex qua nascitur Arctos: Danaen Acrisii, mutatus in aurum; ex qua nascitur Perseus: Europen Phoenicis, mutatus in taurum; ex qua nascitur Minos, et Rhadamanthus Sarpedonque: Eurymedusam Achelai, mutatus in formicam;

ex qua nascitur Myrmidon: Thaliam Aetnam nympham, mutatus in vulturem; ex qua nascuntur apud Siciliam Palixi: Imandram Geneani apud Rhodum, mutatus in imbrem: Cassiopiam, mutatus in virum eius Phoenicem; ex qua nascitur Anchinos: Ledam Thesti, mutatus in cycnum; ex qua nascitur Helena: et iterum eandem, mutatus in stellam; ex qua nascuntur Castor et Pollux: Lamiam, mutatus in upupam: Mnemosynen, mutatus in pastorem; ex qua nascuntur Musae novem: Nemesin, mutatus in anserem: Semelen Cadmiam mutatus in ignem; ex qua nascitur Dionysus," etc.

See also Ps. Justin, *Oratio ad Gentiles* = Ambrose, *Hypomnemata* (Cureton, *Spic. Syr.* pp. 63, 64) for a similar sketch to that of Aristides.

[l. 4 (ܡܒ 11). Pasiphae is an erroneous insertion in the Syriac.

l. 6 (ܡܒ 13). ܣܛܪܐ seems to be an attempt to render *σάτυρον*. In the Syriac of Ambrose (*Spic. Syr.* ܠܛ 16) the Greek word is transliterated.

l. 7 (ܡܒ 14). ܕܣܗܪܐ. Our translator seems to have read ΣΕΛΗΝΗΣ for ΣΕΜΕΛΗΣ.

l. 11 (ܡܒ 19). ܩܣܛܘܪ ܘܦܘܠܘܕܘܩܣ. ܘܐܠܢܐ ܘܦܠܘܕܘܣ. 'Castor and Polydeuces and Helene (ܐܠܢܐ) and Paludus.' This last word is a *vox nihili*; and the confusion has arisen in the following manner. The Greek has 'Castor and Helene and Polydeuces.' The Syriac scribe has written Polydeuces in its more obvious position immediately after Castor, and then the second Polydeuces has suffered corruption.

l. 18 (ܡܓ 6. Gr. p. 105, l. 15). *τῶν θεῶν αὐτῶν* Codd. AW. Syr.

l. 30 (ܡܓ 16). ܘܣܝܡ ܩܘܒܥܐ ܒܪܫܗ in the Syr. alone. Comp. 'cum pilleo Vulcanus et malleo.' Arnob. *adv. nat.* VI. 12.]

l. 31 (ܡܓ 17). For the ornaments made by Hephaestus, and sarcastic Christian remarks thereon, we may cite

Tatian, *Oratio ad Graecos*, c. VIII. *Ὁ γὰρ ἀμφιγυήεις, ὡς εἰκός, ὁ πόρπας καὶ γναμπτὰς ἕλικας δημιουργῶν τοῖς κοροκοσμίοις ἠπάτησε τὴν ἀμήτορα παῖδα καὶ ὀρφανήν* (sc. Ἀθηνᾶν).

[l. 37 (ܡܕ 2). ܦܫܝܚܐ, 'maimed.' The Greek has *κυλλόν*: but it is an impossible epithet for Hermes. The corruption however must have been a very early one. The Pembroke College MS. has *δόλιον* as a suggestion in the margin; but this is merely a conjectural emendation of the seventeenth century. The Latin version has 'uersipellem.' Probably *κυλλὸν* has slipped in from the description of Hephaestus just above. It may be noted however that 'versipellis' = מִרְמָה Prov. xiv. 25, Vulg., where the LXX. has *δόλιος*, which is elsewhere used as an epithet of Hermes. If therefore the Latin really represents a Greek word, and is not a mere guess, *δόλιον* would seem to be appropriate, and it is not very unlike *κυλλόν*.

ܘܕܪܪܐ ('and an athlete'). An addition in the Syr., referring to Hermes as the inventor of the palaestra. Comp. 'curat Mercurius ceromas, pugillatibus et luctationibus praeest,' Arnob. *adv. nat.* III. 23.

p. 43, l. 7 (ܕ 11). The Syr. read Λακεδαίμονα or Λακεδαιμόνιον and omitted υἱόν.

l. 25 (ܗ 7). ὑπὸ τῶν Τιτάνων. Comp. Arnob. *adv. nat.* I. 41, v. 19. The Syr. has the singular.

l. 29 (ܗ 12). ܗܢܐ ܣ̈ܢܝܬܐ ... ܠܒܥܠܕܒ̈ܒܐ. Peculiar to the Syriac. Comp. τά τ' ἐχθρὰ μισεῖν, Eur. *Herc. Fur.* 586.

p. 44, l. 1 (ܗ 21, 22). ܟܢܪܬܐ ܘܢܩܘܫܐ, lit. 'a cithara, and a striker' (cf. ܘ 5). This last word might mean the 'plectrum'; or it might mean another musical instrument. Cf. Arnob. *adv. nat.* VI. 12, 'cum plectro et fidibus Delius.'

The Greek has κιθάραν καὶ ἐπαυθίδα (or ἐπανθίδα, or ἐπαυλίδα). The emendations πληκτίδα and πηκτίδα have little to commend them. The Latin version has 'tibiam.']

l. 31 (ܘ 5). [The paragraph on Rhea and the following one on Proserpine are not in the Greek.] The Fathers not infrequently allude to the myth of Rhea and Atys. [Cf. Tatian, *ad Graecos*, 8, 'Ρέα μὲν γάρ, ἣν οἱ ἀπὸ τῶν Φρυγίων ὀρῶν Κυβέλην φασίν,...διὰ τὸν ἐρώμενον ταύτης Ἄττιν.]

The story is apparently Phrygian in origin, though very similar in its details to forms from the further East. Lucian (*De dea Syra*, 33) describing the three images in the temple at Hierapolis says that the first two are Zeus and Hera, and the third καλέεται δὲ σημήιον καὶ ὑπ' αὐτῶν Ἀσσυρίων οὐδέ τι ὄνομα ἴδιον αὐτῷ ἔθεντο. Baethgen (*Beiträge zur Semitischen Religionsgeschichte*) p. 73 most ingeniously conjectures this to be a misunderstanding of Lucian's; σημεῖον=אתא=עתא which last stands for *Atti* or *Atys*: the name appearing in a variety of forms, sometimes alone, sometimes combined with other deities, and sometimes as a factor in proper names: e.g. in Bardesanes *De Fato* we are told that the men of Edessa down to the time of Abgar used to sacrifice their foreskins to Tharatha: this seems to be a late form עתרעתא=עשתר+עתא or Istar+Atta.

As to the establishment of dances in honour of Atys, these are a characteristic feature of Semitic orgiastic worship. One of the best illustrations is the temple of Baal-Marcod, which stands on a spur of the Lebanon above Beyrout, and where there are many inscriptions from the ancient temple built into the walls of a modern convent. The name implies *Lord of Dances* and in one inscription given by Waddington (Inscr. Syr. No. 1855) is directly paraphrased as κοίρανε κώμων.

[p. 45, l. 11 (ܫ 2). ܕܐܝܬ ܠܗ ܐܪܒܥܐ in the Syriac alone, taken from the formula in l. 9.]

l. 22 (ܫ 13). According to our apologist Isis fled to Byblos in Syria; and this agrees with Plutarch *De Iside et Osiride*, that Byblos was a sanctuary of Isis; now we know from Lucian *De Dea Syra* c. 6 that the great sanctuary at Byblos was a sanctuary of Aphrodite Βυβλίη (cf. Strabo XVI. 2, p. 362 Βύβλος='Αδώνιδος ἱερά). We should therefore have to assume that

Byblos was the centre at once of an Isis-cult and an Aphrodite-cult which is the same thing as an Astarte-cult, for our apologist tells us to equate the Greek Aphrodite to the Syrian Astera. We must then assume either that the two forms of worship existed side by side, or that there had been a fusion of the two cults, the latter hypothesis being favoured by the similarity between the case of Aphrodite weeping for Tammuz and Isis lamenting Osiris. Moreover the confusion extends to the personalities of Osiris and Adonis: and Movers quotes from Stephanus of Byzantium as follows: *'Αμαθοῦς πόλις Κύπρου ἀρχαιοτάτη, ἐν ᾗ Ἄδωνις Ὄσιρις ἐτιμᾶτο ὃν Αἰγύπτιον ὄντα Κύπριοι καὶ Φοίνικες ἰδιοποιοῦντο.*

Whether, then, we pay attention to the dead gods or the wailing goddesses, there is a great similarity in the matter of the two religions. And we have suggested that in the sanctuary at Byblos the two cults may have been carried on side by side. One other question suggests itself, viz. whether they may not both be modifications of some earlier worship. We have some reason for believing that the original Byblos-worship was that of the Assyrian Baaltis, for Philo Byblius says that this city was the gift of Cronos to Baaltis. Now this Baaltis, the Assyrian mother of the gods, appears in the west in a Greek form, first under the name of Mylitta by a common change in the pronunciation of *b* and *m*. But this Mylitta is affirmed by Herodotus to be capable of equation with Aphrodite (I. 131 *καλέουσι δὲ 'Ασσύριοι τὴν 'Αφροδίτην Μύλιττα*) and this would lead us to recognize in the sanctuary at Byblos an original sanctuary of Mylitta.

[p. 46, l. 2 (ܠܛ 6). We should probably read ܕܢܘܙܐ and transfer ܒܠܚܘܕ to the preceding clause.]

l. 3 (ܠܛ 7). The local variation in the Egyptian worship appears in Herodotus and is alluded to by the Christian fathers:

Herod. II. 69. *τοῖσι μὲν δὴ τῶν Αἰγυπτίων ἱροί εἰσι οἱ κροκόδειλοι, τοῖσι δὲ οὔ, ἀλλὰ ἅτε πολεμίους περιέπουσι.*

Justin, *Apol.* I. 24. *ἄλλων ἀλλαχοῦ καὶ δένδρα σεβομένων καὶ ποταμοὺς καὶ μῦς καὶ αἰλούρους καὶ κροκοδείλους καὶ τῶν ἀλόγων ζώων τὰ πολλά.*

Recog. Clement. v. 20. "Nam alii eorum bovem qui Apis dicitur colendum tradidere, alii hircum; alii gattas; nonnulli ibin; quidam serpentem; piscem quoque, et caepas et cloacas, crepitus ventris, pro numinibus habendos esse docuerunt: et alia innumerabilia quae pudet etiam nominare."

[See Mayor's notes to Juv. *Sat.* xv., for a storehouse of references on this point.]

Of the objects of worship mentioned by Aristides, some are rather difficult to identify. The first question that arises is with regard to the animal denoted by ܫܘܪܢܐ. In the Dublin MS. of the Fables of Syntipas, Fable 45, we find

ܫܘܪܢܐ ܐܘܟܡܬ ܦܬܪܐ

The word therefore stands for a cat. The fable to which we have referred is

No. 40 in Landsberger's *Fabeln des Sophos*. The Syriac reference is due to Prof. Bensly.

[ܫܪܘܢܐ = *αἴλουρος* occurs in Lagarde's *Geop.* 116. 19 (Gr. XIV. 4), and the form ܫܘܪܢܐ in *Geop.* 114. 22 (Gr. XIV. 15).]

Twice there is an allusion to sacred fish, once in a general manner, where we should perhaps correct ܢܘܢܐ to ܝܘܢܐ, thus placing the dove with the rest of the sacred birds; and once in a special manner where the name of the fish is given as Shibbuta. What fish is this? Is it the same as the *λεπιδωτὸς* of Herodotus (II. 72)?

νομίζουσι δὲ καὶ τῶν ἰχθύων τὸν καλεύμενον λεπιδωτὸν ἱρὸν εἶναι καὶ τὴν ἔγχελυν.

The name of the fish is found in the Arabic Lexicons as شَبُّوط : and in Freytag it is described as being like a shad (alosa) but three times larger, and is said to be exported from the Euphrates to Aleppo. Cf. Levy, *Neuhebräisches und Chaldäisches Wörterbuch*, IV. pp. 496, 678.

For a similar account of this fish we may refer to a note by Kosegarten in *Z. D. M. G.* IV. 249. Kosegarten merely quotes the Kamus and Freytag, but an editorial note adds that the fish in question is the Latin *rhombus*, i.e. the turbot.

[ܫܠܘܪܐ, 'silurus,' 'the shad-fish' (cf. Mayor's note on Juv. *Sat.* IV. 32). This comes in somewhat inappropriately: and it may have arisen from a misreading of *αἴλουρος*. 'The cat' however is represented lower down by ܫܪܘܢܐ.

ܢܘܢܐ, 'the fish,' is evidently out of place here in the midst of the birds, and indeed it is repeated later on, 'the fish Shibbuta.' It would be easy to emend ܝܘܢܐ, 'the dove'; but all the birds are of the ravenous type. There is just a possibility that ܫܠܐ ܢܘ̈ܢܐ may have been the original word. It occurs in the Pesh. Vers. of Levit. xi. 17, where the corresponding word in the A. V. is 'the cormorant.'

l. 14 (ܝܚ 18). ܥܡ ܚܒܪ̈ܘܬܗܘܢ. The Syriac translator read *ἑταίρων* for *ἑτέρων*.]

l. 27 (ܟ 6). Here the language may be illustrated by a reference to Justin, *Apol.* I. 9, *τί γὰρ δεῖ εἰδόσιν ὑμῖν λέγειν ἃ τὴν ὕλην οἱ τεχνῖται διατιθέασι ξέοντες καὶ τέμνοντες καὶ χωνεύοντες καὶ τύπτοντες;* and *Ep. ad Diogn.* 2, *οὐχ ὃ μὲν αὐτῶν λιθοξόος, ὃ δὲ χαλκεύς, ὃ δὲ ἀργυροκόπος, ὃ δὲ κεραμεὺς ἔπλασεν;*

[p. 47, l. 20 (ܟܐ 15, 16). Our translator has evidently taken *τὴν τῶν θεῶν φυσιολογίαν* in the sense of 'the counting of the natures of the gods.']

p. 49, l. 1 (ܟܠ 21). The description given of the Christians in this chapter recalls in many points the "Teaching of the Apostles." To begin with, we have the golden rule in a negative form, which may be compared with the first chapter of the Teaching, and with a similar Syriac sentence given as a saying of Menander in Land, *Anecdota* I. 69, from Cod. Mus. Britt. 14658, fol. 166 *r*, as follows:

ܟܠ ܡܕܡ ܕܥܠܝܟ ܣܢܐ܂ ܐܢܬ ܠܚܒܪܟ ܠܐ ܬܨܒܐ ܠܡܥܒܕ܂

which is a very different rendering from that of Aristides, and may be suspected from its ascription to Menander to be a translation of some metrical form of the golden rule.

The version in Aristides, from its setting in the text of the Apology, between two precepts against idolatry, viz. idols in the form of man, and meats offered to idols, reminds one of the Codex Bezae which completes the rule of the Council at Jerusalem (Acts xv. 29) by adding the words

καὶ ὅσα μὴ θέλετε ἑαυτοῖς γείνεσθαι, ἑτέρῳ μὴ ποιεῖν.

But whether the sentence stood in this connexion in the primitive Didascalia, we cannot say.

Other parallels will suggest themselves, as when Aristides describes Christian practice in words that seem to answer to

οὐ μοιχεύσεις, οὐ πορνεύσεις, οὐ ψευδομαρτυρήσεις, οὐκ ἀποστερήσεις, οὐκ ἐπιθυμήσεις τὰ τοῦ πλησίον,

which does not differ much from c. II. of the Teaching. The parallelisms, however, are only just sufficient to suggest an acquaintance with the Teaching on the part of Aristides; and his whole presentation of Christian ethics is vastly superior to anything in the Didaché, and can only be paralleled for beauty and spirituality in the pages of Tertullian.

[l. 3 (ܟܕ 1) ܡܒܝܐܝܢ, 'they comfort.' This is a mistranslation of the Greek word *παρακαλοῦσιν*, which in this place clearly means not 'to comfort,' but 'to exhort.']

p. 50, l. 37 (ܟܘ 17). The belief that the world stands by reason of the Christians occurs also in the following passages:

Justin, *Apol.* I. 45. *ἕως ἂν...συντελέσθῃ ὁ ἀριθμὸς τῶν προεγνωσμένων αὐτῷ ἀγαθῶν γινομένων καὶ ἐναρέτων, δι' οὓς καὶ μηδέπω τὴν ἐπικύρωσιν πεποίηται.*

Justin, *Apol.* II. 7. *ὅθεν καὶ ἐπιμένει ὁ θεὸς τὴν σύγχυσιν καὶ κατάλυσιν τοῦ παντὸς κόσμου μὴ ποιῆσαι...διὰ τὸ σπέρμα τῶν χριστιανῶν, ὃ γινώσκει ἐν τῇ φύσει ὅτι αἴτιόν ἐστιν.*

Ep. ad Diogn. 6. *χριστιανοὶ κατέχονται μὲν ὡς ἐν φρουρᾷ τῷ κόσμῳ, αὐτοὶ δὲ συνέχουσι τὸν κόσμον.*

The extract from the Epistle to Diognetus is nearer to the idea of Aristides than the passages quoted from Justin.

[l. 37 (ܟܘ 17). ܘܠܝܬ ܠܗ ܦܠܓܘܬܐ܃ ܕܠܐ... An instance of the so-called pleonastic negative retained from the Greek. Cf. Plato *Hip. min.* 369 D *ἐγώ τοι οὐκ ἀμφισβητῶ μὴ οὐχὶ σὲ εἶναι σοφώτερον ἢ ἐμέ.*]

p. 51, l. 2 (ܟܘ 19). The expression ܡܬܥܪܓܠܝܢ which we have rendered "rolling themselves," occurs again in Melito, *Oration* (Cureton, *Spic. Syr.* p. ܟܛ, 25),

ܡܢܐ ܡܬܥܪܓܠ ܐܢܬ ܥܠ ܐܪܥܐ ܘܡܬܟܫܦ ܐܢܬ:
ܠܨ̈ܘܪܬܐ ܕܠܐ ܡܪܓܫܢ.

("Why rollest thou thyself upon the earth, and offerest supplication to things which are without perception?")

[l. 13 (ܒܝ 7). ܠܘܥܒܐ, 'ridicule,' 'scorn.' This word seems often to be confused with ܠܘܚܫܐ, 'horror,' which occurs as a variant for it, 2 Pet. ii. 18 (compare the Urmi edition of 1846 and the New York edition of 1886): cf. 4 Macc. 14. 1.]

l. 32 (ܒܣ 4). For the expression "gateway of light" cf. Barnab. 18, Ὀδοὶ δύο εἰσὶν διδαχῆς καὶ ἐξουσίας, ἥ τε τοῦ φωτὸς καὶ ἡ τοῦ σκότους, and Justin, *Dial.* 7, εὔχου δέ σοι πρὸ πάντων φωτὸς ἀνοιχθῆναι πύλας· οὐ γὰρ συνοπτα οὐδὲ συννοητὰ πᾶσίν ἐστιν, εἰ μή τῳ θεὸς δῷ συνιέναι καὶ ὁ χριστὸς αὐτοῦ.

l. 36 (ܒܣ 8). The concluding words may be compared with Justin *Dial.* 58, ἐν ᾗπερ μέλλει κρίσει διὰ τοῦ κυρίου μου Ἰησοῦ Χριστοῦ ὁ ποιητὴς τῶν ὅλων θεὸς ποιεῖσθαι.

It will be seen that we have given especial attention to the illustrations furnished to the text of our author by the undoubted writings of Justin and by the Epistle to Diognetus. We have not, however, been able to agree with the opinion of Doulcet in reference to the latter writing, nor with the tradition of Jerome in reference to Justin's imitation of Aristides. It may, however, be taken for granted, from the parallels adduced, that Justin and Aristides are nearly contemporary.

APPENDIX

THE REMAINS OF THE ORIGINAL GREEK

OF

THE APOLOGY OF ARISTIDES

BY

J. ARMITAGE ROBINSON M.A.

FELLOW AND ASSISTANT TUTOR OF CHRIST'S COLLEGE CAMBRIDGE

THE ORIGINAL GREEK OF THE APOLOGY OF ARISTIDES.

While Mr Harris was passing the preceding pages through the press, he kindly allowed me to read the proof sheets of his translation of the Syriac. Shortly afterwards as I was turning over Latin Passionals at Vienna in a fruitless search for a lost MS. of the Passion of S. Perpetua, I happened to be reading portions of the Latin Version of the 'Life of Barlaam and Josaphat,' and presently I stumbled across words which recalled the manner and the thought of Aristides. Turning back to the beginning of a long speech, I found the words: 'Ego, rex, providentia Dei veni in mundum; et considerans celum et terram, mare et solem et lunam, et cetera, admiratus sum ornatum eorum.' The Greek text of 'Barlaam and Josaphat' is printed in Migne's edition of the works of S. John of Damascus: and it was not long before I was reading the actual words of the Apologist himself: Ἐγὼ, *βασιλεῦ, προνοίᾳ θεοῦ ἦλθον εἰς τὸν κόσμον· καὶ θεωρήσας τὸν οὐρανὸν καὶ γῆν καὶ θάλασσαν, ἥλιόν τε καὶ σελήνην καὶ τὰ λοιπὰ, ἐθαύμασα τὴν διακόσμησιν τούτων.* It was with some impatience that I waited for my return to Cambridge, in order to examine the proof sheets again, and so to discover by a comparison of the Syriac Version how much of our author was really in our hands in the original tongue.

To what extent then does the Greek speech in 'Barlaam and Josaphat' correspond to the Syriac Version of the Apology of Aristides? In other words: How far may we claim to have recovered the original Apology in the language in which it was written?

The circumstances under which the Greek has been preserved at all demand first a brief notice. 'The Life of Barlaam and

Joasaph (or Josaphat)' is the title of a religious romance, which, by a tradition dating at the latest from the 11th century, has been connected with the name of S. John of Damascus. It is true that SS. Barlaam and Josaphat find a place in the Calendars of both the Eastern and Western Churches: but it has long been recognised that their 'Life' is a working up of the Indian legend of Sakya Mouni, or Buddha; and a number of the apologues scattered over the piece have also been identified as Eastern stories of a very early date.

The popularity of the book has rarely been equalled in the history of literature. Before the 13th century it had been translated into almost every known language of the world; an Icelandic Version was made about the year 1200 by the order of a Norwegian king; and there is an early English rendering in metre.

It has lately been argued, and I think with success, by Zotenberg[1], that the book is much earlier than the time of S. John of Damascus; and that the matter which it has in common with several of his works is drawn from previous writers such as Gregory Nazianzen and Nemesius. This being so, it may well go back to the 6th century, or perhaps earlier still.

The outline of the story is as follows. An Eastern king, named Abenner, persecutes the Christians, and especially the monks, whom he expels from India. He is childless; but at length the young prince Josaphat is born, and the astrologers, as in the case of Buddha, predict for him an extraordinary greatness. They add however that he will become a Christian. This his father determines to prevent. He encloses him in a magnificent palace; allows none but young and beautiful attendants to approach him; and forbids the mention of sorrow, disease and death, and above all of Christianity. When the prince is grown to man's estate he asks his father to give him liberty. His entreaties are at length successful, as it seems that otherwise his life will be saddened, and the first step will have been taken towards his reception of the forbidden faith. He is allowed to drive out, but the way is carefully prepared beforehand, and guarded from the

[1] *Notice sur le livre de Barlaam et Joasaph*, Paris, 1886. A useful summary of the literature on 'B. and J.' is given by Krumbacher in Iwan von Müller's *Handbuch der alt. Wissensch.* vol. 9, pt. 1, p. 469.

intrusion of sad sights and sounds. At last precaution fails, and he sees one day a lame man and a blind man, and another day a man wrinkled and tottering with age. He inquires whether accidents may befal any man, and whether every man must come at last to miserable old age or death. There is but one answer: and the joy has fled from his life.

A monk of the desert, Barlaam by name, is divinely warned of the prince's condition; and comes disguised as a merchant, and obtains entrance to the prince to shew him a most goodly pearl. In a long discourse, into which Gospel parables and Eastern apologues are skilfully woven, he expounds to him the vanity of the world and the Christian hope of the life to come. In the end the prince is baptized, and Barlaam disappears into the desert. The king, distracted with rage on the one hand and love for his son on the other, casts about for means to shake his faith. A wily counsellor propounds a plan. An old man, who closely resembles Barlaam and who is an admirable actor, is to defend the cause of Christianity in an open debate. He is to make a lame speech, and be easily refuted by the rhetoricians. The prince, seeing his instructor baffled, will renounce his newly accepted faith.

The day comes, and Nachor, for this is the old man's name, appears to personate Barlaam. Josaphat addresses him in vigorous terms, reminding him of the difficulties in which his instructions have involved him, and promising him a miserable fate if he fails to prove his point. Nachor is not reassured by this mode of address; but after some preliminary fencing on the part of the rhetoricians he begins to speak. Such, says our author, was the providence of God, that like Balaam of old he had come to curse, but he ended by blessing with manifold blessings. Or, as he says again, lowering his metaphor; 'He beckoned to the multitude to keep silence, and he opened his mouth, and like Balaam's ass he spake that which he had not purposed to speak; and he said to the king: I, O king, by the providence of God came into the world....'

The Apology of Aristides carried the day: and, to cut the long story short, Nachor himself and finally the king and his people were converted: and at last Josaphat, who in due course succeeds his father, resigns his kingdom and retires to spend his days with Barlaam in the desert[1].

What modifications then were required to fit the Apology for its new surroundings? Surprisingly few.

(1) The king is of course addressed throughout: but this is so in the original piece. Only a short sentence at the end praises the wise choice of the king's son.

(2) The fourfold division of mankind into Barbarians and Greeks, Jews and Christians, was out of place in an Indian court. We find in its stead a triple division—Worshippers of false gods, Jews and Christians: and the first class is subdivided into Chaldeans, Greeks and Egyptians, as being the ringleaders and teachers of heathenism to the rest of the world[2].

(3) A short passage at the close, in which the Christians are defended from the foul charges so often brought against them in the first days, was out of date and consequently has disappeared.

(4) If we add to this that there are traces of compression here and there, and that the description of the Christians at the close is considerably curtailed, we have exhausted the list of substantial modifications which can with certainty be detected.

The substance of the Apology then is for the most part faithfully preserved: but can we say that with the exceptions already named we have the actual Greek words of Aristides himself?

The first and most obvious test to apply is that of comparative length. The Syriac is, speaking roughly, half as long again as the Greek: and this difference is not fully accounted for by the combination in the latter of the preliminary statements about the Jews and the Christians with the fuller descriptions of them given later on, and by the omission of nearly two pages at the close.

[1] A small fragment (below, p. 104), which is omitted from its proper place in Nachor's speech, is embodied in an early part of the book (Bois. p. 49). We thus see that the writer had the Apology before him at the outset of his work, and designed his plot with the definite intention of introducing it.

[2] See, however, below, p. 90; where reasons are given which tend to shew that the Greek has preserved the original triple division, as against the Syriac and the Armenian.

The fact is that the Syriac has a large number of repetitions and not a few additional details which are absent from the Greek. Thus at the end of each description of the several gods and goddesses of the heathen, the Syriac Version points the moral and drives home the inevitable conclusion: and again such histories as those of Kronos and of Isis and Osiris are somewhat more elaborately told in this form of the Apology.

Are we then to conclude that the Syriac translator has enlarged upon his original, and supplemented it here and there from his own resources? Or must we say that the author of 'Barlaam and Josaphat' found the Apology too long for his purpose, and pruned away unnecessary details?

The second hypothesis has a *prima facie* probability, and the general reputation for faithfulness of Syriac translators might point us in the same direction. On the other side it is to be observed that, even when read in the light of the Syriac Version, the Greek form is still felt to be a harmonious and consistent whole: and it certainly does not convey the impression of serious mutilation. The genius of the author, in so framing his plot as perfectly to suit the Apology which he intended to introduce, needs no further praise than is involved in the fact that hitherto no one has had the remotest suspicion that he did not write the speech of Nachor himself. If anything could make his genius appear more extraordinary still, it would be the proof that he had consistently compressed the original document in almost every alternate sentence without leaving any traces of rough handling: but such proof is at present not forthcoming. In the absence of further documents, the question must be decided largely by internal evidence and the minute investigation of the points of difference. But there are two external sources from which light may be thrown upon the problem.

(1) In 1855 Cureton published in his *Spicilegium Syriacum* a treatise bearing the title: 'Hypomnemata, which Ambrose, a chief man of Greece, wrote;' and commencing with the words: 'Do not suppose, men and Greeks, that without fit and just cause is my separation from your customs.' These words are the literal translation of the opening sentence of the *Oratio ad*

Gentiles traditionally ascribed to Justin Martyr: Μὴ ὑπολάβητε, ὦ ἄνδρες Ἕλληνες, ἄλογον ἢ ἀνεπίκριτον εἶναί μου τὸν ἐκ τῶν ὑμετέρων ἐθῶν χωρισμόν.

When we compare the original Greek with the Syriac Version of this document, we find that in point of length they stand to one another exactly as do the Greek and Syriac forms of the Apology of Aristides: that is to say, in either case the Syriac is about half as long again as the Greek. Moreover, as in the case of our Apology, the variation begins to shew itself immediately after the first sentence, which I have quoted. For the Greek continues thus: οὐδὲν γὰρ ἐν αὐτοῖς εὗρον ὅσιον ἢ θεοφιλές. αὐτὰ γὰρ τὰ τῶν ποιητῶν ὑμῶν συνθέματα λύσσης καὶ ἀκρασίας ἐστὶ μνημεῖα. τῷ γὰρ ἐν παιδείᾳ παρ' ὑμῖν προὔχοντι φοιτῶν τις πάντων ἀνθρώπων ἐστὶν ἀργαλεώτατος. πρώτιστα μὲν γάρ φασι τὸν Ἀγαμέμνονα, κ.τ.λ. But the Syriac replaces this by the following, as Cureton renders it: 'For I have investigated the whole of your wisdom of poetry, and rhetoric, and philosophy; and when I found not anything right or worthy of the Deity, I was desirous of investigating the wisdom of the Christians also, and of learning and seeing who they are, and when, and what is this its recent and strange production, or on what good things they rely who follow this wisdom, so as to speak the truth. Men and Greeks, when I had made the enquiry I found not any folly, as in the famous Homer, who says respecting the wars of the two rivals, "for the sake of Helen many of the Greeks perished at Troy, far from their beloved home." For first they say respecting Agamemnon,' &c.

Here then we have a similar problem to that of the Apology of Aristides; and in this case we are not hampered by the consideration that the Greek may possibly have been abbreviated to fit it for incorporation into a religious novel. Few will be disposed to challenge the verdict of Otto[1], that the Syriac translator has so altered and amplified his original as almost to have produced a new work.

We may give one more illustration of the manner in which the translator has proceeded. We have seen already that he has paraded at the outset his independent acquaintance with Homer.

[1] *Justini Opera*, tom. 2, p. xxix.

Where Ulysses is alluded to, later on, the Greek has a sentence full of satire and liable to be misunderstood. Ὁ γὰρ Ἰθακήσιος Λαερτιάδης ἐκ κακίας ἀρετὴν ἐνεπορεύσατο· ὅτι δὲ ἀγαθῆς φρονήσεως ἄμοιρος ἦν, ὁ κατὰ τὰς Σειρῆνας διάπλους ἐδήλωσεν, ὅτε μὴ ἠδυνήθη φρονήσει ἐμφράξαι τὴν ἀκοήν. Corresponding to this we find in the Syriac Version: 'But respecting the guile of Odysseus, son of Laertes, and his murders, who shall tell? For to a hundred and ten suitors in one day his house was a grave, and was filled with dead bodies and blood. And he it is that by his wickedness purchased praises, because by the excellence of his wisdom he was concealed: and he it is that, as ye say, sailed over the sea, and heard the voice of the Sirens, because he stopped his ears with wax.'

The translator then has first supplemented his author by introducing fresh details about Ulysses: and then he has totally missed the meaning of the Greek. He has obviously read it as if it were δι' ἀγαθῆς φρονήσεως ἀμαυρὸς ἦν, 'through the excellence of his wisdom he kept himself in the dark.' Then not seeing the point of φρονήσει ἐμφράξαι, he simply tells us that 'he stopped his ears with wax.' This of course the hero did not do: and the translator has got the Homeric story wrong: nor shall we mend matters much by inserting with Cureton the word 'not' after 'and heard.' We see at any rate plainly enough what was this Syrian's conception of a translator's function when his author seemed obscure.

The parallel between the two Apologies is the more striking, because the line of argument in these *Hypomnemata* vividly recalls parts of Aristides, and the same illustrations of the misdemeanours of the gods frequently reappear in almost the same language. The satire of the so-called Ambrosius is a much keener weapon than the simple narrative of Aristides: but there is not the same intensity of moral earnestness. It is quite credible that the later Apologist had the work of Aristides before him when he wrote, and endeavoured to reproduce the same arguments in what he thought was a more telling manner. Thus he says: Ἀνάγνωτε τῷ Διΐ, ἄνδρες Ἕλληνες, τὸν κατὰ πατρολῳῶν νόμον καὶ τὸ μοιχείας πρόστιμον καὶ τὴν παιδεραστίας αἰσχρότητα (cf. infra p. 109, l. 7). And again: Τί σεμνὸν ἐπιδείκνυται γυνὴ ὅπλοις κεκοσμημένη, κ.τ.λ.

(cf. p. 106, l. 24). And once more: Θέτω τὸν ζῆλον Ἥφαιστος, καὶ μὴ φθονείτω, εἰ πρεσβύτης ὢν καὶ κυλλὸς τὸν πόδα μεμίσητο, Ἄρης δὲ πεφίλητο νέος ὢν καὶ ὡραῖος (cf. p. 105, l. 18).

Enough then has been said to shew that a Syriac translator, finding an early Greek Apology and desiring to reproduce it in his own language, might have no scruple whatever in dealing very freely with his author, in expunging sentences which he was not able or did not care to translate, and in supplementing the original here and there out of his own resources. The Syriac translator of the *Oratio ad Gentiles* has clearly so treated his unknown author; and this fact removes any *a priori* objection to the supposition that the Syriac translator of Aristides has acted in a similar way.

(2) We are fortunate in having an additional source of evidence in the Armenian fragment which contains the opening sentences of the Apology. The Armenian translator has clearly done what we have had some reason to suspect in the case of the Syriac translator. He has dealt freely with his original, adding words and even sentences, and introducing the stock phrases of a later theology. But this, while it diminishes very considerably the amount of the evidence which can be produced from his version, does not materially affect its value as far as it goes. Phrases which are only found in the Armenian, or only found in the Syriac, may be dismissed as possibly the inventions of the respective translators: but there remains a considerable quantity of matter common to the two Versions, which therefore presupposes a Greek original. The question we have to ask is: What is the relation of this common matter to the Greek text now in our hands?

A preliminary point however demands attention: Is the Armenian translated from the Syriac, or is it an independent translation made directly or indirectly from the Greek itself?

A few instances in which the Armenian corresponds with the Greek against the Syriac will suffice to shew that it cannot come from the Syriac as we now have it.

In the opening sentence we have προνοίᾳ and 'providentia' (Arm.) against 'goodness' (Syr.). Immediately afterwards σελήνην and 'luna' (Arm.), which the Syriac omits. Lower down 'rectorem' three times corresponds to parts of διακρατεῖν, but there is nothing to answer to these in the Syriac. In the Christological passage near the end of the fragment, 'una cum Spiritu Sancto' (Arm.) answers to ἐν πνεύματι ἁγίῳ: and here again the Syriac has no equivalent.

Moreover in the description of the Divine nature the Armenian Version says: 'Ei neque colores sunt neque forma,' or as Mr Conybeare renders it 'Colour and form of Him there is not.' This corresponds to the Syriac phrase: 'He has no likeness, nor composition of members.' The Greek fails us here: but we may suppose that the Greek word which has been variously rendered 'colour' and 'likeness' was χρῶμα, as in the passage quoted by Mr Harris from Justin (supra p. 54): *οὐ χρῶμα ἔχον, οὐ σχῆμα.*

We may conclude then that the Armenian Version is not made from the Syriac Version in its present form[1]: and similar arguments could be adduced, if there were any necessity, to shew that the Syriac Version is independent of the Armenian.

I have mentioned already almost all the cases in which the Syriac fails to reproduce in any form matter which is common to the Greek and the Armenian. They scarcely make up between them more than a dozen words. The additional matter found only in the Syriac Version is more considerable.

First, there is the second title which introduces the name of Antoninus Pius, and so conflicts with the first which has the support of the Armenian[2].

Then we have the following phrases:

(*a*) Who is hidden in them and concealed from them: and this is well known, that...

[1] See however p. 90, where the fourfold division of mankind, common to Syr. and Arm., is further criticised.

[2] Mr Harris inclines to accept this second title of the Syriac Version as the true one: see above, pp. 7 ff. But the course of the present argument tends to shew that the Syriac translator has introduced many arbitrary changes on his own account: and this makes me the more unwilling to accept his testimony against that of the Armenian Version, which has moreover the explicit statement of Eusebius to support it. The circumstances under which the Greek has been preserved to us necessitated the omission of the title altogether; so that no direct evidence on the point reaches us from that quarter.

(*b*) And in saying that He is complete, I mean that there is no deficiency in Him.

(*c*) And that which has an end is dissoluble.

(*d*) From man He asks nothing.

(*e*) Who begat...from whom was born...who begat.

(*f*) Of their religion (bis).

(*g*) And it is said that (in the Christological statement)... and clad Himself with...and they say that...who are well known.

I have taken no account of the many places in which the two Versions wander far from each other, and yet seem to have some common basis. Here the Armenian is obviously the worst offender, and its interpolations are far more numerous.

We now turn to the Greek itself in the passage covered by the Armenian fragment, in order to see first of all to what extent what we actually have faithfully represents the Greek words which underlie the Syriac and Armenian Versions.

(1) The first sentence which bears the appearance of compression is the following: *ἀνώτερον πάντων τῶν παθῶν καὶ ἐλαττωμάτων, ὀργῆς τε καὶ λήθης καὶ ἀγνοίας καὶ τῶν λοιπῶν.* This seems to bring together several more expanded phrases witnessed to by the two Versions, which however do not agree with one another sufficiently closely to allow us to make a certain reconstruction.

(2) In the sentence, *ὅπως ἴδωμεν τίνες αὐτῶν μετέχουσι τῆς ἀληθείας καὶ τίνες τῆς πλάνης*, a word, corresponding to 'praefatas' (Arm.) and 'which we have spoken concerning Him' (Syr.), has dropped out before *ἀληθείας*: and instead of *τῆς πλάνης* there must have been a verb in the original; 'ab eis erraverint' (Arm.), 'have erred therefrom' (Syr.). The difference is of course exceedingly slight in itself: but it is important from a critical point of view, when we are testing the faithfulness with which the author of 'Barlaam and Josaphat' has preserved to us the original Apology. We may probably trace in this sentence the influence of an almost identical one, which comes later on, after the preliminary descriptions of the four races have been given. As the Greek combines these descriptions with the fuller

accounts afterwards given, it brings the parallel sentences close together.

(3) The division of mankind into three races, and not four, has been already noticed[1].

(4) It is just at this point that the most serious divergence is found: viz., the omission of the preliminary descriptions of the races, as noted above. This was perhaps the result of the change in the method of their division, which rendered unsuitable the sentences which immediately followed.

Once more, we have to ask how much is there which can be shewn, by the united testimony of the Versions, to have stood in the original Greek, and which yet finds no place in the Greek which has survived.

(1) In the first line both Versions have 'into this world,' while the Greek has *εἰς τὸν κόσμον*: but the demonstrative may perhaps only be an attempt to represent the Greek article. The first real gap is eight lines lower down, where the Versions are very divergent[2], but yet point to some common original. It is probable that the Greek text at this point was difficult or corrupt, and so was omitted altogether by the author of 'Barlaam and Josaphat.' The topic is the difficulty and uselessness of elaborate investigation concerning the Divine nature: and the conclusion is drawn 'that one should fear God and not grieve man' (Syr.), 'utpote unum Deum nos adorare oportet: unumquemque autem nostrum proximum suum sicut semetipsum diligere' (Arm.). To this the Greek has nothing to correspond.

(2) For the list of properties of the Divine nature we have in the Greek merely the compressed sentence, part of which was quoted above. The Versions agree in telling us more fully that 'God is not begotten, not made'; 'without beginning, because that which has a beginning has also an end'; 'without name, because that which has a name belongs to the created'; 'without likeness (Arm. 'colores,' implying *χρῶμα* in the Greek) and composition of members (Arm. 'forma'), for he who possesses this is associated with things created' (Arm. 'mensurabilis est, limiti-

[1] See above, p. 70; and further remarks on p. 90.

[2] The Syriac is untranslateable as it stands.

busque cogitur'); 'neither male nor female' (Arm. adds 'quia cupiditatibus agitatur qui huic est distinctioni obnoxius'); 'the heavens do not contain Him: but the heavens and all things visible and invisible are contained in Him'; 'He has no adversary' (in the reason for this there is fresh discrepancy); 'He is altogether wisdom and understanding.' After this the Greek, as we have it, is again, for the next seven lines, obviously the same as that which lay before the translators.

(3) Now comes the new division of mankind, and the Greek has omitted the following: 'Now the Barbarians reckon— and from Dionysus,' about six lines.

(4) The preliminary accounts of the Jews and the Christians are found in the Greek later on, where they are amalgamated with the fuller descriptions. The account of the Jews agrees fairly well with that given in the Versions, especially in the Armenian. The additions in the Greek will be noticed presently. It adds at the close: *καθάπερ εἷς ἐξ αὐτῶν (τῶν ἀποστόλων) τὰς καθ' ἡμᾶς περιῆλθε χώρας, τὸ δόγμα κηρύττων τῆς ἀληθείας.*

(5) The Christological passage which follows is so important that it will be an advantage to have the three forms side by side.

Οἱ δὲ χριστιανοὶ γενεαλογοῦνται ἀπὸ τοῦ κυρίου Ἰησοῦ Χριστοῦ. οὗτος δὲ ὁ υἱὸς τοῦ θεοῦ τοῦ ὑψίστου ὁμολογεῖται ἐν πνεύματι ἁγίῳ ἀπ' οὐρανοῦ καταβὰς διὰ τὴν σωτηρίαν τῶν ἀνθρώπων· καὶ ἐκ παρθένου ἁγίας γεννηθεὶς, ἀσπόρως τε καὶ ἀφθόρως, σάρκα ἀνέλαβε, καὶ ἀνεφάνη ἀνθρώποις.

The Christians then reckon the beginning of their religion *from Jesus Christ, Who is named the Son of God most High;* and it is said that God *came down from heaven, and from a Hebrew virgin took* and clad Himself with *flesh;* and there dwelt in a daughter *of man the Son of God.*

Christianorum tandem genus a Domino Jesu Christo oritur. Ipse Dei altissimi est Filius, et una cum *Spiritu Sancto* reuelatus est nobis: *de coelis descendit, ex Hebraea uirgine natus,* ex uirgine *carnem assumpsit,* assumptaque *humana* natura *semetipsum Dei Filium reuelauit.*

Here I have distinguished by spaced type or by italics every word, which having a double testimony may be referred to the original Greek. As regards omissions, the Greek omits only the epithet 'Hebrew', which it replaces by the epithet *ἁγία,* and the second reference to 'the Son of God,' where however there is a discrepancy between the two Versions. The Syriac omits *κυρίου,* πνεύματι ἁγίῳ, γεννηθείς, ἀνεφάνη. The Armenian has no omission that can be certainly traced. The additions in each case may be seen at a glance. The Armenian has practically none; though a few lines further down the epithet corresponding to θεοτόκος is applied to the Virgin. The most serious change is that in the Syriac, where the word 'God' is inserted as the subject of the verbs which follow. The passage is one which was more likely than any other in the whole piece to tempt later writers to make changes of their own. It is to be noted that here the Greek in spite of its additions represents the original Apology much more faithfully than the Syriac does.

(6) In the words which follow next the Versions do not agree either with one another, or with the Greek, which has displaced the sentence and gives it a little lower down. But both the Greek and the Syriac appeal to a written Gospel, which the king might read if he chose.

(7) The repetition of the fourfold division of mankind is of course not found in the Greek, and with it has disappeared the problematical sentence: 'To God then ministers wind, and to angels fire; but to demons water, and to men earth.' At this point the Armenian fragment ends.

What then is the result of our investigation of this opening passage, in which alone we have a triple testimony to the contents of the original Apology?

(1) There is one serious modification (if, indeed, we have not here the original) in the Greek, as it is preserved to us; but it was necessitated by the conditions of its reproduction in its new surroundings.

(2) There is one serious displacement in the Greek; but this was almost necessitated by the modification just mentioned.

(3) The description of the Divine nature is very much abbreviated in the Greek; but no word occurs in it which has not the support of the Versions.

(4) In the Christological passage which we examined in detail the Greek was seen to preserve the original statements, though with the addition of the later phrase ἀσπόρως τε καὶ ἀφθόρως.

(5) The Syriac Version is often loose and inaccurate: it drops a phrase here and there; and it makes insertions by way of explanation or of supplement, and sometimes in such a way as to convey a wholly false conception of the original.

We learn then to expect for the remainder of the Apology that the Greek, as we have it, will as a rule give us the actual words of Aristides, except in the very few places in which modification was obviously needed. Where the Syriac presents us with matter which has no counterpart whatever in the Greek, we shall hesitate to pronounce that the Greek is defective, unless we are able to suggest a good reason for the omission, or to authenticate the Syriac from some external source[1].

The Greek Text of 'Barlaam and Josaphat.'

It is remarkable that this work, which at one time enjoyed such extraordinary popularity, should not have found its way into print in its original language before the present century. The Latin Version wrongly attributed to Georgius Trapezuntius, but really, as the MSS. of it prove, of a much earlier date, was printed, together with various works of S. John of Damascus, at Basel in 1539: but it was reserved to Boissonade to publish the Greek Text for the first time in the fourth volume of his *Anecdota*, which appeared at Paris in 1832.

Boissonade apologises for the meagreness of his *apparatus criticus* on the ground that an edition was expected almost immediately from Schmidt and Kopitar the librarian of the Imperial Library at Vienna. This edition, however, never appeared. Out of seventeen MSS. preserved in the Library at Paris, Boissonade used throughout but two, 903 and 1128, which he refers to as A and C. He gives occasional readings from two others, 904 and 907, which he names B and D. In the portion of the book which specially concerns us, viz. the speech of Nachor, C is defective for about 10 of Boissonade's pages, and the testimony of D is frequently

[1] Cf. infra, p. 90.

recorded. From time to time readings are also quoted from the Latin Version.

This very inadequate text has been reprinted in Migne's *Patrologia Graeca*, tom. 96, in the third volume of the works of S. John of Damascus: but we have gained nothing by the reproduction except new blunders.

In the *Wiener Jahrbücher für Deutsche Literatur* (lxxii. 274, lxxiii. 176) Schubart has given some description of the Vienna MSS., and a list of the principal variants contained in them.

Lastly, Zotenberg[1] has made a useful list of about 60 MSS., and has constructed a critical text of certain passages of special interest. Nothing however has been attempted as yet in the way of a genealogical classification of the MSS.; a work which will involve great labour, but which is essential to the production of a satisfactory edition.

In editing the Remains of the Apology of Aristides I have used three MSS., which were kindly placed at my disposal in Cambridge. I have recorded their variants with a greater completeness than is necessary for my present purpose, in order to aid a future editor of the whole treatise in assigning them without further trouble to their proper families.

(1) I have to thank Miss Algerina Peckover of Wisbech for kindly sending to the University Library a MS. in her possession, which apparently belongs to the beginning of the eleventh century. This Codex is specially interesting for the pictures which a later hand has drawn in the margin, sometimes in ink and sometimes in colours. It is unfortunately defective at the beginning and at the end. It commences with the words *τῇ προνοίᾳ τοῦ δημιουργοῦ φωτιζόμενα* (Bois. p. 48), and ends with *καὶ ἐν ὁδῷ τῶν ἐντολῶν σου ἠξίωσας τὸν δρόμον τέλε* (Bois. p. 357). Unhappily it has been corrected very largely throughout, and it is frequently impossible to discover the original readings: those which are obviously by a later hand I have marked as W^2.

(2) The authorities of Magdalen College, Oxford, with a like generosity allowed me to use their codex, Gr. 4, side by side with

[1] *Notice sur le livre de B. et J.*, pp. 3—5.

the Wisbech MS. in our Library. This bears the date 1064. It contains besides: a Life of S. Basil, a tract on Images, the Martyrdom of SS. Galaction and Episteme, a tract on Penalties, and a work of Anastasius Sinaiticus. It has remained for the most part uncorrected.

(3) In the Library of Pembroke College, Cambridge, there is a MS. of the 17th century, the readings of which are of sufficient interest to be recorded for the present in spite of its late date.

In my *apparatus criticus* these MSS. are referred to by the letters W, M and P respectively. I have now and then recorded readings from the Vienna MSS. collated by Schubart, using the signs V_{21}, V_{102}, &c., where the figures correspond with Schubart's numbers. Wherever I have differed from the text of Boissonade, I have recorded his readings, and sometimes I have expressly mentioned his MSS., A, C and D. I have given in the margin of the Greek text the reference to Boissonade's pages. Where it seemed desirable I have recorded readings of the Latin Version, taking them from the Basel edition of 1539 mentioned above.

The Bearing of the Apology on the Canon.

There are but few references to the Books of Scripture in the Apology of Aristides, which thus stands in striking contrast with the works of Justin. On two occasions the Emperor is referred to Christian writings. In the first case a written Gospel is distinctly implied, as the matter in hand is the outline of our Lord's Life; the words in the Greek are[1]: οὗ τὸ κλέος τῆς παρουσίας ἐκ τῆς παρ' αὐτοῖς καλουμένης εὐαγγελικῆς ἁγίας γραφῆς ἔξεστί σοι γνῶναι, βασιλεῦ, ἐὰν ἐντύχῃς (p. 110, l. 21). The second reference is more general, and possibly includes Books outside the Canon: ταῖς γραφαῖς ἐγκύψας τῶν χριστιανῶν εὑρήσεις, κ.τ.λ. (p. 111, l. 24; cf. Syr. supra p. 50 fin.). There are no direct quotations from the New Testament, although the Apologist's diction is undoubtedly coloured at times by the language of the Apostolic writers.

(1) The opening sentence recalls the words of 2 Macc. vii. 28: ἀξιῶ σε, τέκνον, ἀναβλέψαντα εἰς τὸν οὐρανὸν καὶ τὴν γῆν, καὶ τὰ

[1] For the Syriac see above, p. 36 fin. 'This is taught from that Gospel,' &c.

ἐν αὐτοῖς πάντα ἰδόντα, γνῶναι ὅτι ἐξ οὐκ ὄντων ἐποίησεν αὐτὰ ὁ θεός.

(2) p. 100, l. 11. *δι' αὐτοῦ δὲ τὰ πάντα συνέστηκεν.* Cf. Col. i. 17, *καὶ τὰ πάντα ἐν αὐτῷ συνέστηκεν* (cf. *δι' αὐτοῦ* in i. 16).

(3) p. 101, l. 6. *καὶ ἤρξαντο σέβεσθαι τὴν κτίσιν παρὰ τὸν κτίσαντα αὐτούς.* This is clearly based on Rom. i. 25: *καὶ ἐσεβάσθησαν καὶ ἐλάτρευσαν τῇ κτίσει παρὰ τὸν κτίσαντα.* The addition of *αὐτούς* is interesting. The Syriac translator renders: 'and they began to serve created things instead of the Creator of them'; he is probably led to make the change by the recollection of the Syriac Version (Pesh.) in this passage, where the word 'Creator' has the suffix of the fem. plural.

(4) p. 104, l. 2. *σοφοὶ λέγοντες εἶναι ἐμωράνθησαν.* Cf. Rom. i. 22: *φάσκοντες εἶναι σοφοὶ ἐμωράνθησαν.*

(5) p. 107, l. 12. *ὅθεν λαμβάνοντες οἱ ἄνθρωποι ἀφορμὴν ἀπὸ τῶν θεῶν αὐτῶν, ἔπραττον πᾶσαν ἀνομίαν καὶ ἀσέλγειαν καὶ ἀσέβειαν.* These words are a kind of echo, although in a different sense, of Rom. vii. 8: *ἀφορμὴν δὲ λαβοῦσα ἡ ἁμαρτία διὰ τῆς ἐντολῆς κατειργάσατο ἐν ἐμοὶ πᾶσαν ἐπιθυμίαν.*

(6) p. 109, l. 12. *νυνὶ δὲ οἱ νόμοι καλοί εἰσι καὶ δίκαιοι.* Here again we seem to feel the influence of the same chapter; Rom. vii. 12, 16, *ὥστε ὁ μὲν νόμος ἅγιος, καὶ ἡ ἐντολὴ ἁγία καὶ δικαία καὶ ἀγαθή...σύνφημι τῷ νόμῳ ὅτι καλός* (cf. 1 Tim. i. 8).

(7) p. 109, l. 26. *οὗτοι γάρ, τοῦ Ἀβραὰμ ὄντες ἀπόγονοι καὶ Ἰσαὰκ καὶ Ἰακὼβ, παρῴκησαν εἰς Αἴγυπτον· ἐκεῖθεν δὲ ἐξήγαγεν αὐτοὺς ὁ θεὸς ἐν χειρὶ κραταιᾷ καὶ ἐν βραχίονι ὑψηλῷ.* The first part of this sentence has affinities with Heb. xi. 8, 9, *πίστει Ἀβραάμ...παρῴκησεν εἰς γῆν τῆς ἐπαγγελίας...μετὰ Ἰσαὰκ καὶ Ἰακώβ.* And the whole may be compared with Acts xiii. 17, *ἐν τῇ παροικίᾳ ἐν γῇ Αἰγύπτου, καὶ μετὰ βραχίονος ὑψηλοῦ ἐξήγαγεν αὐτοὺς ἐξ αὐτῆς.* The second part of the phrase however is not attested by the Syr. and Arm. Versions, and may possibly have been introduced by the author of 'Barlaam and Josaphat' from Ps. cxxxvi. 11, 12.

(8) p. 110, l. 2. *τοὺς ἀπεσταλμένους πρὸς αὐτοὺς προφήτας καὶ δικαίους ἀπέκτειναν.* This is a combination of words found in S. Matt. xiii. 17, *πολλοὶ προφῆται καὶ δίκαιοι*, and S. Matt. xxiii.

37 (cf. S. Luke xiii. 34) *ἡ ἀποκτείνουσα τοὺς προφήτας, καὶ λιθοβολοῦσα τοὺς ἀπεσταλμένους πρὸς αὐτήν.* But here again we cannot be sure that we have the words of Aristides himself. This last remark applies also to the phrase, *ἀλλ' οὐ κατ' ἐπίγνωσιν* (p. 110, l. 9), which comes from Rom. x. 2.

(9) p. 110, l. 19. *θανάτου ἐγεύσατο* clearly comes from Heb. ii. 9; but the Syr. simply has 'He died,' and the Arm. has nothing at all to correspond. Hence we cannot be certain that these are the words of Aristides. They probably have replaced the statement preserved in the Syr. 'He was pierced by the Jews.' Throughout this great Christological passage it is worth noting how the actual phrases of the N. T. are not introduced.

(10) p. 111, l. 30. *οὐ γὰρ ἀνθρώπων ῥήματα λαλοῦσιν, ἀλλὰ τὰ τοῦ θεοῦ.* With this we may perhaps compare 1 Thess. ii. 13, *ἐδέξασθε οὐ λόγον ἀνθρώπων ἀλλὰ, καθὼς ἀληθῶς ἐστὶν, λόγον θεοῦ*[1].

The Apology and the Didaché.

A source from which our author has drawn part of his description of the life and conduct of the Christians is the Two Ways, though it may well be doubted whether he knew it in the form preserved to us in the Didaché.

The passage in question runs as follows in the Apology (c. xv.): *Οὐ μοιχεύουσιν, οὐ πορνεύουσιν, οὐ ψευδομαρτυροῦσιν, οὐκ ἐπιθυμοῦσι τὰ ἀλλότρια· τιμῶσι πατέρα καὶ μητέρα· καὶ τοὺς*

[1] The following parallels may also be noted: p. 111, l. 17, 1 Thess. ii. 10; p. 111, l. 29, Apoc. xv. 3; p. 108, l. 2 (ἀσυνέτων), and p. 110, l. 1 (ἀχάριστοι), Rom. i. 21; p. 109, l. 30, Rom. ix. 22; p. 111, l. 26 (οὐκ ἀπ' ἐμαυτοῦ λέγω), Joh. vii. 17, xii. 49. Moreover there seems to be some relation between our Apology and several chapters of the Book of Wisdom, beginning with the personal statement of c. vii. 1: *εἰμὶ μὲν κἀγὼ θνητὸς ἄνθρωπος κ.τ.λ.* Comp. esp. vii. 15 *ἐμοὶ δὲ δῴη ὁ θεὸς εἰπεῖν κατὰ γνώμην...αὐτὸς γάρ μοι ἔδωκε τῶν ὄντων γνῶσιν ἀψευδῆ, εἰδέναι σύστασιν κόσμου καὶ ἐνέργειαν στοιχείων κ.τ.λ.*...(ix. 1) *ὁ ποιήσας τὰ πάντα ἐν λόγῳ σου κ.τ.λ.*...(xii. 24) *τῶν πλάνης ὁδῶν μακρότερον ἐπλανήθησαν, θεοὺς ὑπολαμβάνοντες τὰ καὶ ἐν ζῴοις κ.τ.λ.*... (xiii. 2) *ἀλλ' ἢ πῦρ ἢ πνεῦμα ἢ ταχινὸν ἀέρα ἢ κύκλον ἄστρων ἢ βίαιον ὕδωρ ἢ φωστῆρας οὐρανοῦ πρυτάνεις κόσμου θεοὺς ἐνόμισαν...ὁ κατασκευάσας αὐτὰ δυνατώτερός ἐστιν... ταλαίπωροι δὲ καὶ ἐν νεκροῖς αἱ ἐλπίδες αὐτῶν κ.τ.λ....ἐν τοίχῳ ἔθηκεν αὐτὸ ἀσφαλισάμενος σιδήρῳ...ὅτι ἀδυνατεῖ ἑαυτῷ βοηθῆσαι κ.τ.λ.*

πλησίον φιλοῦσι· δίκαια κρίνουσιν· ὅσα οὐ θέλουσιν αὐτοῖς γίνεσθαι ἑτέρῳ οὐ ποιοῦσι· τοὺς ἀδικοῦντας αὐτοὺς παρακαλοῦσι καὶ προσφιλεῖς αὐτοὺς ἑαυτοῖς ποιοῦσι· τοὺς ἐχθροὺς εὐεργετεῖν σπουδάζουσι· πραεῖς εἰσὶ καὶ ἐπιεικεῖς· ἀπὸ πάσης συνουσίας ἀνόμου καὶ ἀπὸ πάσης ἀκαθαρσίας ἐγκρατεύονται· χήραν οὐχ ὑπερορῶσιν, ὀρφανὸν οὐ λυποῦσιν· ὁ ἔχων τῷ μὴ ἔχοντι ἀνεπιφθόνως ἐπιχορηγεῖ· ξένον ἐὰν ἴδωσιν, ὑπὸ στέγην εἰσάγουσι, καὶ χαίρουσιν ἐπ' αὐτῷ, ὡς ἐπὶ ἀδελφῷ ἀληθινῷ· οὐ γάρ, κ.τ.λ.

The following parallels may be adduced from the Didaché:

c. ii. *οὐ μοιχεύσεις...οὐ πορνεύσεις... οὐκ ἐπιθυμήσεις τὰ τοῦ πλησίον...οὐ ψευδομαρτυρήσεις.*

c. i. *ἀγαπήσεις...τὸν πλησίον σου.*

c. iv. *κρινεῖς δικαίως.*

c. i. *πάντα δὲ ὅσα ἐὰν θελήσῃς μὴ γίνεσθαί σοι, καὶ σὺ ἄλλῳ μὴ ποίει.*

c. iv. *εἰρηνεύσεις δὲ μαχομένους.*

c. iii. *ἴσθι δὲ πραΰς.*

To these we may perhaps add, as parallel to the last of the sentences cited above:

c. iv. *οὐκ ἀποστραφήσῃ τὸν ἐνδεόμενον, συγκοινωνήσεις δὲ πάντα τῷ ἀδελφῷ σου.*

It may also be noted that the whole passage is prefaced by the words: *ἔχουσι τὰς ἐντολὰς αὐτοῦ τοῦ κυρίου Ἰησοῦ Χριστοῦ... καὶ ταύτας φυλάττουσι.* Compare Did. c. iv.: *οὐ μὴ ἐγκαταλίπῃς ἐντολὰς κυρίου, φυλάξεις δὲ κ.τ.λ.*

When we turn to the Epistle of Barnabas we find there the same parallels which have been quoted from the Didaché, with two exceptions; viz., *οὐ ψευδομαρτυρήσεις*, and the negative form of the Golden Rule.

On the other hand, we find in Barn. c. xix.: *ἡ οὖν ὁδὸς τοῦ φωτός ἐστιν αὕτη· ἐάν τις θέλων ὁδὸν ὁδεύειν ἐπὶ τὸν ὡρισμένον τόπον, κ.τ.λ.*: with which we may compare Apol. c. xvi.: *ὄντως οὖν αὕτη ἐστὶν ἡ ὁδὸς τῆς ἀληθείας, ἥτις τοὺς ὁδεύοντας αὐτὴν εἰς τὴν αἰώνιον χειραγωγεῖ βασιλείαν.* And the two phrases about the widow and the orphan, which found no parallel in the Didaché, may be compared with Barn. c. xx.: *χήρᾳ καὶ ὀρφανῷ οὐ προσέχοντες.* Compare also Barn. c. xix.: *διὰ λόγου κοπιῶν καὶ πορευόμενος εἰς τὸ παρακαλέσαι* with Apol. c. xv. (quoted above) *τοὺς ἀδικοῦντας αὐτοὺς παρακαλοῦσι.*

It is possible then that here we have a witness to the earlier Two Ways, which has been variously embodied in the Didaché and the Epistle of Barnabas.

Some support may be given to this view when we observe that the wording of the negative form of the Golden Rule in our Apology has a greater affinity to the famous interpolations in Codex Bezae than to the clause in the Didaché. This appears partly from the position of the first negative, and partly from the use of *ἕτερος* rather than *ἄλλος*.

Let us bring the various texts together:

Acts xv. 20. *ὅσα μὴ θέλουσιν ἑαυτοῖς γείνεσθαι, ἑτέροις μὴ ποιεῖτε.*

Acts xv. 29. *ὅσα μὴ θέλουσιν ἑαυτοῖς γείνεσθαι, ἑτέρῳ μὴ ποιεῖν.*

Apol. c. xv. *ὅσα οὐ θέλουσιν αὐτοῖς γίνεσθαι, ἑτέρῳ οὐ ποιοῦσιν.*

Did. c. i. *πάντα δὲ ὅσα ἐὰν θελήσῃς μὴ γίνεσθαί σοι, καὶ σὺ ἄλλῳ μὴ ποίει.*

It is hardly possible therefore to believe that Aristides can have drawn this precept directly from the Didaché in the form in which we know it.

The Apology and the Preaching of Peter.

At the close of the Apology Aristides challenges the Emperor to examine the writings of the Christians, from which he declares that the materials for his defence are drawn: p. 111, l. 23: *καὶ ἵνα γνῷς, βασιλεῦ, ὅτι οὐκ ἀπ᾽ ἐμαυτοῦ ταῦτα λέγω, ταῖς γραφαῖς ἐγκύψας τῶν χριστιανῶν εὑρήσεις οὐδὲν ἔξω τῆς ἀληθείας με λέγειν*: or, as it is more fully said in the Syriac Version: 'Take now their writings and read in them, and lo! ye will find that not of myself have I brought these things forward nor as their advocate have I said them, but as I have read in their writings, these things I firmly believe,' &c.

We have seen already that he refers to a written Gospel for his statements as to the life and work of our Lord. We have also seen that he has drawn part of his description of the conduct of the Christians from the 'Two Ways.' Moreover the Book of

Wisdom seems to have influenced his method and his language in several parts of his work.

The following investigation will tend to shew that he owes a still greater debt to a work now lost, which exercised a considerable influence upon the writings of the second century.

The Preaching of Peter (*κήρυγμα Πέτρου*) is classed by Eusebius (*H. E.* III. 3) together with his Acts, his Gospel and his Apocalypse as outside the Canon of writings accepted by the universal Church (*οὐδ' ὅλως ἐν καθολικοῖς ἴσμεν παραδεδομένα*). He goes on to say of these four books that none of the early writers or of his contemporaries used quotations from them. This statement is however incorrect: for Clement of Alexandria again and again quotes from both the Preaching and the Apocalypse, as authoritative works. The Preaching of Peter then was one of those books which, like the Didaché, the Epistle of Barnabas and the Shepherd of Hermas, at one time claimed a place in the Canon; though its claim was disallowed, even more emphatically perhaps than the claims of these other competitors.

We must in the first instance gather together all the fragments which can be assigned with certainty to this work[1]. For the sake of clearness I have arranged them in the order in which it will be most easy to compare them with our Apology.

Clem. Al. Strom. VI. 39 ff. *Γινώσκετε οὖν ὅτι εἷς θεός ἐστιν, ὃς ἀρχὴν πάντων ἐποίησεν καὶ τέλους ἐξουσίαν ἔχων, καὶ ὁ ἀόρατος ὃς τὰ πάντα ὁρᾷ, ἀχώρητος ὃς τὰ πάντα χωρεῖ, ἀνεπιδεὴς οὗ τὰ πάντα ἐπιδέεται καὶ δι' ὃν ἔστιν*[2]*· ἀκατάληπτος, ἀέναος, ἄφθαρτος, ἀποίητος, ὃς τὰ πάντα ἐποίησεν λόγῳ δυναμέως αὐτοῦ*[3].

Τοῦτον τὸν θεὸν σέβεσθε μὴ κατὰ τοὺς Ἕλληνας[4]*· ὅτι ἀγνοίᾳ*

[1] Hilgenfeld (*N. T. extra Can.* pp. 56 ff.), to whose work I need scarcely acknowledge my indebtedness, has brought together under the head of Πέτρου (καὶ Παύλου) κήρυγμα, various fragments of the *Didascalia Petri*, &c. The fact that these find no parallels in Aristides will give a new reason for keeping them separate.

[2] *Apol.* c. i. *αὐτὸν οὖν λέγω εἶναι θεὸν τὸν συστησάμενον τὰ πάντα καὶ διακρατοῦντα ...ἀπροσδεῆ...πάντες δὲ αὐτοῦ χρῄζουσιν.*

[3] c. i. 'Now I say that God is not begotten, not made: a constant nature,... immortal, complete, and incomprehensible...the heavens do not contain Him; but the heavens and all things visible and invisible are contained in Him' (Syr.).

c. iv. *ἄφθαρτος...καὶ ἀόρατος, αὐτὸς δὲ πάντα ὁρᾷ.*

c. xiv. *τὸν ἀόρατον καὶ πάντα ὁρῶντα καὶ πάντα δημιουργήσαντα δεῖ θεὸν σέβεσθαι.*

[4] cc. viii. ff.

φερόμενοι καὶ μὴ ἐπιστάμενοι τὸν θεὸν[1] *(ὡς ἡμεῖς κατὰ τὴν γνῶσιν τὴν τελείαν), ὧν ἔδωκεν αὐτοῖς ἐξουσίας εἰς χρῆσιν*[2] *μορφώσαντες*[3] *ξύλα καὶ λίθους, χαλκὸν καὶ σίδηρον, χρυσὸν καὶ ἄργυρον, τῆς ὕλης αὐτῶν καὶ χρήσεως τὰ δοῦλα τῆς ὑπάρξεως ἀναστήσαντες σέβονται· καὶ ἃ δέδωκεν αὐτοῖς εἰς βρῶσιν ὁ θεὸς, πετεινὰ τοῦ ἀέρος καὶ τῆς θαλάσσης τὰ νηκτὰ καὶ τῆς γῆς τὰ ἑρπετὰ καὶ τὰ θηρία σὺν κτήνεσι τετραπόδοις τοῦ ἀγροῦ, γαλᾶς τε καὶ μῦς, αἰλούρους τε καὶ κύνας καὶ πιθήκους*[4]*· καὶ τὰ ἴδια βρώματα βρωτοῖς*[5] *θύματα θύουσιν, καὶ νεκρὰ νεκροῖς*[6] *προσφέροντες ὡς θεοῖς ἀχαριστοῦσι τῷ θεῷ διὰ τούτων ἀρνούμενοι αὐτὸν εἶναι*[7].

Μηδὲ *κατὰ Ἰουδαίους σέβεσθε, καὶ γὰρ ἐκεῖνοι μόνοι οἰόμενοι τὸν θεὸν γινώσκειν οὐκ ἐπίστανται, λατρεύοντες ἀγγέλοις καὶ ἀρχαγγέλοις, μηνὶ καὶ σελήνῃ· καὶ ἐὰν μὴ σελήνη φανῇ, σάββατον οὐκ ἄγουσι τὸ λεγόμενον πρῶτον, οὐδὲ ἄζυμα οὔτε ἑορτὴν οὔτε μεγάλην ἡμέραν*[8].

Ὥστε καὶ ὑμεῖς ὁσίως καὶ δικαίως μανθάνοντες ἃ παραδίδομεν ὑμῖν φυλάσσεσθε[9], *καινῶς τὸν θεὸν διὰ τοῦ χριστοῦ σεβόμενοι. εὕρομεν γὰρ ἐν ταῖς γραφαῖς, καθὼς ὁ κύριος λέγει· Ἰδοὺ διατίθεμαι ὑμῖν καινὴν διαθήκην, οὐχ ὡς διεθέμην τοῖς πατράσιν ὑμῶν ἐν ὄρει* Χωρήβ. *νέαν ὑμῖν διέθετο· τὰ γὰρ* Ἑλλήνων *καὶ* Ἰουδαίων *παλαιά, ὑμεῖς δὲ οἱ καινῶς αὐτὸν τρίτῳ γένει σεβόμενοι* Χριστιανοί[10].

[1] c. iii. *μὴ εἰδότες θεὸν ἐπλανήθησαν.*

[2] c. v. *καὶ αὐτὸ γὰρ εἰς χρῆσιν τῶν ἀνθρώπων γέγονε, καὶ κατακυριεύεται ὑπ' αὐτῶν* (et saepius).

[3] c. iii. *ὧν καὶ μορφώματά τινα ποιήσαντες ὠνόμασαν ἐκτύπωμα τοῦ οὐρανοῦ, κ.τ.λ.... καὶ συγκλείσαντες ναοῖς προσκυνοῦσι.*

[4] c. xii. *τινὲς γὰρ αὐτῶν ἐσεβάσθησαν πρόβατον...τινὲς δὲ τὸν αἴλουρον καὶ τὸν κύνα καὶ τὸν λύκον καὶ τὸν πίθηκον, κ.τ.λ.*

[5] c. xii. *ἄλογα ζῶα παρεισήγαγον θεοὺς εἶναι, χερσαῖά τε καὶ ἔνυδρα...ὁρῶντες γὰρ τοὺς θεοὺς αὐτῶν βιβρωσκομένους ὑπὸ ἑτέρων ἀνθρώπων*...(this confirms Potter's emendation *βρωτοῖς* for *βροτοῖς*.) [6] c. iii. *σεβόμενοι ἀγάλματα νεκρά.*

[7] c. xiv. *ἀγνώμονες καὶ αὐτοὶ φανέντες καὶ ἀχάριστοι...ἀρνοῦνται τὸν υἱὸν τοῦ θεοῦ.*

[8] c. xiv. 'The Jews...suppose in their minds that they are serving God, but... their service is to angels and not to God, in that they observe sabbaths and new moons and the passover and the great fast and the fast, and circumcision, and cleanness of meats.' (Syr.)

[9] c. xv. *τὰ γὰρ προστάγματα αὐτοῦ ἀσφαλῶς φυλάττουσιν, ὁσίως καὶ δικαίως ζῶντες.*

[10] c. xvi. 'And this people is truly a new people,' &c. (Syr.)

c. ii. *φανερὸν...ὅτι τρία γένη εἰσὶν ἀνθρώπων ἐν τῷδε τῷ κόσμῳ· ὧν εἰσὶν οἱ τῶν παρ' ὑμῖν λεγομένων θεῶν προσκυνηταί, καὶ Ἰουδαῖοι, καὶ χριστιανοί.* 'There are four races of men in this world: Barbarians and Greeks, Jews and Christians.' (Syr.)

Ibid. 48. (*ὁ κύριός φησι πρὸς τοὺς μαθητὰς μετὰ τὴν ἀνάστασιν*) *Ἐξελεξάμην ὑμᾶς δώδεκα μαθητάς, κρίνας ἀξίους ἐμοῦ* (*οὓς ὁ κύριος ἠθέλησεν καὶ ἀποστόλους πιστοὺς ἡγησάμενος εἶναι*), *πέμπων ἐπὶ τὸν κόσμον εὐαγγελίσασθαι τοὺς κατὰ τὴν οἰκουμένην ἀνθρώπους*[1], *γινώσκειν ὅτι εἷς θεός ἐστιν, διὰ τῆς τοῦ χριστοῦ πίστεως ἐμῆς δηλοῦντας τὰ μέλλοντα, ὅπως οἱ ἀκούσαντες καὶ πιστεύσαντες σωθῶσιν, οἱ δὲ μὴ πιστεύσαντες ἀκούσαντες μαρτυρήσωσιν, οὐκ ἔχοντες ἀπολογίαν εἰπεῖν Οὐκ ἠκούσαμεν.* (*τί οὖν; οὐχὶ καὶ ἐν Ἅιδου ἡ αὐτὴ γέγονεν οἰκονομία;*)[2]

Ibid. 43. *ἐὰν μὲν οὖν τις θελήσῃ τοῦ Ἰσραὴλ μετανοήσας διὰ τοῦ ὀνόματός μου πιστεύειν ἐπὶ τὸν θεόν, ἀφεθήσονται αὐτῷ αἱ ἁμαρτίαι. μετὰ δώδεκα ἔτη ἐξέλθετε εἰς τὸν κόσμον, μή τις εἴπῃ Οὐκ ἠκούσαμεν.*

Ibid. 48. *ὅσα ἐν ἀγνοίᾳ τις ὑμῶν ἐποίησεν μὴ εἰδὼς σαφῶς τὸν θεόν, ἐὰν ἐπιγνοὺς μετανοήσῃ, πάντα αὐτῷ ἀφεθήσεται τὰ ἁμαρτήματα*[3].

Ibid. 128. *ἡμεῖς δὲ ἀναπτύξαντες τὰς βίβλους ἃς εἴχομεν τῶν προφητῶν, ἃ μὲν διὰ παραβολῶν, ἃ δὲ δι᾽ αἰνιγμάτων, ἃ δὲ αὐθεντικῶς καὶ αὐτολεξεὶ τὸν χριστὸν Ἰησοῦν ὀνομαζόντων, εὕρομεν καὶ τὴν παρουσίαν αὐτοῦ καὶ τὸν θάνατον καὶ τὸν σταυρὸν καὶ τὰς λοιπὰς κολάσεις πάσας ὅσας ἐποίησαν αὐτῷ οἱ Ἰουδαῖοι*[4], *καὶ τὴν ἔγερσιν καὶ τὴν εἰς οὐρανοὺς ἀνάληψιν πρὸ τοῦ Ἱεροσόλυμα κτισθῆναι, καθὼς ἐγέγραπτο. ταῦτα πάντα ἃ ἔδει αὐτὸν παθεῖν, καὶ μετ᾽ αὐτὸν ἃ ἔσται. ταῦτα οὖν ἐπιγνόντες ἐπιστεύσαμεν τῷ θεῷ διὰ τῶν γεγραμμένων εἰς αὐτόν*[5].

ἔγνωμεν γὰρ ὅτι ὁ θεὸς αὐτὰ προσέταξεν ὄντως[6], *καὶ οὐδὲν ἄτερ γραφῆς λέγομεν*[7].

[1] c. xv. *οὗτος δώδεκα ἔσχε μαθητάς, οἳ μετὰ τὴν ἐν οὐρανοῖς ἄνοδον αὐτοῦ ἐξῆλθον εἰς τὰς ἐπαρχίας τῆς οἰκουμένης καὶ ἐδίδαξαν κ.τ.λ.*

[2] c. ii. 'He had twelve disciples, in order that a certain dispensation of His might be fulfilled' (Syr.); c. xv. *κατ᾽ οἰκονομίαν μεγάλην.*

[3] c. xvi. 'And when it chances that one of them turns...he confesses to God, saying, In ignorance I did these things: and he cleanses his heart, and his sins are forgiven him, because he did them in ignorance in former time' (Syr.).

[4] c. ii. 'He was pierced by the Jews' (Syr.).

[5] c. xvi. 'As I have read in their writings, these things I firmly believe, and those things also that are to come' (Syr.).

[6] c. xv. *καθὼς κύριος ὁ θεὸς αὐτοῖς προσέταξεν...ὄντως οὖν αὕτη κ.τ.λ.* (c. xvi).

[7] c. xvi. *καὶ ἵνα γνῷς, βασιλεῦ, ὅτι οὐκ ἀπ᾽ ἐμαυτοῦ ταῦτα λέγω, ταῖς γραφαῖς ἐγκύψας τῶν χριστιανῶν, εὑρήσεις οὐδὲν ἔξω τῆς ἀληθείας με λέγειν.*

I have given above in full (with one exception; Clem. Strom. i. 182, *νόμος καὶ λόγος ὁ κύριος*) all the indisputable fragments of the Preaching of Peter[1]: and the parallels adduced from the Apology of Aristides shew that there is an intimate connexion between the two documents.

Before going further into the interesting problem of the reconstruction of the Preaching, let us inquire what light these parallels throw upon the relation of the Syriac Version to the Greek text of the Apology.

(1) Several passages of the Syriac Version, quoted above in the notes, which are wanting in the Greek as we now have it, are authenticated by their similarity to portions of the Preaching.

Of these the most important are: (*a*) the worship of angels attributed to the Jews; (*b*) the description of the Christians as a 'new people'; (*c*) the confession of the converted heathen; (*d*) the attribution of our Lord's sufferings to the Jews. Especially valuable are (*a*) and (*c*), as giving us ground for believing that the great closing section of the Syriac Version, which is so curtailed in the Greek, is substantially the writing of Aristides himself.

(2) On the other hand, the division into three races, which we find in the Greek, has the support of the famous *τρίτῳ γένει* of the Preaching. The fourfold division of the Syriac and Armenian Versions (Barbarians and Greeks, Jews and Christians) comes therefore under grave suspicion: and the more we examine it, the less primitive it appears. For to the Greek mind the Jews were themselves Barbarians: see, for example, Clem. Strom. vi. 44, *νόμος μὲν καὶ προφῆται βαρβάροις, φιλοσοφία δὲ Ἕλλησι*: and Orig. c. Cels. i. 2, *ἑξῆς βάρβαρόν φησιν ἄνωθεν εἶναι τὸ δόγμα, δηλονότι τὸν Ἰουδαϊσμόν*. Moreover there seems to be no parallel to this fourfold classification of races in early Christian literature.

The Preaching of Peter is quoted by Heracleon (Orig. Comm. in Joan. xiii. 17), and we shall see that possibly it was used by

[1] The context of the quotations in Clement may sometimes give us, in the light thrown by the Apology, further materials for the reconstruction of the Preaching. Thus Strom. vi. 127, *ὅταν τις τὸν υἱὸν τοῦ θεοῦ τοῦ τὰ πάντα πεποιηκότος σάρκα ἀνειληφότα καὶ ἐν μήτρᾳ παρθένου κυοφορηθέντα, καθὸ γεγέννηται τὸ αἰσθητὸν αὐτοῦ σαρκίον, ἀκολούθως δὲ καθὸ γέγονεν τοῦτο πεπονθότα καὶ ἀνιστάμενον ὁ μὲν λέγει, οἱ δὲ ἀκούουσιν, κ.τ.λ.*, has several points of resemblance with Apol. c. xv., *οὗτος δὲ ὁ υἱὸς τοῦ θεοῦ τοῦ ὑψίστου ὁμολογεῖται...ἐκ παρθένου ἁγίας γεννηθεὶς...σάρκα ἀνέλαβε, κ.τ.λ.*

Celsus. It seems also to have been in the hands of the unknown writer of the Epistle to Diognetus. Moreover in the Sibylline Oracles we have several passages which seem to be based on it. Some of these are especially interesting, as shewing coincidences with our Apology, though not with the existing fragments of the Preaching[1].

Now if three or four extant works can be shewn to have drawn materials from a document, which is known to us now only by a few fragments, there is obviously a possibility that the lost document may be to some extent critically reconstructed by a consideration of common matter found in any two of the works, which may accordingly have been taken from the document in question. To attempt to do this fully for the Preaching of Peter would be beyond our present scope: but we may fairly consider here what contributions to such a reconstruction are afforded by our Apology, which has apparently made so free a use of it.

Let us begin with those passages which either the Preaching or the Apology have in common with *the Sibylline Oracles*. I shall not attempt a discrimination between the various writings which are gathered under the name of the Sibyl, but shall simply give references to Alexandre's edition of 1869.

Prooem. 7 ff.

Εἶς θεὸς, ὃς μόνος ἄρχει, ὑπερμεγέθης, ἀγένητος,
παντοκράτωρ, ἀόρατος, ὁρῶν μόνος αὐτὸς ἅπαντα,
αὐτὸς δ' οὐ βλέπεται θνητῆς ὑπὸ σαρκὸς ἁπάσης.

* * *

αὐτὸν τὸν μόνον ὄντα σέβεσθ' ἡγήτορα κόσμου,
ὃς μόνος εἰς αἰῶνα καὶ ἐξ αἰῶνος ἐτύχθη,
αὐτογενὴς, ἀγένητος, ἅπαντα κρατῶν διαπαντός.

* * *

[1] The Gnostic Acts of Thomas are frequently indebted to the Preaching of Peter, as may be seen by the following passages: c. 1, *διείλαμεν τὰ κλίματα τῆς οἰκουμένης κ.τ.λ.*: c. 15, *καὶ εἰπεῖν μὲν ὡς δεῖ οὐ δύναμαι, ἃ δὲ χωρῶ λέγειν περὶ αὐτοῦ, κ.τ.λ.*: c. 28, *οὐκ ἔχει τις λόγον ἀπολογίας μέλλων παρ' αὐτοῦ κρίνεσθαι, ὡς μὴ ἀκούσας*: c. 36, *οὐδὲ θυσιῶν δέεται ἵνα αὐτῷ θύσῃς*: c. 38, *ἀλλὰ παραβλέπει ὑμῶν τὰ παραπτώματα ἃ κατὰ ἄγνοιαν ἦτε πεποιηκότες*: c. 55, *τῶν πράξεων ὧν διεπράξασθε χωρὶς γνώσεως...πιστεύσατε...καὶ ἀφίησιν ὑμῖν τὰ πρὸ τού του πεπραγμένα ἁμαρτήματα*: c. 56, *μὴ λογίσῃ ἡμῶν τὰ παραπτώματα καὶ τὰ πρῶτα σφάλματα, ἃ διεπραξάμεθα ἐν ἀγνοίᾳ ὄντες* (see too the argument from prophecy in the same chapter).

ἀλλὰ θεὸς μόνος εἷς πανυπέρτατος, ὃς πεποίηκεν
οὐρανὸν, ἠέλιόν τε καὶ ἀστέρας, ἠδὲ σελήνην,
καρποφόρον γαῖάν τε καὶ ὕδατος οἴδματα πόντου.

* * *

ἡμῖν τε κτήνη ὑπέταξεν πάντα βροτοῖσιν,
πάντων θ' ἡγητῆρα κατέστησεν θεότευκτον,
ἀνδρὶ δ' ὑπέταξεν, κ.τ.λ.

* * *

αἰσχύνθητε γαλᾶς καὶ κνώδαλα θειοποιοῦντες.
οὐ μανίη καὶ λύσσα φρενῶν [αἴσθησιν ἀφαιρεῖ],
εἰ λοπάδας κλέπτουσι θεοὶ, συλοῦσι δὲ χύτρας;

* * *

προσκυνέοντες ὄφεις, κύνας, αἰλούρους, ἀνόητοι,
καὶ πετεηνὰ σέβεσθε, καὶ ἑρπετὰ θηρία γαίης,
καὶ λίθινα ξόανα, καὶ ἀγάλματα χειροποίητα,
κὰν παρόδοισι λίθων συγχώματα· ταῦτα σέβεσθε,
ἄλλα τε πολλὰ μάταια, ἃ δή κ' αἰσχρὸν ἀγορεύειν.

Bk. iii. 9 ff.

τίπτε μάτην πλάζεσθε, καὶ οὐκ εὐθεῖαν ἀταρπὸν
βαίνετε, ἀθανάτου κτίστου μεμνημένος αἰεί;
εἷς θεός ἐστι μόναρχος, ἀθέσφατος, αἰθέρι ναίων,
αὐτοφυὴς, ἀόρατος, ὁρῶν μόνος αὐτὸς ἅπαντα.
ὃν χείρ γ' οὐκ ἐποίησε λιθοξόος, οὐδ' ἀπὸ χρυσοῦ
τέχνης ἀνθρώπου φαίνει τύπος, οὐδ' ἐλέφαντος.

* * *

τίς γὰρ θνητὸς ἐὼν κατιδεῖν δύναται θεὸν ὄσσοις;
ἢ τίς χωρήσει κἂν τοὔνομα μοῦνον ἀκοῦσαι
οὐρανίου μεγάλοιο θεοῦ, κόσμον κρατέοντος;
ὃς λόγῳ ἔκτισε πάντα, καὶ οὐρανὸν ἠδὲ θάλασσαν,
ἠέλιόν τ' ἀκάμαντα, σελήνην τε πλήθουσαν,
ἄστρα τε, κ.τ.λ.

* * *

οὐ σέβετ', οὐδὲ φοβεῖσθε θεὸν, ματαίως δὲ πλανᾶσθε
προσκυνέοντες ὄφεις τε, καὶ αἰλούροισι θύοντες,
εἰδώλοις τ' ἄλλοις, λιθίνοις θ' ἱδρύμασι φωτῶν,
καὶ ναοῖς ἀθέοισι καθεζόμενοι πρὸ θυράων,
τηρεῖτε τὸν ἐόντα θεὸν, ὃς πάντα φυλάσσει.

Bk. viii. 375 ff.

ἀρχὴν καὶ τέλος οἶδα, ὃς οὐρανὸν ἔκτισα καὶ γῆν,
μοῦνος γὰρ θεός εἰμι, καὶ οὐκ ἔστι θεὸς ἄλλος.
εἰκόνα θεσπίζουσιν ἐμὴν, ληφθεῖσαν ἀφ' ὕλης,
χειρί τε μορφώσαντες ἐπ' εἰδώλοισιν ἀναύδοις
δοξάζουσι λιταῖς καὶ θρησκείαισιν ἀνάγνοις.
τὸν κτίστην προλιπόντες ἀσελγείαις ἐλάτρευσαν.

* * *

οὐ χρήζω θυσιῶν, οὐ σπονδῶν ὑμετεράων.

* * *

ταῦτα γὰρ, εἰς μνήμην βασιλήων ἠδὲ τυράννων,
δαίμοσι ποιήσουσι νεκροῖς, ὡς οὐρανίοισι.

When with these passages before us we read over again the early sections of the Preaching and the parallels to them which I have quoted from Aristides, we shall feel that we have here something more than ordinary commonplaces about the unity of God and the folly of idolatry. Again, when we compare together the first and second groups of passages from the Sibylline Books, we shall be led to ask for a common basis which shall explain their resemblances. Neither seems to be a direct imitation of the other: each presents us with words and phrases not found in the other, but accounted for at once on the supposition that either the Preaching of Peter or our own Apology lies in the background. Thus in the first we have *παντοκράτωρ, ἀγένητος, γαλᾶς, πετεηνὰ καὶ ἑρπετά, ἃ δή κ' αἰσχρὸν ἀγορεύειν.* In the second, *τοὔνομα, λόγῳ ἔκτισε, ναοῖς...τηρεῖτε.*

Moreover the mention of Creation by the Word guides us to the Preaching, in preference to the Apology, in which this finds no place: and the phrases which are found in the Apology, but not in the Preaching, need not cause us difficulty when we remember how very fragmentary is our knowledge of the latter document.

In fact we may at once begin a tentative reconstruction, and say that the Preaching probably contained

(1) *παντοκράτωρ* and *ἀγένητος* as epithets of the Deity;

(2) the verb *διακρατεῖν* of His continuous action upon created things;

(3) the statement that the Deity has no outward image, and no name;

(4) that God created 'heaven, earth and sea, sun, moon and stars';

(5) that these were made for the sake of Man;

(6) among objects of false worship, ὄφεις, and other things disgraceful even to name in such a connexion;

(7) a reference to the folly of guarding the Deity.

From the lines in the eighth Book we may add:

(8) the desertion of the Creator for the creature;

(9) that God has no need of sacrifice and oblation.

Another passage of the Sibylline writings bears a striking resemblance to our Apology. This is the commencement of the fourth Book[1], of which Alexandre says: 'Liber hic Christianorum Sibyllinorum antiquissimus est habendus, scriptus nempe primo saeculo.' It opens with lines which recall much of what has been already cited, dealing with the attributes of the Creator. It then gives a brief description of the men who shall one day inhabit the earth (ll. 25 ff.). We may select the following passages:

ὅσσοι δὴ στέρξουσι θεὸν μέγαν, εὐλογέοντες
πρὶν φαγέειν πιέειν τε, πεποιθότες εὐσεβέῃσιν.

* * *

οὐδ' ἄρ' ἐπ' ἀλλοτρίῃ κοίτῃ πόθον αἰσχρὸν ἔχοντες,
οὔτ' ἐπὶ ἄρσενος ὕβριν ἀπεχθέα τε στυγερήν τε.
ὧν τρόπον εὐσεβίην τε καὶ ἤθεα ἀνέρες ἄλλοι
οὔποτε μιμήσονται, ἀναιδείην ποθέοντες·
ἀλλ' αὐτοὺς χλεύῃ τε γέλωτί τε μυχθίζοντες,
νήπιοι ἀφροσύνῃσιν, ἐπιψεύσονται ἐκείνοις,
ὅσσ' αὐτοὶ ῥέξουσιν, ἐπίψογα καὶ κακὰ ἔργα.

With reference to the first of these passages, we may remember that in the description of the Christians in c. xv. we saw that Aristides uses the 'Two Ways': but at the end of his account he adds words which remind us forcibly of the Preaching of Peter: *ὁσίως καὶ δικαίως ζῶντες, καθὼς κύριος ὁ θεὸς αὐτοῖς προσέταξεν*: and then he goes on: *εὐχαριστοῦντες αὐτῷ κατὰ πᾶσαν ὥραν ἐν παντὶ βρώματι καὶ ποτῷ καὶ τοῖς λοιποῖς ἀγαθοῖς.*

[1] It is not unimportant to observe that this Book has also remarkable affinities with the *Apocalypse* of Peter.

With regard to the second passage, there is a still more striking parallel in c. xvii., preserved to us only in the Syriac Version. 'The Greeks then, O king, because they practise foul things in sleeping with males, and with mother and sister and daughter, turn the ridicule of their foulness upon the Christians; but the Christians are honest and pious,' etc.

These coincidences are worth noting even if we are not prepared, with our present knowledge, to suppose that they send us back for their explanation to the Preaching of Peter[1].

Next let us turn to *the Epistle to Diognetus*. As soon as the Armenian fragment of Aristides was discovered, it was observed that it had points in common with this anonymous Epistle. The coincidences have multiplied greatly with our larger knowledge of the Apology. Several of them have been quoted by Mr Harris in his notes, but it is necessary for our present purpose to bring them together again under one view. I shall do this in the briefest possible form, giving in the footnotes references to such parallels in the Apology as have not already been quoted above.

Ep. ad Diog. c. 1. οὔτε τοὺς νομιζομένους ὑπὸ τῶν Ἑλλήνων θεοὺς λογίζονται, οὔτε τὴν Ἰουδαίων δεισιδαιμονίαν φυλάσσουσι ...καὶ τί δήποτε καινὸν τοῦτο γένος ἢ ἐπιτήδευμα εἰσῆλθεν εἰς τὸν βίον νῦν καὶ οὐ πρότερον.

παρὰ τοῦ θεοῦ, τοῦ καὶ τὸ λέγειν καὶ τὸ ἀκούειν ἡμῖν χορηγοῦντος, αἰτοῦμαι δοθῆναι ἐμοὶ μὲν εἰπεῖν οὕτως[2] κ.τ.λ.

c. 2. ὡς ἂν καὶ λόγου καινοῦ...ἀκροατὴς ἐσόμενος.

οὐχ ὁ μέν τις λίθος ἐστὶν ὅμοιος τῷ πατουμένῳ, ὁ δ' ἐστὶ χαλκὸς οὐ κρείσσων τῶν εἰς τὴν χρῆσιν ἡμῖν κεχαλκευμένων σκευῶν, ὁ δὲ ξύλον ἤδη καὶ σεσηπός, ὁ δὲ ἄργυρος χρῄζων ἀνθρώπου τοῦ φυλάξαντος ἵνα μὴ κλαπῇ, ὁ δὲ σίδηρος κ.τ.λ.

εἰς τὴν μορφὴν τούτων ἐκτυπωθῆναι[3] κ.τ.λ.

[1] With the thought contained in the passage last quoted, compare Just. Apol. ii. 12: Αἰδέσθητε, αἰδέσθητε, ἃ φανερῶς πράττετε εἰς ἀναιτίους ἀναφέροντες, καὶ τὰ προσόντα καὶ ἑαυτοῖς καὶ τοῖς ὑμετέροις περιβάλλοντες τούτοις ὧν οὐδὲν οὐδ' ἐπὶ ποσὸν μετουσία ἐστί. But here the notion of ridicule, which we find in Aristides and in the Sibyl, is wanting.

[2] *Ap.* c. ii. τούτων οὕτως εἰρημένων περὶ θεοῦ, καθὼς ἐμὲ ἐχώρησε περὶ αὐτοῦ λέγειν.

[3] *Ap.* c. iii. ὧν καὶ μορφώματά τινα ποιήσαντες ὠνόμασαν ἐκτύπωμα κ.τ.λ.

τοὺς δὲ ἀργυρέους καὶ χρυσοῦς ἐγκλείσαντες ταῖς νυξὶ, καὶ ταῖς ἡμέραις φύλακας παρακαθιστάντες, ἵνα μὴ κλαπῶσιν[1].

c. 3. ἑξῆς δὲ περὶ τοῦ μὴ κατὰ τὰ αὐτὰ Ἰουδαίοις θεοσεβεῖν...Ἰουδαῖοι τοίνυν...καλῶς θεὸν ἕνα τῶν πάντων σέβειν, καὶ δεσπότην ἀξιοῦσι φρονεῖν· εἰ δὲ τοῖς προειρημένοις ὁμοιοτρόπως[2] τὴν θρησκείαν προσάγουσιν αὐτῷ ταύτην, διαμαρτάνουσιν.

ὁ γὰρ ποιήσας τὸν οὐρανὸν καὶ τὴν γῆν καὶ πάντα τὰ ἐν αὐτοῖς, καὶ πᾶσιν ἡμῖν χορηγῶν ὧν προσδεόμεθα, οὐδενὸς ἂν αὐτὸς προσδέοιτο τούτων ὧν τοῖς οἰομένοις διδόναι παρέχει αὐτός. οἱ δέ γε θυσίας κ.τ.λ.

c. 4. ἀλλὰ μὴν τό γε περὶ τὰς βρώσεις αὐτῶν ψοφοδεὲς, καὶ τὴν περὶ τὰ σάββατα δεισιδαιμονίαν, καὶ τὴν τῆς περιτομῆς ἀλαζονείαν, καὶ τὴν τῆς νηστείας καὶ νουμηνίας εἰρωνείαν, κ.τ.λ.

τό τε γὰρ τῶν ὑπὸ τοῦ θεοῦ κτισθέντων εἰς χρῆσιν ἀνθρώπων, κ.τ.λ.

τὸ δὲ παρεδρεύοντας αὐτοὺς ἄστροις καὶ σελήνῃ τὴν παρατήρησιν τῶν μηνῶν καὶ τῶν ἡμερῶν ποιεῖσθαι, κ.τ.λ.

c. 6. χριστιανοὶ κατέχονται μὲν ὡς ἐν φρουρᾷ τῷ κόσμῳ, αὐτοὶ δὲ συνέχουσι τὸν κόσμον[3].

c. 7. οὐ γὰρ ἐπίγειον, ὡς ἔφην, εὕρημα τοῦτ' αὐτοῖς παρεδόθη, οὐδὲ θνητὴν ἐπίνοιαν φυλάσσειν οὕτως ἀξιοῦσιν ἐπιμελῶς, οὐδὲ ἀνθρωπίνων οἰκονομίαν μυστηρίων πεπίστευνται. ἀλλ' αὐτὸς ἀληθῶς ὁ παντοκράτωρ καὶ παντοκτίστης καὶ ἀόρατος θεὸς, αὐτὸς...τὸν λόγον τὸν ἅγιον...ἐνίδρυσε καὶ ἐγκατεστήριξε ταῖς καρδίαις αὐτῶν[4].

c. 8. οἱ μέν τινες πῦρ ἔφασαν εἶναι τὸν θεὸν (οὗ μέλλουσι χωρήσειν αὐτοὶ, τοῦτο καλοῦσι θεὸν), οἱ δὲ ὕδωρ, οἱ δ' ἄλλο τι τῶν στοιχείων τῶν ἐκτισμένων ὑπὸ θεοῦ.

[1] *Ap.* c. iii. συγκλείσαντες ναοῖς...τηροῦσιν ἀσφαλῶς ἵνα μὴ κλαπῶσιν.

[2] *Ap.* c. xiv. καὶ εἰσὶ παρόμοιοι τῶν ἐθνῶν.

[3] *Ap.* c. xvi. 'And I have no doubt that the world stands by reason of the intercession of the Christians' (Syr.).

[4] *Ap.* c. xv. οὗτοί εἰσιν οἱ ὑπὲρ πάντα τὰ ἔθνη τῆς γῆς εὑρόντες τὴν ἀλήθειαν· γινώσκουσι γὰρ τὸν θεὸν κτίστην καὶ δημιουργὸν τῶν ἁπάντων...ἔχουσι τὰς ἐντολὰς...ἐν ταῖς καρδίαις κεχαραγμένας.

c. 10. *ὁ γὰρ θεὸς τοὺς ἀνθρώπους ἠγάπησε, δι' οὓς ἐποίησε τὸν κόσμον, οἷς ὑπέταξε πάντα τὰ ἐν τῇ γῇ.*

ὃς, ἃ παρὰ τοῦ θεοῦ λαβὼν ἔχει, ταῦτα τοῖς ἐπιδεομένοις χορηγῶν, θεὸς γίνεται τῶν λαμβανόντων, οὗτος μιμητής ἐστι θεοῦ[1].

We cannot account for these parallels by merely supposing that Aristides had the Epistle to Diognetus before him: for there are many points in common between Aristides and the Preaching of Peter, such as the worship of angels ascribed to the Jews, which do not appear in the Epistle. Nor will the converse hypothesis hold good. For, to take one instance out of several, the phrase in the Epistle *μὴ κατὰ τὰ αὐτὰ Ἰουδαίοις θεοσεβεῖν* is directly parallel to *μηδὲ κατὰ Ἰουδαίους σέβεσθε* in the Preaching; but it has no counterpart in form in the Apology.

Here again then we are guided to the hypothesis that the Preaching lies behind both of these works. Can we gain anything further in the way of its reconstruction?

Taking up some of our former points (see p. 93) we are confirmed in thinking that the Preaching contained

(1) *παντοκράτωρ* as an epithet of the Deity.

(2) the statement that God created 'heaven and earth and all that is therein.'

(3) that these were made for the sake of Man; and we may add 'placed in subjection under him.' (Cf. Or. Sibyl. *Prooem.*, quoted above.)

(4) a reference to the folly of guarding the Deity.

(5) that God has no need of sacrifices.

We may perhaps go on to add

(6) a statement that God must give the power to speak rightly of Him.

(7) a reference to circumcision and meats in treating of the Jews.

(8) the position of the Christians as sustaining the world.

(9) the fixing of God's commandments in their hearts.

[1] *Ap.* c. i. 'He is God of all, who made all for the sake of man' (Syr.).

[2] *Ap.* c. xiv. 'They imitate God by reason of the love which they have for man: for they have compassion on the poor,' &c. (Syr.).

(10) a reasoned condemnation of the worship of fire, water and other elements.

(11) the imitation of God consists in beneficence.

Mr Harris has collected (pp. 23 ff.) several instances of contact between the Apology of Aristides and *the True Word of Celsus;* and he has suggested that Celsus may have had the Apology in his hands when he wrote his attack upon Christianity. We are now in a position to see that most of the coincidences which have been pointed out would be accounted for by the supposition that it was the Preaching of Peter itself, and not our Apology, which, like 'Jason and Papiscus' and other apocryphal writings, supplied the materials of his attack.

It will be more satisfactory to present the evidence in full as we have done in the previous cases, even at the risk of some repetition. I shall follow the order of Origen's reply.

Orig. *c. Cels.* I. 4. *κοινὸν εἶναι καὶ πρὸς τοὺς ἄλλους φιλοσόφους, ὡς οὐ σεμνόν τι καὶ καινὸν μάθημα.* Cf. II. 5 *μηδὲν δὲ καινὸν ἐν τούτοις διδάσκεσθαι φαίνων χριστιανοὺς, οἴεται ἀνατρέπειν χριστιανισμόν.* Also IV. 14 *λέγω δὲ οὐδὲν καινὸν, ἀλλὰ πάλαι δεδογμένα* (i.e. he does not claim novelty for his view, as they do for theirs).

I. 23. *τῷ ἡγησαμένῳ σφῶν ἑπόμενοι Μωϋσῇ...ἕνα ἐνόμισαν εἶναι θεόν.*

I. 26. *λέγων αὐτοὺς σέβειν ἀγγέλους καὶ γοητείᾳ προσκεῖσθαι, ἧς ὁ Μωϋσῆς αὐτοῖς γέγονεν ἐξηγητής. ποῦ γὰρ τῶν γραμμάτων Μωϋσέως εὗρε τὸν νομοθέτην παραδιδόντα σέβειν ἀγγέλους...ἐπαγγέλλεται δὲ διδάξειν ἑξῆς, πῶς καὶ Ἰουδαῖοι ὑπὸ ἀμαθίας ἐσφάλησαν ἐξαπατώμενοι*[1] (cf. v. 6).

...περὶ τοῦ σωτῆρος ἡμῶν, ὡς γενομένου ἡγεμόνος τῇ καθὸ χριστιανοί ἐσμεν γενέσει ἡμῶν· καί φησιν αὐτὸν πρὸ πάνυ ὀλίγων ἐτῶν τῆς διδασκαλίας ταύτης καθηγήσασθαι, νομισθέντα ὑπὸ χριστιανῶν υἱὸν εἶναι τοῦ θεοῦ[2].

I. 28. *πρῶτον δὲ ὡς πλασαμένου αὐτοῦ τὴν ἐκ παρθένου γένεσιν.*

[1] *Ap.* c. xiv.

[2] *Ap.* c. xv. οἱ δὲ χριστιανοὶ γενεαλογοῦνται ἀπὸ τοῦ κυρίου Ἰησοῦ Χριστοῦ. οὗτος δὲ ὁ υἱὸς τοῦ θεοῦ τοῦ ὑψίστου ὁμολογεῖται...καὶ ἐκ παρθένου ἁγίας γεννηθεὶς.

I. 49 f. *ἀλλ' εἶπεν ὁ ἐμὸς προφήτης ἐν Ἱεροσολύμοις ποτὲ, ὅτι ἥξει θεοῦ υἱὸς, τῶν ὁσίων κριτὴς, καὶ τῶν ἀδίκων κολαστής... τί μᾶλλον σὺ ἢ ἄλλοι μυρίοι, οἱ μετὰ τὴν προφητείαν γενόμενοι, εἰσὶ περὶ ὧν ταῦτα προεφητεύετο ;*

III. 19. *μηδὲν σεμνότερον τράγων καὶ κυνῶν, τῶν παρ' Αἰγυπτίοις, εἰσάγοντας ἐν ταῖς περὶ τοῦ Ἰησοῦ διηγήσεσιν.*

III. 22. *ἐν τῷ καθ' ἡμῶν λόγῳ Διοσκούρους καὶ Ἡρακλέα καὶ Ἀσκληπιὸν καὶ Διόνυσον ὀνομάζει...καί φησιν οὐκ ἀνέχεσθαι μὲν ἡμᾶς τούτους νομίζειν θεοὺς, ὅτι ἄνθρωποι ἦσαν... τὸν δὲ Ἰησοῦν ἀποθανόντα, κ.τ.λ.*

IV. 23. *καὶ ἡμῖν πάντα ὑποβέβληται, γῆ καὶ ὕδωρ καὶ ἀὴρ καὶ ἄστρα, καὶ ἡμῶν ἕνεκα πάντα, καὶ ἡμῖν δουλεύειν τέτακται.* (Cf. IV. 99, *οὔκουν ἀνθρώπῳ πεποίηται τὰ πάντα.*)

Besides these parallels there are several instances in which Celsus seems to turn a weapon used by the Christians back upon themselves: e.g., I. 54, *ὀνειδίζει τῷ σωτῆρι ἐπὶ τῷ πάθει, ὡς μὴ βοηθηθέντι ὑπὸ τοῦ πατρὸς, ἢ μὴ δυνηθέντι ἑαυτῷ βοηθῆσαι*[1]. II. 9, *καίτοι θεὸν, φησὶν, ὄντα φεύγειν ἐνῆν, οὔτε δεθέντα ἀπάγεσθαι, κ.τ.λ.* So again in III. 42, his reply to the charge of corruptibility brought against idols is that flesh is still more corruptible: *παραβάλλων τὰς ἀνθρωπίνας τοῦ Ἰησοῦ σάρκας χρυσῷ καὶ ἀργύρῳ καὶ λίθῳ, ὅτι αὗται ἐκείνων φθαρτότεραι.* And in III. 76 we seem to hear the echo of Christian words in: *ὅμοιον ποιεῖν τὸν ἐν ἡμῖν διδάσκαλον, ὡς εἴ τις μεθύων εἰς μεθύοντας παριὼν κακηγορεῖ τοὺς νήφοντας ὡς μεθύοντας*[2].

It is not easy on the evidence here collected to say whether it was the Preaching of Peter or the Apology of Aristides which lay before Celsus, but we can hardly doubt that it must have been one or the other. The statement that the world was made for the sake of man does not find a place in the recognised fragments of the Preaching; but we have given good reasons for believing that it was contained in it. On the other hand, the Apology gives no starting point for the attack of Celsus on Jewish prophecies about the Messiah, whereas the Preaching laid great stress on this point (see above, p. 89).

[1] *Ap.* c. x. *εἰ οὖν Διόνυσος σφαγεὶς οὐκ ἠδυνήθη ἑαυτῷ βοηθῆσαι...πῶς ἂν εἴη θεός ;* (et passim). Cf. *δέσμιος* and *δραπέτης* in the same chapter.

[2] *Ap.* c. xvi. *ὁδεύοντες γὰρ ἐν σκότει προσρήσσονται ἑαυτοῖς ὡς μεθύοντες.*

APOLOGIA ARISTIDIS

VT APVD HISTORIAM BARLAAM ET JOSAPHAT CONSERVATVR.

I. Ἐγώ, βασιλεῦ, προνοίᾳ θεοῦ ἦλθον εἰς τὸν κόσμον· καὶ 239
θεωρήσας τὸν οὐρανὸν καὶ τὴν γῆν καὶ τὴν θάλασσαν, ἥλιόν τε καὶ σελήνην καὶ τὰ λοιπά, ἐθαύμασα τὴν διακόσμησιν τούτων. ἰδὼν δὲ τὸν κόσμον καὶ τὰ ἐν αὐτῷ πάντα, ὅτι κατὰ ἀνάγκην κινεῖται, συνῆκα τὸν κινοῦντα καὶ διακρατοῦντα εἶναι θεόν· πᾶν γὰρ τὸ κινοῦν ἰσχυρότερον τοῦ κινουμένου, καὶ τὸ διακρατοῦν ἰσχυρότερον τοῦ διακρατουμένου ἐστίν. αὐτὸν οὖν λέγω εἶναι θεὸν τὸν συστησάμενον τὰ πάντα καὶ διακρατοῦντα, ἄναρχον καὶ ἀΐδιον, ἀθάνατον καὶ ἀπροσδεῆ, ἀνώτερον πάντων τῶν παθῶν καὶ ἐλαττωμάτων, ὀργῆς τε καὶ λήθης καὶ ἀγνοίας καὶ τῶν λοιπῶν. δι' αὐτοῦ δὲ τὰ πάντα συνέστηκεν. οὐ χρήζει θυσίας καὶ σπονδῆς, οὐδέ τινος πάντων τῶν φαινομένων· πάντες δὲ αὐτοῦ χρήζουσι.

II. Τούτων οὕτως εἰρημένων περὶ θεοῦ, καθὼς ἐμὲ ἐχώρησε περὶ αὐτοῦ λέγειν, ἔλθωμεν καὶ ἐπὶ τὸ ἀνθρώπινον γένος, ὅπως ἴδωμεν τίνες αὐτῶν μετέχουσι τῆς ἀληθείας καὶ τίνες τῆς 240
πλάνης. φανερὸν γάρ ἐστιν ἡμῖν, ὦ βασιλεῦ, ὅτι τρία γένη εἰσὶν ἀνθρώπων ἐν τῷδε τῷ κόσμῳ· ὧν εἰσὶν οἱ τῶν παρ' ὑμῖν λεγομένων θεῶν προσκυνηταί, καὶ Ἰουδαῖοι, καὶ χριστιανοί· αὐτοὶ δὲ πάλιν οἱ τοὺς πολλοὺς σεβόμενοι θεοὺς εἰς τρία διαιροῦνται γένη, Χαλδαίους τε καὶ Ἕλληνας καὶ Αἰγυπτίους·

2 καὶ τὴν γῆν καὶ τὴν] MP; καὶ γῆν καὶ Bois; γῆν καὶ W; sed cf. p. 101, l. 8 ἥλιόν τε] P Bois; ἥλιον MW 5 κινεῖται] κινοῦνται M 6 ἰσχυρώτερον M (et l. 7) 7, 8 θεὸν εἶναι M 11 θυσιῶν M 12 σπονδῆς] Bois; *libamine* lat; σπονδὰς PW; σπονδῶν M om. τινος MP Bois; sed *aliquo* lat 15 ἐπὶ] περὶ W 18 ἀνθρώπων] P Bois syr; om. MW lat ὑμῖν] ὑμῶν P Bois 21 διαίρονται P

οὗτοι γὰρ γεγόνασιν ἀρχηγοὶ καὶ διδάσκαλοι τοῖς λοιποῖς ἔθνεσι τῆς τῶν πολυωνύμων θεῶν λατρείας καὶ προσκυνήσεως.

III. Ἴδωμεν οὖν τίνες τούτων μετέχουσι τῆς ἀληθείας καὶ τίνες τῆς πλάνης.

Οἱ μὲν γὰρ Χαλδαῖοι, μὴ εἰδότες θεὸν, ἐπλανήθησαν ὀπίσω τῶν στοιχείων, καὶ ἤρξαντο σέβεσθαι τὴν κτίσιν παρὰ τὸν κτίσαντα αὐτούς· ὧν καὶ μορφώματά τινα ποιήσαντες ὠνόμασαν ἐκτύπωμα τοῦ οὐρανοῦ καὶ τῆς γῆς καὶ τῆς θαλάσσης, ἡλίου τε καὶ σελήνης, καὶ τῶν λοιπῶν στοιχείων ἢ φωστήρων, καὶ συγκλείσαντες ναοῖς προσκυνοῦσι θεοὺς καλοῦντες, οὓς καὶ τηροῦσιν ἀσφαλῶς ἵνα μὴ κλαπῶσιν ὑπὸ λῃστῶν, καὶ οὐ συνῆκαν ὅτι πᾶν τὸ τηροῦν μεῖζον τοῦ τηρουμένου ἐστὶ, καὶ ὁ ποιῶν μείζων ἐστὶ τοῦ ποιουμένου. εἰ γὰρ ἀδυνατοῦσιν οἱ θεοὶ αὐτῶν περὶ τῆς ἰδίας σωτηρίας, πῶς ἄλλοις σωτηρίαν χαρίσονται; πλάνην οὖν μεγάλην ἐπλανήθησαν οἱ Χαλδαῖοι, σεβόμενοι ἀγάλματα νεκρὰ καὶ ἀνωφελῆ. καὶ θαυμάζειν μοι ἐπέρχεται, ὦ βασιλεῦ, πῶς οἱ λεγόμενοι φιλόσοφοι αὐτῶν οὐδ' ὅλως συνῆκαν ὅτι καὶ αὐτὰ τὰ στοιχεῖα φθαρτά ἐστιν. εἰ δὲ τὰ στοιχεῖα φθαρτά ἐστι καὶ ὑποτασσόμενα κατὰ ἀνάγκην,
241 πῶς εἰσὶ θεοί; εἰ δὲ τὰ στοιχεῖα οὐκ εἰσὶ θεοὶ, πῶς τὰ ἀγάλματα, ἃ γέγονεν εἰς τιμὴν αὐτῶν, θεοὶ ὑπάρχουσιν;

IV. Ἔλθωμεν οὖν, ὦ βασιλεῦ, ἐπ' αὐτὰ τὰ στοιχεῖα, ὅπως ἀποδείξωμεν περὶ αὐτῶν ὅτι οὐκ εἰσὶ θεοὶ, ἀλλὰ φθαρτὰ καὶ ἀλλοιούμενα, ἐκ τοῦ μὴ ὄντος παραχθέντα προστάγματι τοῦ ὄντως θεοῦ, ὅς ἐστιν ἄφθαρτός τε καὶ ἀναλλοίωτος καὶ ἀόρατος· αὐτὸς δὲ πάντα ὁρᾷ, καὶ καθὼς βούλεται ἀλλοιοῖ καὶ μεταβάλλει. τί οὖν λέγω περὶ τῶν στοιχείων;

Οἱ νομίζοντες τὸν οὐρανὸν εἶναι θεὸν πλανῶνται. ὁρῶμεν γὰρ αὐτὸν τρεπόμενον καὶ κατὰ ἀνάγκην κινούμενον, καὶ ἐκ πολλῶν συνεστῶτα· διὸ καὶ κόσμος καλεῖται. κόσμος δὲ κατασκευή ἐστι τινὸς τεχνίτου· τὸ κατασκευασθὲν δὲ ἀρχὴν καὶ

2 πολυονύμων P 4 τίνες] + τῶν M 5 μὴ] οἱ μὴ Bois 6 om. τῶν M 7 κτίσαντα] + καὶ ποιήσαντα P 8 ἐκτύπωμα] MPV_{omn}; *figuram* lat; ἐκτυπώματα W Bois καὶ (sec)] ἢ MP 11 τηροῦσιν] συντηροῦντες M 14 om. ἰδίας P 14, 15 χαρίσωνται W* 18 om. καὶ M 18, 19 om. φθαρτά ἐστιν. εἰ δὲ τὰ στοιχεῖα W 18—20 om. φθαρτά ἐστιν. εἰ—θεοί; εἰ δὲ τὰ στοιχεῖα P 24 ἀλλοιούμενα] ἀπολύμενα W ὄντος] ὄντως W* 25 ὄντως] ὄντος PW^2 26 ὁρῶν P 30 om. καὶ PW lat

τέλος ἔχει. κινεῖται δὲ ὁ οὐρανὸς κατὰ ἀνάγκην σὺν τοῖς αὐτοῦ φωστῆρσι· τὰ γὰρ ἄστρα τάξει καὶ διαστήματι φερόμενα ἀπὸ σημείου εἰς σημεῖον, οἱ μὲν δύνουσιν, οἱ δὲ ἀνατέλλουσι, καὶ κατὰ καιροὺς πορείαν ποιοῦνται τοῦ ἀποτελεῖν θέρη καὶ χειμῶνας, καθὰ ἐπιτέτακται αὐτοῖς παρὰ τοῦ θεοῦ, καὶ οὐ παραβαίνουσι τοὺς ἰδίους ὅρους, κατὰ ἀπαραίτητον φύσεως ἀνάγκην, σὺν τῷ οὐρανίῳ κόσμῳ. ὅθεν φανερόν ἐστι μὴ εἶναι τὸν οὐρανὸν θεὸν, ἀλλ' ἔργον θεοῦ.

Οἱ δὲ νομίζοντες τὴν γῆν εἶναι θεὰν ἐπλανήθησαν. ὁρῶμεν γὰρ αὐτὴν ὑπὸ τῶν ἀνθρώπων ὑβριζομένην καὶ κατακυριευομένην, σκαπτομένην καὶ φυρομένην καὶ ἄχρηστον γινομένην. ἐὰν γὰρ ὀπτηθῇ, γίνεται νεκρά· ἐκ γὰρ τοῦ ὀστράκου φύεται οὐδέν. ἔτι δὲ καὶ ἐὰν ἐπὶ πλέον βραχῇ, φθείρεται καὶ αὐτὴ καὶ οἱ καρποὶ 242 αὐτῆς. καταπατεῖται δὲ ὑπό τε ἀνθρώπων καὶ τῶν λοιπῶν ζώων, αἵμασι φονευομένων μιαίνεται, διορύσσεται, γεμίζεται νεκρῶν, θήκη γίνεται σωμάτων. τούτων οὕτως ὄντων, οὐκ ἐνδέχεται τὴν γῆν εἶναι θεὰν, ἀλλ' ἔργον θεοῦ εἰς χρῆσιν ἀνθρώπων.

V. Οἱ δὲ νομίζοντες τὸ ὕδωρ εἶναι θεὸν ἐπλανήθησαν. καὶ αὐτὸ γὰρ εἰς χρῆσιν τῶν ἀνθρώπων γέγονε, καὶ κατακυριεύεται ὑπ' αὐτῶν, μιαίνεται καὶ φθείρεται, καὶ ἀλλοιοῦται ἑψόμενον καὶ ἀλλασσόμενον χρώμασι, καὶ ὑπὸ τοῦ κρύους πηγνύμενον, καὶ αἵμασι μολυνόμενον, καὶ εἰς πάντων τῶν ἀκαθάρτων πλύσιν ἀγόμενον. διὸ ἀδύνατον τὸ ὕδωρ εἶναι θεὸν, ἀλλ' ἔργον θεοῦ.

Οἱ δὲ νομίζοντες τὸ πῦρ εἶναι θεὸν πλανῶνται. τὸ γὰρ πῦρ ἐγένετο εἰς χρῆσιν ἀνθρώπων, καὶ κατακυριεύεται ὑπ' αὐτῶν, περιφερόμενον ἐκ τόπου εἰς τόπον εἰς ἕψησιν καὶ ὄπτησιν παντοδαπῶν κρεῶν, ἔτι δὲ καὶ νεκρῶν σωμάτων· φθείρεται δὲ καὶ κατὰ πολλοὺς τρόπους, ὑπὸ τῶν ἀνθρώπων σβεννύμενον. διὸ οὐκ ἐνδέχεται τὸ πῦρ εἶναι θεὸν, ἀλλ' ἔργον θεοῦ.

Οἱ δὲ νομίζοντες τὴν τῶν ἀνέμων πνοὴν εἶναι θεὰν πλανῶνται.

1 οὐρανὸς] + καὶ W · αὐτοῦ] ἑαυτοῦ PW 3 δύουσιν Bois ἀνατέλουσι MW 5 καθὰ] καθ' ὃ W 11 om. σκαπτομένην Bois (sed C habet) φυρομένην] Bois; φυρουμένην PW; φρουρουμένην CM 11, 12 om. γινομένην—ὀπτηθῇ P 12 ἐκ γὰρ] καθότι ἐκ W om. τοῦ P 15 om. γεμίζεται Bois (sed C habet) 16 νεκρωθήκη P 19 om. τῶν PW 20 ἑψούμενον MPW 22 om. καὶ αἵμασι μολυνόμενον Bois V_{21} 22, 23 om. καὶ εἰς πάντων—ἀγόμενον M 24, 25 τὸ γὰρ πῦρ ἐγένετο εἰς χρῆσιν] καὶ αὐτὸ γὰρ εἰς χρῆσιν ἐγένετο Bois V_{21} 25 χρῆσιν] χρίσιν M 28 om. καὶ W σβενύμενον W

φανερὸν γάρ ἐστιν ὅτι δουλεύει ἑτέρῳ, καὶ χάριν τῶν ἀνθρώπων κατεσκεύασται ὑπὸ τοῦ θεοῦ πρὸς μεταγωγὴν πλοίων καὶ συγκομιδὰς τῶν σιτικῶν, καὶ εἰς λοιπὰς αὐτῶν χρείας· αὔξει τε καὶ λήγει κατ' ἐπιταγὴν θεοῦ. διὸ οὐ νενόμισται τὴν τῶν ἀνέμων πνοὴν εἶναι θεάν, ἀλλ' ἔργον θεοῦ.

VI. Οἱ δὲ νομίζοντες τὸν ἥλιον εἶναι θεὸν πλανῶνται. ὁρῶμεν γὰρ αὐτὸν κινούμενον κατὰ ἀνάγκην καὶ τρεπόμενον, καὶ
243 μεταβαίνοντα ἀπὸ σημείου εἰς σημεῖον, δύνοντα καὶ ἀνατέλλοντα, τοῦ θερμαίνειν τὰ φυτὰ καὶ βλαστὰ εἰς χρῆσιν τῶν ἀνθρώπων, ἔτι δὲ καὶ μερισμὸν ἔχοντα μετὰ τῶν λοιπῶν ἀστέρων, καὶ ἐλάττονα ὄντα τοῦ οὐρανοῦ πολύ, καὶ ἐκλείποντα τοῦ φωτός, καὶ μηδεμίαν αὐτοκράτειαν ἔχοντα. διὸ οὐ νενόμισται τὸν ἥλιον εἶναι θεόν, ἀλλ' ἔργον θεοῦ.

Οἱ δὲ νομίζοντες τὴν σελήνην εἶναι θεὰν πλανῶνται. ὁρῶμεν γὰρ αὐτὴν κινουμένην κατὰ ἀνάγκην καὶ τρεπομένην, καὶ μεταβαίνουσαν ἀπὸ σημείου εἰς σημεῖον, δύνουσάν τε καὶ ἀνατέλλουσαν εἰς χρῆσιν τῶν ἀνθρώπων, καὶ ἐλάττονα οὖσαν τοῦ ἡλίου, αὐξομένην τε καὶ μειουμένην, καὶ ἐκλείψεις ἔχουσαν. διὸ οὐ νενόμισται τὴν σελήνην εἶναι θεάν, ἀλλ' ἔργον θεοῦ.

VII. Οἱ δὲ νομίζοντες τὸν ἄνθρωπον εἶναι θεὸν πλανῶνται. ὁρῶμεν γὰρ αὐτὸν κινούμενον κατὰ ἀνάγκην, καὶ τρεφόμενον καὶ γηράσκοντα, καὶ μὴ θέλοντος αὐτοῦ. καὶ ποτὲ μὲν χαίρει, ποτὲ δὲ λυπεῖται, δεόμενος βρώματος καὶ ποτοῦ καὶ ἐσθῆτος. εἶναι δὲ αὐτὸν ὀργίλον καὶ ζηλωτὴν καὶ ἐπιθυμητήν, καὶ μεταμελόμενον, καὶ ἐλαττώματα πολλὰ ἔχοντα. φθείρεται δὲ κατὰ πολλοὺς τρόπους, ὑπὸ στοιχείων καὶ ζώων, καὶ τοῦ ἐπικειμένου αὐτῷ θανάτου. οὐκ ἐνδέχεται οὖν εἶναι τὸν ἄνθρωπον θεόν, ἀλλ' ἔργον θεοῦ.

Πλάνην οὖν μεγάλην ἐπλανήθησαν οἱ Χαλδαῖοι, ὀπίσω τῶν ἐπιθυμημάτων αὐτῶν. σέβονται γὰρ τὰ φθαρτὰ στοιχεῖα καὶ
244 τὰ νεκρὰ ἀγάλματα, καὶ οὐκ αἰσθάνονται ταῦτα θεοποιούμενοι.

1 *ἑτέρῳ*] *θεῷ* C 3 *συγκομηδὰς* M; *uentilationem* lat *σιτίων* Bois $V_{71.\,102}$ *αὐξουμένην* P 10 *μερισμὸν*] W; *diuisionem* lat; *μερισμοὺς* MP Bois 16, 17 *ἀνατέλουσαν* M 17 *χρῆσιν*] W; *χρείαν* MP Bois 18 *αὐξουμένην* MPW Bois 22 *καὶ ποτὲ μὲν χαίρει*] deficit C usque ad *καὶ εἰσὶ παράνομοι* p. 110, l. 10 23 *βρώματος*] *βρωμάτων* Bois; *ἄρτου* W; *cibo* lat 24 *ἐπιθυμητὴν καὶ ζηλωτὴν* M 25 *μετάμελον* W; *μεταβαλλόμενον* P *πολλὰ ἐλαττώματα* Bois 27 *ὑποκειμένου* W; *imminente* lat 30 *ἐπιθυμιῶν* P

VIII. Ἔλθωμεν οὖν ἐπὶ τοὺς Ἕλληνας, ἵνα ἴδωμεν εἴ τι φρονοῦσι περὶ θεοῦ. οἱ οὖν Ἕλληνες σοφοὶ λέγοντες εἶναι ἐμωράνθησαν χεῖρον τῶν Χαλδαίων, παρεισάγοντες θεοὺς πολλοὺς γεγενῆσθαι, τοὺς μὲν ἄρρενας, τὰς δὲ θηλείας, παντοίων παθῶν καὶ παντοδαπῶν δημιουργοὺς ἀνομημάτων. [οὓς ἐκεῖνοι αὐτοὶ [49] ἐξέθεντο μοιχοὺς εἶναι καὶ φονεῖς, ὀργίλους καὶ ζηλωτὰς καὶ θυμαντικούς, πατροκτόνους καὶ ἀδελφοκτόνους, κλέπτας καὶ ἅρπαγας, χωλοὺς καὶ κυλλούς, καὶ φαρμακούς, καὶ μαινομένους· καὶ τούτων τινὰς μὲν τετελευτηκότας, τινὰς δὲ κεκεραυνωμένους καὶ δεδουλευκότας ἀνθρώποις, καὶ φυγάδας γενομένους, καὶ κοπτομένους καὶ θρηνουμένους, καὶ εἰς ζῶα μεταμορφουμένους ἐπὶ πονηραῖς καὶ αἰσχραῖς πράξεσιν.] ὅθεν γελοῖα καὶ μωρὰ καὶ ἀσεβῆ παρεισήγαγον οἱ Ἕλληνες, βασιλεῦ, ῥήματα, τοὺς μὴ ὄντας προσαγορεύοντες θεούς, κατὰ τὰς ἐπιθυμίας αὐτῶν τὰς πονηράς, ἵνα, τούτους συνηγόρους ἔχοντες τῆς κακίας, μοιχεύωσιν, ἁρπάζωσι, φονεύωσι, καὶ τὰ πάνδεινα ποιῶσιν. εἰ γὰρ οἱ θεοὶ αὐτῶν τοιαῦτα ἐποίησαν, πῶς καὶ αὐτοὶ οὐ τοιαῦτα πράξουσιν; ἐκ τούτων οὖν τῶν ἐπιτηδευμάτων τῆς πλάνης συνέβη τοῖς ἀνθρώποις πολέμους ἔχειν συχνούς, καὶ σφαγὰς καὶ αἰχμαλωσίας πικράς.

IX. Ἀλλὰ καὶ καθ' ἕκαστον τῶν θεῶν αὐτῶν εἰ θελήσομεν ἐλθεῖν τῷ λόγῳ, πολλὴν ὄψει τὴν ἀτοπίαν· ὅπως παρεισάγεται αὐτοῖς πρὸ πάντων θεὸς Κρόνος, καὶ τούτῳ θύουσι τὰ ἴδια τέκνα· ὃς ἔσχε παῖδας πολλοὺς ἐκ τῆς Ῥέας, καὶ μανεὶς ἤσθιε τὰ ἴδια τέκνα. φασὶ δὲ τὸν Δία κόψαι αὐτοῦ τὰ ἀναγκαῖα καὶ βαλεῖν εἰς τὴν θάλασσαν, ὅθεν Ἀφροδίτη μυθεύεται γεννᾶσθαι. δήσας οὖν τὸν ἴδιον πατέρα ὁ Ζεὺς ἔβαλεν εἰς τὸν Τάρταρον. ὁρᾷς 245 τὴν πλάνην καὶ ἀσέλγειαν ἣν παρεισάγουσι κατὰ τοῦ θεοῦ

1 οὖν] καὶ PW; *itaque* lat 3 πολλοὺς θεοὺς Bois 4 τὰς] τοὺς Bois; *alios* lat 5 αὐτοὶ ἐκεῖνοι M 6 φωνεῖς, ὀργήλους M 7 καὶ ἀδελφοκτόνους] om. P syr; καὶ ἀδελφοκτώνους M 8 χωλοὺς—μαινομένους] καὶ ἐξωλεῖς κακῶν P κυλλοὺς] κοιλοὺς M 9 καικεραυνωμένους M; κεραυνωμένους P 10, 11 καὶ κοπτ. καὶ θρην.] post κεκεραυνωμένους Bois 12 πράξεσιν] μίξεσιν Bois 15, 16 μοιχεύσωσιν, ἁρπάξωσι, φονεύσωσι M 16 πάνδεινα] πάντα δεινὰ P; δεινὰ πάντα M; *omnia mala* lat 18 πράξωσιν PW + εἰ γὰρ οἱ θεοὶ αὐτῶν ἄφρονες, πῶς οὐχὶ καὶ αὐτοὶ ὅμοιοι αὐτοῖς ἔσονται W 19 τοὺς ἀνθρώπους Bois 21 om. καὶ PW lat 22 ὅπως] ὁ πρῶτος coniecit Bois; *inducitur enim* lat 23 θεὸς] + ὁ λεγόμενος Bois θύσωσι P 24 ἴσθιε M 25 τὸν Δία κόψαι] τοῦτον διακόψαι W² 26 ἀφροδίτην W Bois μηθύεται M; μυθύεσθαι Bois 27 ἔβαλλεν W²

αὐτῶν; ἐνδέχεται οὖν θεὸν εἶναι δέσμιον καὶ ἀπόκοπον; ὦ τῆς ἀνοίας· τίς τῶν νοῦν ἐχόντων ταῦτα φήσειεν;

Δεύτερος παρεισάγεται ὁ Ζεὺς, ὃν φασὶ βασιλεῦσαι τῶν θεῶν αὐτῶν, καὶ μεταμορφοῦσθαι εἰς ζῶα, ὅπως μοιχεύσῃ θνητὰς γυναῖκας. παρεισάγουσι γὰρ τοῦτον μεταμορφούμενον εἰς ταῦρον πρὸς Εὐρώπην, καὶ εἰς χρυσὸν πρὸς Δανάην, καὶ εἰς κύκνον πρὸς Λήδαν, καὶ εἰς σάτυρον πρὸς Ἀντιόπην, καὶ εἰς κεραυνὸν πρὸς Σεμέλην· εἶτα γενέσθαι ἐκ τούτων τέκνα πολλὰ, Διόνυσον καὶ Ζῆθον καὶ Ἀμφίονα καὶ Ἡρακλῆν καὶ Ἀπόλλωνα καὶ Ἄρτεμιν καὶ Περσέα, Κάστορά τε καὶ Ἑλένην καὶ Πολυδεύκην,
246 καὶ Μίνωα καὶ Ῥαδάμανθυν καὶ Σαρπηδόνα, καὶ τὰς ἐννέα θυγατέρας ἃς προσηγόρευσαν Μούσας. εἶθ' οὕτως παρεισάγουσι τὰ κατὰ τὸν Γανυμήδην. συνέβη οὖν, βασιλεῦ, τοῖς ἀνθρώποις μιμεῖσθαι ταῦτα πάντα, καὶ γίνεσθαι μοιχοὺς καὶ ἀρρενομανεῖς, καὶ ἄλλων δεινῶν ἔργων ἐργάτας, κατὰ μίμησιν τοῦ θεοῦ αὐτῶν. πῶς οὖν ἐνδέχεται θεὸν εἶναι μοιχὸν ἢ ἀνδροβάτην, ἢ πατροκτόνον;

X. Σὺν τούτῳ δὲ καὶ Ἥφαιστόν τινα παρεισάγουσι θεὸν εἶναι, καὶ τοῦτον χωλὸν, καὶ κρατοῦντα σφῦραν καὶ πυρόλαβον, καὶ χαλκεύοντα χάριν τροφῆς. ἆρα ἐπενδεής ἐστιν; ὅπερ οὐκ ἐνδέχεται θεὸν εἶναι χωλὸν οὐδὲ προσδεόμενον ἀνθρώπων.

Εἶτα τὸν Ἑρμῆν παρεισάγουσι θεὸν εἶναι ἐπιθυμητὴν καὶ κλέπτην καὶ πλεονέκτην καὶ μάγον †καὶ κυλλὸν† καὶ λόγων ἑρμηνευτήν. ὅπερ οὐκ ἐνδέχεται θεὸν εἶναι τοιοῦτον.

Τὸν δὲ Ἀσκληπιὸν παρεισάγουσι θεὸν εἶναι, ἰατρὸν ὄντα καὶ κατασκευάζοντα φάρμακα καὶ σύνθεσιν ἐμπλάστρων, χάριν τροφῆς· ἐπενδεὴς γὰρ ἦν· ὕστερον δὲ κεραυνοῦσθαι αὐτὸν ὑπὸ τοῦ Διὸς διὰ Τυνδάρεων Λακεδαίμονος υἱὸν, καὶ ἀποθανεῖν. εἰ

2 τῶν] τὸν W*   3, 4 τῶν θεῶν] τὸν θεὸν P   8 σημέλην P   9 ἀμφίωνα P   ἡρακλῆ M   ἀπόλωνα MW   10 κάστωρα P   πολυδευκῆ M   11 μήνωα PW   om. καὶ (prim.) P   σαρπιδόνα M   ἐνέα W*   12 παρειάγουσι P   13 γανυμίδην P   συνέβη] σέβη M   14 om. ταῦτα πάντα καὶ γίνεσθαι P   15 om. ἔργων M   τοῦ θεοῦ] τῶν θεῶν AW syr; *dei sui* lat   18 τούτῳ] τούτοις W²   παρεισάγουσί τινα M   20 ἐπιδεής W Bois   21 οὐδὲ] καὶ P Bois   23 κυλὸν W; *uersipellem* lat   23, 24 om. καὶ μάγον—ἑρμηνευτήν M   24 εἶναι] + τὸν P; + χωλὸν (κυλὸν W²) οὐδὲ προσδεόμενον ἀνθρώπων· ὅπερ οὐκ ἐνδέχεται θεὸν εἶναι W   25 ἀσκήπιον M   27 ἐπιδεὴς W   28 τυνδάρεων] Bois; τυνδάρεω M; τυνδάρεως W²P; τοινδάρεως AW*; *Darii* lat

δὲ Ἀσκληπιὸς θεὸς ὢν καὶ κεραυνωθεὶς οὐκ ἠδυνήθη ἑαυτῷ βοηθῆσαι, πῶς ἄλλοις βοηθήσει;

Ἄρης δὲ παρεισάγεται θεὸς εἶναι πολεμιστὴς καὶ ζηλωτής, 247
καὶ ἐπιθυμητὴς θρεμμάτων καὶ ἑτέρων τινῶν· ὕστερον δὲ αὐτὸν μοιχεύοντα τὴν Ἀφροδίτην δεθῆναι αὐτὸν ὑπὸ τοῦ νηπίου Ἔρωτος καὶ ὑπὸ Ἡφαίστου. πῶς οὖν θεὸς ἦν ὁ ἐπιθυμητὴς καὶ πολεμιστὴς καὶ δέσμιος καὶ μοιχός;

Τὸν δὲ Διόνυσον παρεισάγουσι θεὸν εἶναι, νυκτερινὰς ἄγοντα ἑορτὰς καὶ διδάσκαλον μέθης, καὶ ἀποσπῶντα τὰς τῶν πλησίον γυναῖκας, καὶ μαινόμενον καὶ φεύγοντα· ὕστερον δὲ αὐτὸν σφαγῆναι ὑπὸ τῶν Τιτάνων. εἰ οὖν Διόνυσος σφαγεὶς οὐκ ἠδυνήθη ἑαυτῷ βοηθῆσαι, ἀλλὰ καὶ μαινόμενος ἦν καὶ μέθυσος καὶ δραπέτης, πῶς ἂν εἴη θεός;

Τὸν δὲ Ἡρακλῆν παρεισάγουσι μεθυσθῆναι καὶ μανῆναι, καὶ τὰ ἴδια τέκνα σφάξαι, εἶτα πυρὶ ἀναλωθῆναι καὶ οὕτως ἀποθανεῖν. πῶς δ' ἂν εἴη θεός, μέθυσος καὶ τεκνοκτόνος, καὶ κατακαιόμενος; ἢ πῶς ἄλλοις βοηθήσει, ἑαυτῷ βοηθῆσαι μὴ δυνηθείς;

XI. Τὸν δὲ Ἀπόλλωνα παρεισάγουσι θεὸν εἶναι ζηλωτήν, ἔτι δὲ καὶ τόξον καὶ φαρέτραν κρατοῦντα, ποτὲ δὲ καὶ κιθάραν καὶ †ἐπαυθίδα†, καὶ μαντευόμενον τοῖς ἀνθρώποις χάριν μισθοῦ. ἆρα ἐπενδεής ἐστιν; ὅπερ οὐκ ἐνδέχεται θεὸν εἶναι ἐνδεῆ καὶ ζηλωτὴν καὶ κιθαρῳδόν.

Ἄρτεμιν δὲ παρεισάγουσιν ἀδελφὴν αὐτοῦ εἶναι, κυνηγὸν οὖσαν, καὶ τόξον ἔχειν μετὰ φαρέτρας· καὶ ταύτην ῥέμβεσθαι
κατὰ τῶν ὀρέων μόνην μετὰ τῶν κυνῶν, ὅπως θηρεύσῃ ἔλαφον 248
ἢ κάπρον. πῶς οὖν ἔσται θεὸς ἡ τοιαύτη γυνὴ καὶ κυνηγὸς καὶ ῥεμβομένη μετὰ τῶν κυνῶν;

Ἀφροδίτην δὲ λέγουσι καὶ αὐτὴν θεὰν εἶναι μοιχαλίδα. ποτὲ γὰρ ἔσχε μοιχὸν τὸν Ἄρην, ποτὲ δὲ Ἀγχίσην, ποτὲ δὲ Ἄδωνιν, οὗτινος καὶ τὸν θάνατον κλαίει, ζητοῦσα τὸν ἐραστὴν

1 ἠδυνήθει M αὐτῷ W 4 ἐπιθυμίτης M θρεμμάτων] χρημάτων V_{102}; χρημάτων θρεμμάτων W; *ouium* lat 6 ἦν] ἐστιν P Bois 12 om. ἀλλὰ M 14 ἡρακλῆ M 17 βοηθήσει] + ὁ W 19 ἀπόλωνα W² 20 om. καὶ (prim.) MW κρατεῖν M om. καὶ (tert.) W κιθάρα M 21 ἐπαυθίδα] W Bois; ἐπανθίδα M; ἐπαυλίδα P; *tibiam* lat; πηκτίδα coniecit Bois 23 ἐνδεῆ καὶ ζηλωτὴν] ζηλωτήν, ἐνδεῆ P 25 ἔχειν] ἔχον M 26 om. τῶν (sec.) W θηρεύσει P Bois 27 om. οὖν P 30 ἀγχίσιν PW* 31 ἀδώνην MP οὗτινος] αὕτη W²

αὐτῆς· ἣν λέγουσιν καὶ εἰς Ἅδου καταβαίνειν, ὅπως ἐξαγοράσῃ τὸν Ἄδωνιν ἀπὸ τῆς Περσεφόνης. εἶδες, ὦ βασιλεῦ, μείζονα ταύτης ἀφροσύνην· θεὰν παρεισάγειν τὴν μοιχεύουσαν καὶ θρηνοῦσαν καὶ κλαίουσαν;

Ἄδωνιν δὲ παρεισάγουσι θεὸν εἶναι κυνηγόν, καὶ τοῦτον βιαίως ἀποθανεῖν πληγέντα ὑπὸ τοῦ ὑός, καὶ μὴ δυνηθέντα βοηθῆσαι τῇ ταλαιπωρίᾳ αὐτοῦ. πῶς οὖν τῶν ἀνθρώπων φροντίδα ποιήσεται ὁ μοιχὸς καὶ κυνηγὸς καὶ βιοθάνατος;

Ταῦτα πάντα καὶ πολλὰ τοιαῦτα καὶ πολλῷ πλεῖον αἰσχρότερα καὶ πονηρὰ παρεισήγαγον οἱ Ἕλληνες, βασιλεῦ, περὶ τῶν θεῶν αὐτῶν, ἃ οὔτε λέγειν θέμις, οὔτ' ἐπὶ μνήμης ὅλως φέρειν· ὅθεν λαμβάνοντες οἱ ἄνθρωποι ἀφορμὴν ἀπὸ τῶν θεῶν αὐτῶν, ἔπραττον πᾶσαν ἀνομίαν καὶ ἀσέλγειαν καὶ ἀσέβειαν, καταμιαίνοντες γῆν τε καὶ ἀέρα ταῖς δειναῖς αὐτῶν πράξεσιν.

249 XII. Αἰγύπτιοι δέ, ἀβελτερώτεροι καὶ ἀφρονέστεροι τούτων ὄντες, χεῖρον πάντων τῶν ἐθνῶν ἐπλανήθησαν. οὐ γὰρ ἠρκέσθησαν τοῖς τῶν Χαλδαίων καὶ Ἑλλήνων σεβάσμασιν, ἀλλ' ἔτι καὶ ἄλογα ζῶα παρεισήγαγον θεοὺς εἶναι χερσαῖά τε καὶ ἔνυδρα, καὶ τὰ φυτὰ καὶ βλαστά, καὶ ἐμιάνθησαν ἐν πάσῃ μανίᾳ καὶ ἀσελγείᾳ χεῖρον πάντων τῶν ἐθνῶν ἐπὶ τῆς γῆς.

Ἀρχαίως γὰρ ἐσέβοντο τὴν Ἶσιν, ἔχουσαν ἀδελφὸν καὶ ἄνδρα τὸν Ὄσιριν, τὸν σφαγέντα ὑπὸ τοῦ ἀδελφοῦ αὐτοῦ τοῦ Τυφῶνος. καὶ διὰ τοῦτο φεύγει ἡ Ἶσις μετὰ Ὥρου τοῦ υἱοῦ αὐτῆς εἰς Βύβλον τῆς Συρίας, ζητοῦσα τὸν Ὄσιριν, καὶ πικρῶς θρηνοῦσα, ἕως ηὔξησεν ὁ Ὧρος καὶ ἀπέκτεινε τὸν Τυφῶνα. οὔτε οὖν ἡ Ἶσις ἴσχυσε βοηθῆσαι τῷ ἰδίῳ ἀδελφῷ καὶ ἀνδρί· οὔτε ὁ Ὄσιρις σφαζόμενος ὑπὸ τοῦ Τυφῶνος ἠδυνήθη ἀντιλαβέσθαι ἑαυτοῦ· οὔτε Τυφῶν ὁ ἀδελφοκτόνος, ἀπολλύμενος ὑπὸ τοῦ Ὥρου καὶ τῆς Ἴσιδος, εὐπόρησε ῥύσασθαι ἑαυτὸν τοῦ

1 ἣν] ὃν W* 2 ἴδες W 3 μοιχευομένην W² 5 ἀδώνην M 6 υἱὸς W δυνηθῆναι MP 7 βοηθῆσαι post αὐτοῦ P αὐτοῦ] ἑαυτοῦ Bois 8 ποιήσηται PW βιαιοθάνατος M 9 πλείονα P; *plura* lat 10 παρεισάγουσιν M; παρήγαγον P 12 τῶν] τοῦ P 14 καὶ] + τὸν P 15 ἀβελτερώτεροι] M Bois; ἀβελτώτεροι DW*; ἀβελτότεροι APW² 18 ἄλογα] ἄλλα M παρήγαγον W 20 ἐπὶ τῆς γῆς] ἐπὶ γῆς M; τῶν ἐπὶ τῆς γῆς P; ἐπλανήθησαν W 21 ἀρχαίως] ἀρχῆθεν Bois; *in principio* lat ἀδελφὴν W 23 om. τοῦ (prior.) Bois μετὰ] + τοῦ τύφωνος καὶ W 24 βίβλον MPW* om. καὶ P Bois 25 θρηνοῦσα] θανοῦσα W 27 om. ὁ M 28 ἀπολλύμενος] Bois; ἀπολλόμενος MPW

θανάτου. καὶ ἐπὶ τοιούτοις ἀτυχήμασι γνωρισθέντες αὐτοὶ θεοὶ ὑπὸ τῶν ἀσυνέτων Αἰγυπτίων ἐνομίσθησαν· οἵτινες, μηδ' 250
ἐν τούτοις ἀρκεσθέντες ἢ τοῖς λοιποῖς σεβάσμασι τῶν ἐθνῶν, καὶ τὰ ἄλογα ζῷα παρεισήγαγον θεοὺς εἶναι.

Τινὲς γὰρ αὐτῶν ἐσεβάσθησαν πρόβατον, τινὲς δὲ τράγον, ἕτεροι δὲ μόσχον καὶ τὸν χοῖρον, ἄλλοι δὲ τὸν κόρακα καὶ τὸν ἱέρακα καὶ τὸν γῦπα καὶ τὸν ἀετὸν, καὶ ἄλλοι τὸν κροκόδειλον, τινὲς δὲ τὸν αἴλουρον καὶ τὸν κύνα, καὶ τὸν λύκον καὶ τὸν πίθηκον, καὶ τὸν δράκοντα καὶ τὴν ἀσπίδα, καὶ ἄλλοι τὸ κρόμυον καὶ τὸ σκόροδον καὶ ἀκάνθας, καὶ τὰ λοιπὰ κτίσματα. καὶ οὐκ αἰσθάνονται οἱ ταλαίπωροι περὶ πάντων τούτων ὅτι οὐδὲν ἰσχύουσιν. ὁρῶντες γὰρ τοὺς θεοὺς αὐτῶν βιβρωσκομένους ὑπὸ ἑτέρων ἀνθρώπων καὶ καιομένους καὶ σφαττομένους καὶ σηπομένους, οὐ συνῆκαν περὶ αὐτῶν ὅτι οὐκ εἰσὶ θεοί.

XIII. Πλάνην οὖν μεγάλην ἐπλανήθησαν οἵ τε Αἰγύπτιοι καὶ οἱ Χαλδαῖοι καὶ οἱ Ἕλληνες τοιούτους παρεισάγοντες θεοὺς, καὶ ἀγάλματα αὐτῶν ποιοῦντες, καὶ θεοποιούμενοι τὰ κωφὰ καὶ ἀναίσθητα εἴδωλα. καὶ θαυμάζω πῶς ὁρῶντες τοὺς θεοὺς αὐτῶν ὑπὸ τῶν δημιουργῶν πριζομένους καὶ πελεκουμένους, καὶ κολοβουμένους, παλαιουμένους τε ὑπὸ τοῦ χρόνου καὶ ἀναλυομένους καὶ χωνευομένους, οὐκ ἐφρόνησαν περὶ αὐτῶν ὅτι οὐκ εἰσὶ θεοί. ὅτε γὰρ περὶ τῆς ἰδίας σωτηρίας οὐδὲν ἰσχύουσι, πῶς τῶν ἀνθρώπων πρόνοιαν ποιήσονται; ἀλλ' οἱ ποιηταὶ αὐτῶν καὶ φιλόσοφοι, τῶν τε Χαλδαίων καὶ Ἑλλήνων καὶ Αἰγυπτίων, θελήσαντες τοῖς ποιήμασιν αὐτῶν καὶ συγγραφαῖς σεμνῦναι τοὺς παρ' αὐτοῖς θεοὺς, μειζόνως τὴν αἰσχύνην αὐτῶν ἐξεκάλυψαν καὶ γυμνὴν πᾶσι προὔθηκαν. εἰ γὰρ τὸ σῶμα τοῦ ἀνθρώπου πολυμερὲς ὂν οὐκ ἀποβάλλεταί τι τῶν ἰδίων μελῶν, ἀλλὰ πρὸς πάντα τὰ μέλη ἀδιάρρηκτον ἕνωσιν ἔχον ἑαυτῷ ἐστὶ σύμφωνον, 251
πῶς ἐν φύσει θεοῦ μάχη καὶ διαφωνία ἔσται τοσαύτη; εἰ γὰρ

2, 3 μηδ' ἐν] μηδὲ W 4 om. θεοὺς εἶναι MW*; *deos esse* lat 7 κορκόδηλον W 8 om. τὸν (prim.) PW ἔλουρον W* om. τὸν (sec.) MPW 9 πίθηκα W καὶ τὸν δράκοντα] δράκοντα δὲ P; om. τὸν M 10 κρόμμυον M σκόρδον M ἀκάνθας] Bois; ἄκανθα PW; ἄκανθον M; *spinas* lat 11 ᾐσθάνοντο P 14 σηπομένους] + καὶ P 16 om. οἱ (sec.) W 19 πελεκωμένους Bois 19, 20 om. καὶ κολοβουμένους Bois 20 κολοβωμένους MP 20, 21 ἀναλλοιουμένους καὶ χονευομένους P 26 παρ' αὐτῶν P 29 ἔχων W* 30 τοσαύτη ἔσται PW

μία φύσις τῶν θεῶν ὑπῆρχεν, οὐκ ὤφειλεν θεὸς θεὸν διώκειν, οὔτε σφάζειν, οὔτε κακοποιεῖν· εἰ δὲ οἱ θεοὶ ὑπὸ θεῶν ἐδιώχθησαν καὶ ἐσφάγησαν, καὶ ἡρπάγησαν καὶ ἐκεραυνώθησαν, οὐκ ἔτι μία φύσις ἐστὶν, ἀλλὰ γνῶμαι διῃρημέναι, πᾶσαι κακοποιοί· ὥστε οὐδεὶς ἐξ αὐτῶν ἐστὶ θεός. φανερὸν οὖν ἐστὶν, ὦ βασιλεῦ, πλάνην εἶναι πᾶσαν τὴν περὶ τῶν θεῶν φυσιολογίαν.

Πῶς δὲ οὐ συνῆκαν οἱ σοφοὶ καὶ λόγιοι τῶν Ἑλλήνων ὅτι νόμους θέμενοι κρίνονται ὑπὸ τῶν ἰδίων νόμων; εἰ γὰρ οἱ νόμοι δίκαιοί εἰσιν, ἄδικοι πάντως οἱ θεοὶ αὐτῶν εἰσὶ, παράνομα ποιήσαντες, ἀλληλοκτονίας καὶ φαρμακείας καὶ μοιχείας καὶ κλοπὰς καὶ ἀρσενοκοιτίας. εἰ δὲ καλῶς ἔπραξαν ταῦτα, οἱ νόμοι ἄρα ἄδικοί εἰσι, κατὰ τῶν θεῶν συντεθέντες. νυνὶ δὲ οἱ νόμοι καλοί εἰσι καὶ δίκαιοι, τὰ καλὰ ἐπαινοῦντες καὶ τὰ κακὰ ἀπαγορεύοντες· τὰ δὲ ἔργα τῶν θεῶν αὐτῶν παράνομα· παράνομοι ἄρα οἱ θεοὶ αὐτῶν, καὶ ἔνοχοι πάντες θανάτου καὶ ἀσεβεῖς οἱ τοιούτους θεοὺς παρεισάγοντες. εἰ μὲν γὰρ μυθικαὶ αἱ περὶ αὐτῶν ἱστορίαι, οὐδέν εἰσιν εἰ μὴ μόνον λόγοι· εἰ δὲ φυσικαὶ, οὐκ ἔτι θεοί εἰσιν οἱ ταῦτα ποιήσαντες καὶ παθόντες· εἰ δὲ ἀλληγορικαὶ, μῦθοί εἰσι καὶ οὐκ ἄλλο τι.

252 XIV. Ἀποδέδεικται τοίνυν, ὦ βασιλεῦ, ταῦτα πάντα τὰ πολύθεα σεβάσματα πλάνης ἔργα καὶ ἀπωλείας ὑπάρχειν. οὐ χρὴ γὰρ θεοὺς ὀνομάζειν ὁρατοὺς καὶ μὴ ὁρῶντας· ἀλλὰ τὸν ἀόρατον καὶ πάντα ὁρῶντα καὶ πάντα δημιουργήσαντα δεῖ θεὸν σέβεσθαι.

Ἔλθωμεν οὖν, ὦ βασιλεῦ, καὶ ἐπὶ τοὺς Ἰουδαίους, ὅπως ἴδωμεν τί φρονοῦσι καὶ αὐτοὶ περὶ θεοῦ. οὗτοι γὰρ, τοῦ Ἀβραὰμ ὄντες ἀπόγονοι καὶ Ἰσαὰκ καὶ Ἰακὼβ, παρῴκησαν εἰς Αἴγυπτον· ἐκεῖθεν δὲ ἐξήγαγεν αὐτοὺς ὁ θεὸς ἐν χειρὶ κραταιᾷ καὶ ἐν βραχίονι ὑψηλῷ διὰ Μωσέως τοῦ νομοθέτου αὐτῶν, καὶ τέρασι πολλοῖς καὶ σημείοις ἐγνώρισεν αὐτοῖς τὴν ἑαυτοῦ δύναμιν.

1 ὑπεῖρχεν ὠκ M διώκην M 2 εἰ] Οἱ M (Ο rubr.) οἱ] supra lin. e pri. manu M 4 κακοποιαί PW² 5 φανερὰν W om. ἐστὶν MW 7 ὅτι] + καὶ οἱ coniecit Bois 9 πάντως] πάντες W om. εἰσὶ W* 10 φαρμακίας P Bois 11 ἀρσενοκοιτείας M 14 εἰ τὰ ἔργα δὲ M 15 ἄρα] + καὶ P 17, 18 om. εἰ μὴ—θεοί εἰσιν M 18 ταῦτα] τοιαῦτα M 20 ἀποδέδεικται cum preced. W 21 ὑπάρχει W² 22 γὰρ] οὖν Bois 23 πάντα ὁρῶντα καὶ πάντα] πάντα ὁρῶντα καὶ πάντας P; πάντας Bois 24 σέβεσθαι θεόν Bois 26, 27 ὄντες τοῦ ἀβραὰμ P 27 om. καὶ (prior) P ἰσαὰκ] + τε P Bois

ἀλλά, ἀγνώμονες καὶ αὐτοὶ φανέντες καὶ ἀχάριστοι, πολλάκις ἐλάτρευσαν τοῖς τῶν ἐθνῶν σεβάσμασι, καὶ τοὺς ἀπεσταλμένους πρὸς αὐτοὺς προφήτας καὶ δικαίους ἀπέκτειναν. εἶτα ὡς εὐδόκησεν ὁ υἱὸς τοῦ θεοῦ ἐλθεῖν ἐπὶ τῆς γῆς, ἐμπαροινήσαντες εἰς αὐτὸν προέδωκαν Πιλάτῳ τῷ ἡγεμόνι τῶν Ῥωμαίων καὶ σταυρῷ κατεδίκασαν, μὴ αἰδεσθέντες τὰς εὐεργεσίας αὐτοῦ, καὶ τὰ ἀναρίθμητα θαύματα ἅπερ ἐν αὐτοῖς εἰργάσατο· καὶ ἀπώλοντο τῇ ἰδίᾳ παρανομίᾳ. σέβονται γὰρ καὶ νῦν τὸν θεὸν μόνον παντοκράτορα, ἀλλ' οὐ κατ' ἐπίγνωσιν· τὸν γὰρ χριστὸν ἀρνοῦνται τὸν υἱὸν τοῦ θεοῦ, καὶ εἰσὶ παρόμοιοι τῶν ἐθνῶν, κἂν ἐγγίζειν πως τῇ ἀληθείᾳ δοκῶσιν, ἧς ἑαυτοὺς ἐμάκρυναν. ταῦτα περὶ τῶν Ἰουδαίων.

XV. Οἱ δὲ χριστιανοὶ γενεαλογοῦνται ἀπὸ τοῦ κυρίου Ἰησοῦ Χριστοῦ. οὗτος δὲ ὁ υἱὸς τοῦ θεοῦ τοῦ ὑψίστου ὁμολογεῖται ἐν πνεύματι ἁγίῳ ἀπ' οὐρανοῦ καταβὰς διὰ τὴν σωτηρίαν τῶν 253
ἀνθρώπων· καὶ ἐκ παρθένου ἁγίας γεννηθείς, ἀσπόρως τε καὶ ἀφθόρως, σάρκα ἀνέλαβε, καὶ ἀνεφάνη ἀνθρώποις, ὅπως ἐκ τῆς πολυθέου πλάνης αὐτοὺς ἀνακαλέσηται. καὶ τελέσας τὴν θαυμαστὴν αὐτοῦ οἰκονομίαν, διὰ σταυροῦ θανάτου ἐγεύσατο ἑκουσίᾳ βουλῇ κατ' οἰκονομίαν μεγάλην· μετὰ δὲ τρεῖς ἡμέρας ἀνεβίω καὶ εἰς οὐρανοὺς ἀνῆλθεν. οὗ τὸ κλέος τῆς παρουσίας ἐκ τῆς παρ' αὐτοῖς καλουμένης εὐαγγελικῆς ἁγίας γραφῆς ἔξεστί σοι γνῶναι, βασιλεῦ, ἐὰν ἐντύχῃς. οὗτος δώδεκα ἔσχε μαθητάς, οἳ μετὰ τὴν ἐν οὐρανοῖς ἄνοδον αὐτοῦ ἐξῆλθον εἰς τὰς ἐπαρχίας τῆς οἰκουμένης, καὶ ἐδίδαξαν τὴν ἐκείνου μεγαλωσύνην· καθάπερ εἷς ἐξ αὐτῶν τὰς καθ' ἡμᾶς περιῆλθε χώρας, τὸ δόγμα κηρύττων τῆς ἀληθείας. ὅθεν οἱ εἰσέτι διακονοῦντες τῇ δικαιοσύνῃ τοῦ κηρύγματος αὐτῶν καλοῦνται χριστιανοί.

Καὶ οὗτοί εἰσιν οἱ ὑπὲρ πάντα τὰ ἔθνη τῆς γῆς εὑρόντες τὴν ἀλήθειαν· γινώσκουσι γὰρ τὸν θεὸν κτίστην καὶ δημιουργὸν τῶν ἁπάντων ἐν υἱῷ μονογενεῖ καὶ πνεύματι ἁγίῳ, καὶ ἄλλον

1 ἀχάριστοι] ἄχρηστοι Bois 3, 4 ηὐδώκησεν P 5 om. τῷ M ἡγημόνι P 7 καὶ] διὸ P Bois 8 θεὸν τὸν μόνον Bois 9 παντοκράτωρα PW* 10 παρόμοιοι] παρόμηοι M; παράνομοι W* τοῖς ἔθνεσι Bois κἂν] καὶ W² 11 δοκῶσιν W* 14 om. ὁ P 17 ἀδιαφθόρως W² 18 αὐτοὺς πλάνης P 19 αὐτοῦ] + μεγάλην W θανάτον W 20 μεγάλιν W 22 om. ἁγίας M 23 om. γνῶναι W τύχῃς W* ἔσχε δώδεκα P 25 μεγαλοσύνην PW* 29 om. οἱ P 30 θεὸν] + εἶναι W² 31 μονογενῆ PW²

θεὸν πλὴν τούτου οὐ σέβονται. ἔχουσι τὰς ἐντολὰς αὐτοῦ τοῦ
κυρίου Ἰησοῦ Χριστοῦ ἐν ταῖς καρδίαις κεχαραγμένας, καὶ
ταύτας φυλάττουσι, προσδοκῶντες ἀνάστασιν νεκρῶν καὶ ζωὴν
τοῦ μέλλοντος αἰῶνος. οὐ μοιχεύουσιν, οὐ πορνεύουσιν, οὐ
ψευδομαρτυροῦσιν, οὐκ ἐπιθυμοῦσι τὰ ἀλλότρια, τιμῶσι πατέρα
καὶ μητέρα, καὶ τοὺς πλησίον φιλοῦσι, δίκαια κρίνουσιν, ὅσα οὐ
θέλουσιν αὐτοῖς γίνεσθαι ἑτέρῳ οὐ ποιοῦσι, τοὺς ἀδικοῦντας
αὐτοὺς παρακαλοῦσι καὶ προσφιλεῖς αὐτοὺς ἑαυτοῖς ποιοῦσι, ܟܕ
τοὺς ἐχθροὺς εὐεργετεῖν σπουδάζουσι, πραεῖς εἰσὶ καὶ ἐπιεικεῖς,
254 ἀπὸ πάσης συνουσίας ἀνόμου καὶ ἀπὸ πάσης ἀκαθαρσίας
ἐγκρατεύονται, χήραν οὐχ ὑπερορῶσιν, ὀρφανὸν οὐ λυποῦσιν·
ὁ ἔχων τῷ μὴ ἔχοντι ἀνεπιφθόνως ἐπιχορηγεῖ· ξένον ἐὰν
ἴδωσιν, ὑπὸ στέγην εἰσάγουσι, καὶ χαίρουσιν ἐπ' αὐτῷ ὡς
ἐπὶ ἀδελφῷ ἀληθινῷ· οὐ γὰρ κατὰ σάρκα ἀδελφοὺς ἑαυτοὺς
καλοῦσιν, ἀλλὰ κατὰ ψυχήν. ἕτοιμοί εἰσιν ὑπὲρ Χριστοῦ
τὰς ψυχὰς αὐτῶν προέσθαι· τὰ γὰρ προστάγματα αὐτοῦ
ἀσφαλῶς φυλάττουσιν, ὁσίως καὶ δικαίως ζῶντες, καθὼς
κύριος ὁ θεὸς αὐτοῖς προσέταξεν, εὐχαριστοῦντες αὐτῷ κατὰ ܟܗ
πᾶσαν ὥραν ἐν παντὶ βρώματι καὶ ποτῷ καὶ τοῖς λοιποῖς
ἀγαθοῖς.

XVI. Ὄντως οὖν αὕτη ἐστὶν ἡ ὁδὸς τῆς ἀληθείας, ἥτις τοὺς
ὁδεύοντας αὐτὴν εἰς τὴν αἰώνιον χειραγωγεῖ βασιλείαν, τὴν
ἐπηγγελμένην παρὰ Χριστοῦ ἐν τῇ μελλούσῃ ζωῇ. καὶ ἵνα ܟܘ
γνῷς, βασιλεῦ, ὅτι οὐκ ἀπ' ἐμαυτοῦ ταῦτα λέγω, ταῖς γραφαῖς
ἐγκύψας τῶν χριστιανῶν εὑρήσεις οὐδὲν ἔξω τῆς ἀληθείας με
λέγειν.

Καλῶς οὖν συνῆκεν ὁ υἱός σου, καὶ δικαίως ἐδιδάχθη τοῦ
λατρεύειν ζῶντι θεῷ καὶ σωθῆναι εἰς τὸν μέλλοντα ἐπέρχεσθαι
αἰῶνα. μεγάλα γὰρ καὶ θαυμαστὰ τὰ ὑπὸ τῶν χριστιανῶν
λεγόμενα καὶ πραττόμενα· οὐ γὰρ ἀνθρώπων ῥήματα λαλοῦσιν,
ἀλλὰ τὰ τοῦ θεοῦ. τὰ δὲ λοιπὰ ἔθνη πλανῶνται, καὶ πλανῶσιν

1 τούτου] αὐτοῦ W 2 ἐγκεχαραγμένας P 5 τῶν ἀλλοτρίων M 6, 7 αὐτοῖς οὐ θέλουσι W 7 ποιοῦσι] + καὶ P 8 αὐτοὺς (prior.)] αὐτοῖς W om. ἑαυτοῖς W 9 om. εἰσὶ W 12 ἀφθόνως P Bois 13 αὐτῷ] αὐτοῖς W[2] 14 ἑαυτοὺς ἀδελφοὺς W 15 ψυχήν] πνεῦμα V_{21} Bois; *animam* lat 16 αὐτῶν] ἑαυτῶν W 18 om. ὁ θεὸς W 19 ποτῷ] πόματι M 22 χειραγωγεῖ] + οὐρανῶν W[2] 27 ἐδιδάχθην W om. τοῦ Bois 28 σωθῆναι] συνθεῖναι W[2] 31 om. τὰ (prior.) P

ἑαυτούς· ὁδεύοντες γὰρ ἐν σκότει προσρήσσονται ἑαυτοῖς ὡς μεθύοντες.

XVII. Ἕως ὧδε ὁ πρὸς σέ μου λόγος, βασιλεῦ, ὁ ὑπὸ τῆς ἀληθείας ἐν τῷ νοΐ μου ὑπαγορευθείς. διὸ παυσάσθωσαν οἱ ἀνόητοί σου σοφοὶ ματαιολογοῦντες κατὰ τοῦ κυρίου· συμφέρει γὰρ ὑμῖν θεὸν κτίστην σέβεσθαι καὶ τὰ ἄφθαρτα αὐτοῦ 255
ἐνωτίζεσθαι ῥήματα, ἵνα, κρίσιν ἐκφυγόντες καὶ τιμωρίας, ζωῆς ἀνωλέθρου δειχθείητε κληρονόμοι.

1 προσρήσσοντες P 6 ἡμῖν W ἄφθαρτα] ἄφραστα W 7 τιμωρίας] MPW²; *tormenta* lat; τιμωρίαν W* Bois 8 ἀνολέθρου M

INDEX OF GREEK WORDS.

INDEX OF SUBJECT MATTER.

www.ingramcontent.com/pod-product-compliance
Lightning Source LLC
Chambersburg PA
CBHW051941160426
43198CB00013B/2255

* 9 7 8 1 5 9 2 4 4 8 4 7 0 *

ܫܠܡ ܒܪܘܚܐ

ܕܐܪܣܛܛܠܝܣ ܦܝܠܣܘܦܐ.

ܐܪܝܣܛܝܕܣ

ܬܘܒ ܡܦܩ ܒܪܘܚܐ ܕܥܒܕ ܐܪܝܣܛܝܕܣ ܦܝܠܘܣܘܦܐ. ܩܕܡ ܗܕܪܝܢܘܣ ܡܠܟܐ܆ ܥܠ ܫ̈ܘܦ ܕܠܝܬ ܐܠܗܐ: ܐܘܚܕ ܟܠ ܩܣܪ ܛܝܛܘܣ ܗܕܪܝܢܘܣ ܐܢܛܘܢܝܢܘܣ. ܣ̈ܒܝܣܛܐ ܘܡܪ̈ܚܡܢܐ. ܡܢ ܡܪܩܝܢܘܣ ܐܪܝܣܛܝܕܣ ܦܝܠܘܣܘܦܐ ܕܐܬ̈ܢܝܐ ܀

ܐܢܐ ܐܘ̄ ܡܠܟܐ ܒܛܝܒܘܬܗ ܕܐܠܗܐ ܐܬܝܬ ܠܥܠܡܐ ܗܢܐ. ܘܟܕ ܐܬܒܩܝܬ ܒܫܡܝܐ ܘܒܐܪܥܐ. ܘܒܝ̈ܡܡܐ. ܘܚܙܝܬ ܠܫܡܫܐ ܘܠܫܪܟܐ ܕܬܘܩ̈ܢܐ. ܐܬܕܡܪܬ ܒܬܩܢܘܬܗ ܕܥܠܡܐ. ܐܣܬܟܠܬ ܕܝܢ. ܕܗܘ ܥܠܡܐ ܘܟܠ ܕܒܗ܆ ܕܡܢ ܥܘܝܢܐ ܕܐܚܪܢܐ ܡܬܬܙܝܥܝܢ. ܘܐܣܬܟܠܬ܆ ܕܗܘ ܕܡܙܝܥ ܠܗܘܢ ܐܠܗܐ ܐܝܬܘܗܝ. ܕܟܣܐ ܒܗܘܢ ܘܚܒܝܫ ܡܢܗܘܢ. ܘܝܕܝܥܐ ܗܝ ܕܗܘ ܕܡܙܝܥ ܚܝܠܬܢ ܡܢ ܗܘ ܕܡܬܬܙܝܥ. ܘܕܐܬܒܥܐ ܠܡܥܩܒ ܥܠܘܗܝ ܕܗܘܝܘ ܡܕܒܪܢܐ ܕܟܠ. ܕܐܝܟܢ ܐܝܬܘܗܝ܆ ܗܕܐ ܓܝܪ ܡܬܚܙܝܐ ܠܝ܆ ܠܐ ܡܬܕܪܟܢܐ ܓܝܪ ܐܝܬܘܗܝ ܒܟܝܢܗ: ܘܕܐܬܒܨܐ ܥܠ ܫܪܝܪܘܬܐ ܕܡܕܒܪܢܘܬܗ ܐܝܟ ܕܐܕܪܟܝܗ ܠܟܠܗ. ܠܐ ܡܘܬܪܐ ܠܝ. ܠܐ ܓܝܪ ܐܢܫ ܡܫܟܚ ܕܡܫܡܠܝܐܝܬ ܢܕܪܟܝܗ ܀ ܐܡܪ ܐܢܐ ܕܝܢ ܥܠ ܗܘ ܡܕܒܪܢܗ ܕܥܠܡܐ: ܕܐܝܬܘܗܝ ܐܠܗܐ ܕܟܠ. ܕܥܒܕ ܟܠ ܡܛܠ ܒܪ ܐܢܫܐ.

---

2. A ܕ seems to have been deleted before ܥܠ.

ܘܡܬܚܫܚܐ ܠܗ ܕܡܕܡ ܦܘܫܐ. ܕܐܝܟ ܕܢܣܒ ܠܐܠܗܐ. ܠܒܪ ܐܢܫܐ ܕܝܢ ܠܐ ܢܒܥܐ ܀

ܐܡܪ ܐܢܐ ܕܝܢ ܕܐܠܗܐ ܐܝܬܘܗܝ ܠܐ ܝܠܝܕܐ. ܠܐ ܥܒܝܕܐ. ܟܝܢܐ ܩܝܘܡܐ ܕܠܐ ܫܘܪܝ. ܘܕܠܐ ܫܘܠܡ. ܠܐ ܡܝܘܬܐ. ܫܡܠܝܐ ܘܠܐ ܡܬܒܨܪܢܐ. ܡܫܡܠܝܐ ܕܝܢ ܕܐܡܪܬ ܗܕܐ ܗܝ. ܕܠܝܬ ܒܗ ܒܨܝܪܘܬܐ. ܘܠܐ ܣܢܝܩ ܠܡܕܡ. ܟܠܡܕܡ ܕܝܢ ܒܠܘܗܝ ܣܢܝܩ. ܘܕܐܡܪܬ ܕܐܝܬܘܗܝ ܕܠܐ ܫܘܪܝ ܗܕܐ ܗܝ: ܕܟܠ ܕܐܝܬ ܠܗ ܫܘܪܝܐ ܐܦ ܫܘܠܡܐ ܐܝܬ ܠܗ. ܘܗܘ ܕܐܝܬ ܠܗ ܫܘܠܡܐ ܡܬܫܪܝܢܐ ܐܝܬܘܗܝ. ܫܡܐ ܠܝܬ ܠܗ. ܟܠ ܓܝܪ ܡܕܡ ܕܐܝܬ ܠܗ ܫܡܐ. ܒܢܬܐ ܐܝܬܘܗܝ ܕܒܪܝܬܐ. ܕܡܘܬܐ ܠܝܬ ܠܗ. ܘܐܦ ܠܐ ܪܘܟܒܐ ܕܗܕܡܐ. ܡܢ ܓܝܪ ܕܗܕܐ ܩܢܐ. ܒܢܬܐ ܐܝܬܘܗܝ ܕܥܒܕܐ. ܠܐ ܕܟܪܐ ܐܝܬܘܗܝ ܐܦܠܐ ܢܩܒܬܐ. ܫܡܝܐ ܠܐ ܡܚܝܕܝܢ ܠܗ. ܐܠܐ ܫܡܝܐ ܘܟܠ ܕܡܬܚܙܝܐ ܘܕܠܐ ܡܬܚܙܝܢ ܒܗ ܡܚܝܕܝܢ. ܕܠܩܘܒܠܗ ܠܝܬ ܠܗ. ܠܐ ܓܝܪ ܐܝܬ ܐܢܫ ܕܫܠܝܛ ܡܢܗ. ܚܡܬܐ ܘܪܘܓܙܐ ܠܐ ܩܢܐ. ܠܝܬ ܓܝܪ ܡܕܡ ܕܡܨܝܐ ܕܢܩܘܡ ܠܘܩܒܠܗ܀ ܛܥܝܘ ܘܡܬܚܫܚܘܬܐ ܠܝܬ ܒܟܝܢܗ. ܟܠܗ ܓܝܪ ܒܟܠܗ ܣܘܟܠܬܐ ܐܝܬܘܗܝ ܘܦܘܠܚܢܐ ܘܒܗ ܡܩܝܡ ܟܠ ܕܡܩܝܡ. ܠܐ ܣܢܝܩ ܕܒܚܬܐ ܘܢܘܩܝܐ. ܐܦ ܠܐ ܚܕܐ ܡܢ ܐܝܠܝܢ ܕܡܬܚܙܝܢ. ܡܢ ܐܢܫ ܡܕܡ ܠܐ ܫܐܠ. ܟܠ ܢܩܫ ܕܝܢ ܡܢܗ ܫܐܠܝܢ܀

ܡܛܠ ܗܟܝܠ ܕܐܬܐܡܪ ܠܟܘܢ ܡܢܝ ܥܠ ܐܠܗܐ:

22. ܢܩܫ] Cod. ܢܦܫ.

ܒܟܐ ܕܐܬܒܣܡܬ ܦܘܪܢܣܝ̈ܗ ܕܬܦܠܠ ܠܟܠܗܘܢ܀ ܢܐܬܐ ܠܡ ܗܟܢܐ ܓܝܪ ܠܒܣܡܐ ܕܒܢܝ̈ܢܫܐ. ܐܡܒܢܐ ܕܢܙܒ ܕܐܬܠܝ ܡܢܗܘܢ ܐܫܬܕܪ ܦܬܘܬܐ ܡܢ ܫܪܪܐ. ܗܢܐ ܕܐܡܪܝܢ ܠܟܠܗܘܢ. ܘܐܬܠܝ ܦܬܚܝܢ ܡܢ ܐܝܕܘܗܝ܀

ܗܕܐ ܓܠܝܐ ܗܝ ܠܟܘܢ ܐܘ ܦܠܣܐ. ܕܓܢ̈ܣܐ ܕܒܢܝ̈ܢܫܐ ܒܠܫܢܐ ܗܢܝܢ. ܐܬܝܗܘܢ ܐܪ̈ܒܥܐ. ܒܪ̈ܝܬܐ. ܘܦܘ̈ܢܝܐ. ܡܗ̈ܕܝܐ ܘܒܪ̈ܘܛܢܝܐ.

ܒܪ̈ܝܬܐ ܗܟܝܠ ܣܓܕܝܢ ܐܝܟ ܠܒܣܡܐ ܕܕܝܠܗܘܢ. ܡܢ ܦܘܠܚܗ ܘܡܢ ܪܐܫ ܘܡܪܥܐ ܕܐܠܗ̈ܝܗܘܢ.

ܡ̈ܠܝܐ ܕܝܢ ܡܢ ܐܠܗܘܗܝ: ܗܘ ܕܡܬܐܡܪ ܕܐܬܩܘܡܘ ܡܢ ܕܡܘܗ. ܡܢ ܐܠܗܘܗܝ ܕܝܢ ܐܬܬܠܝܕ ܐܠܗܘ ܘܡܫܬܡܗ. ܫܪܟܐ ܕܝܢ ܕܠܐܕܐ. ܡܢ ܐܢܫܐ ܘܡܢ ܦܪܘܢܝܗ. ܠܚܪܬܐ ܕܝܢ ܡܢ ܕܢܫܐ ܡܬܝܪܐ. ܘܡܢ ܡܪܕܘܬܐ ܘܡܢ ܕܢܘܚܗܘ܀

ܡܒܘܓܝܐ ܕܝܢ ܣܓܕܝܢ ܐܝܟ ܠܒܣܡܗܘܢ. ܡܢ ܐܟܪܝܣ ܗܢܐ ܕܐܘܠܝ ܠܐܣܘܣ: ܕܡܠܟܐ ܐܬܬܠܝ ܡܟܘܒ. ܕܗܘ ܗܢܐ ܐܘܠܝ ܦܪܣܝܐ ܒܢܝܐ. ܕܗܘܝܢ ܐܬܬܬܩܒܘ ܡܢ ܗܘܪܢܐ ܒܡܕܝܢ. ܘܬܡܢ ܐܬܩܒܪܘ ܒܠܒܣܐ ܕܒܢܝܢܐ. ܡܢ ܗܘ ܗܐܡܪ ܢܒܣܡܘܢ. ܠܚܪܬܐ ܕܝܢ ܐܫܬܡܗܘ ܡܗ̈ܕܝܐ܀

ܒܪ̈ܘܛܢܝܐ ܗܟܝܠ ܣܓܕܝܢ ܥܘܕܪ ܕܕܝܠܗܘܢ. ܡܢ ܡܥܒܕ ܡܥܒܕܢܐ. ܘܗܘ ܗܢܐ ܡܫܬܡܗ ܒܫܡ ܕܐܠܗܐ ܦܠܣܐ. ܘܡܬܐܡܪ ܕܢܦܩ ܐܠܗܐ ܡܢ ܫܡܝܐ. ܘܡܢ ܒܬܘܠܬܐ ܒܪܬܐ ܫܦܠ ܘܠܒܫ ܒܣܪܐ. ܘܒܩܢ ܒܒܪܬ ܐܢܫܐ

---

13. ܡܪܕܘܬܐ ܘܡܢ] Cod. ܡܪܕܘ ܘܡܢ.

ܒܪܗ ܕܐܠܗܐ. ܗܕܐ ܡܢ ܣܒܪܬܐ ܗܝ ܕܩܕܡ ܩܠܝܠ ܙܒܢܐ ܐܡܝܪܐ ܐܝܟ ܕܐܡܪܝܢ܆ ܕܐܬܟܪܙܬ ܡܬܩܠܣܐ. ܗܘ ܕܐܦ ܐܢܬܘܢ ܐܢ ܬܩܪܘܢ ܒܗ ܬܕܪܟܘܢ ܚܝܠܐ ܕܥܠܝܗ܆ ܗܘ ܗܟܝܠ ܗܢܐ ܝܫܘܥ. ܡܢ ܫܪܒܬܐ ܕܥܒܪܝܐ ܐܬܝܠܕ. ܘܗܘܘ ܠܗ ܕܝܢ ܬܠܡܝܕܐ ܬܪܥܣܪ ܐܝܟܢܐ ܕܡܕܒܪܢܘܬܗ ܡܕܡ ܬܫܬܡܠܐ. ܗܘ ܗܢܐ ܡܢ ܝܗܘܕܝܐ ܐܙܕܩܦ. ܘܡܝܬ ܘܐܬܩܒܪ. ܘܐܡܪܝܢ ܕܡܢ ܒܬܪ ܬܠܬܐ ܝܘܡܝܢ ܩܡ ܘܐܣܬܠܩ ܠܫܡܝܐ. ܘܗܝܕܝܢ ܢܦܩܘ ܬܠܡܝܕܐ ܗܠܝܢ ܬܪܥܣܪ ܒܡܕܝܢܬܐ ܝܕܝܥܬܐ ܕܒܥܠܡܐ. ܘܥܠ ܪܒܘܬܗ ܕܗܘ ܡܠܦܝܢ ܗܘܘ܆ ܒܟܠܗ ܡܟܝܟܘܬܐ ܘܢܟܦܘܬܐ. ܘܡܛܠ ܗܕܐ ܐܦ ܐܝܠܝܢ ܕܝܘܡܢ ܠܗܢ ܟܪܘܙܘܬܐ ܡܫܡܫܝܢ. ܟܪܝܣܛܝܢܐ ܡܬܩܪܝܢ ܕܐܫܬܡܥܘܢ ܠܛܒܒܐ. ܐܝܬܝܗܘܢ ܗܟܝܠ ܐܪܒܥܐ ܓܢ̈ܣܐ ܕܒܢܝܢܫܐ܆ ܐܝܟ ܕܩܕܡܬ ܐܡܪܬ. ܒܪ̈ܒܪܝܐ ܘܝܘ̈ܢܝܐ. ܝܗܘ̈ܕܝܐ ܘܟܪܣܛܝ̈ܢܐ.

ܠܐܠܗܐ ܗܟܝܠ ܡܫܡܫܐ ܪܘܚܢܝܐ ܘܠܡܠܐܟ̈ܐ ܢܘܪܐ. ܠܪ̈ܘܚܐ ܕܝܢ ܩ̈ܫܝܐ. ܘܠܒܢ̈ܝ ܐܢܫܐ ܐܪܥܐ. ܀ ܀

ܢܫܪܐ ܗܟܝܠ ܡܢ ܒܪ̈ܒܪܝܐ܆ ܘܒܐܝܕܐ ܒܐܝܕܐ ܢܐܬܐ ܠܘܬ ܫܪܟܐ ܕܥܡ̈ܡܐ܆ ܐܝܟܢܐ ܕܢܚܙܐ ܕܐܝܠܝܢ ܡܢܗܘܢ ܐܚܝܕܝܢ ܫܪܪܐ ܕܥܠ ܐܠܗܐ. ܘܐܝܠܝܢ ܡܢܗܘܢ ܛܥܝܘܬܐ ܀

ܒܪ̈ܒܪܝܐ ܗܟܝܠ ܡܛܠ ܕܠܐ ܐܕܪܟܘܗܝ ܠܐܠܗܐ. ܛܥܘ ܒܐܣܛܘܟܣܐ. ܘܫܪܝܘ ܕܢܦܠܚܘܢ ܠܒܪ̈ܝܬܐ ܚܠܦ ܒܪܘܝܗܝܢ ܘܡܛܠܬܗ ܕܗܕܐ ܥܒܕܘ ܕܡ̈ܘܬܐ ܘܚܒܫܘ ܒܗܝܟܠܐ. ܘܗܐ ܣܓܕܝܢ ܠܗܘܢ ܘܗܐ ܢܛܪܝܢ ܠܗܘܢ ܒܙܗܝܪܘܬܐ ܪܒܬܐ. ܕܐܠܗ̈ܝܗܘܢ ܡܢ ܠܓܢ̈ܒܐ ܠܐ ܢܬܓܢܒܘܢ. ܘܠܐ ܐܣܬܟܠܘ

ܒܪ̈ܒܢܐ. ܕܟܠ ܐܝܟܢܐ ܕܢܛܪ ܐܢܘܢ ܗܘ ܡܢ ܗܘ ܕܡܬܒܛܪ. ܘܟܠ ܡܢ ܕܒܪܐ ܐܢܘܢ ܗܘ ܡܢ ܗܘ ܡܒܕܩ ܕܡܬܒܪܝܐ. ܐܢ ܗܘ ܗܟܝܠ ܕܐܠܗ̈ܝܗܘܢ ܡܫ̈ܠܡܝܢ ܠܦܘܪܥܢܐ ܕܢܟ̈ܣܘܗܝ ܐܝܟܢܐ ܢܦܪܥܘܢ ܠܒܢܝ̈ܢܫܐ ܦܘܪܥܢܐ. ܛܥܝܘܬܐ ܗܟܝܠ ܪܒܬܐ ܛܥܘ ܟܠܕ̈ܝܐ: ܕܦܠܚܘ ܠܨ̈ܠܡܐ ܡܝ̈ܬܐ ܕܐܝܬܝܗܘܢ ܠܗܘܢ ܕܠܐ ܡܘܬܪܢ.

ܘܐܬܐ ܠܢ ܕܐܬܕܒܪ ܐܘ ܡܠܟܐ ܥܠ ܦܝܠܘܣܘܦܝܗܘܢ: ܕܐܝܟܢܐ ܐܦ ܗܢܘܢ ܛܥܘ: ܘܫܡ̈ܗܘܢ ܐܠܗ̈ܐ ܠܐܣܛܘܟܣܐ ܕܐܬܥܒܕ ܠܐܝܩܪܐ ܕܐܣܛܘܟܣܐ. ܘܠܐ ܐܣܬܟܠܘ ܫܢ̈ܝܢܐ ܕܐܦ ܗܢܘܢ ܐܣܛܘ̈ܟܣܐ ܡܬܚ̈ܒܠܢܐ ܐܝܬܝܗܘܢ ܘܡܫܬܚܠܦܢܐ. ܡܢܬܐ ܓܝܪ ܩܠܝܠ ܡܢܗ ܕܐܣܛܘܟܣܐ: ܐܢ ܡܫܬܪܝܐ ܐܘ ܡܬܚܒܠܐ. ܟܘܠܗ ܡܫܬܪܝܐ ܘܡܬܚܒܠ. ܐܢ ܗܟܝܠ ܗܢܘܢ ܐܣܛܘ̈ܟܣܐ ܡܫܬܪ̈ܝܢ ܘܡܬܚܒܠܝܢ ܘܡܬܥ̈ܒܕܝܢ ܕܢܬܥܒܕܘܢ ܠܐܚܪܢܐ ܕܡܥܒܐ ܡܢܗܘܢ: ܘܠܐ ܐܝܬܝܗܘܢ ܒܟܝܢܗܘܢ ܐܠܗ̈ܐ: ܐܝܟܢܐ ܗܝ ܠܕ̈ܒܚܬܐ ܕܐܬܥܒܕ ܠܐܝܩܪܗܘܢ ܦܪܝܡ ܐܠܗܐ. ܪܒܐ ܗܝ ܗܟܝܠ ܛܥܝܘܬܐ ܕܐܡܪܘ ܦܝܠܘܣܘܦܝܗܘܢ ܥܠ ܡܫ̈ܬܡܫܢܝܗܘܢ ⁘

ܢܦܩܘܟ ܡܛܠ ܐܘ ܡܠܟܐ ܥܠܝܗܘܢ ܕܥܠܝܗܘܢ ܕܐܣܛܘܟܣܐ. ܐܝܟ ܕܢܚܘܐ ܥܠܝܗܘܢ ܕܠܐ ܐܝܬܝܗܘܢ ܐܠܗ̈ܐ: ܐܠܐ ܒܪܝܬܐ ܡܬܚܒܠܢܝܬܐ ܘܡܫܬܚܠܦܢܝܬܐ: ܕܐܝܬܝܗ̇ ܒܕܡܘܬܗ ܕܒܪܢܫܐ. ܐܠܗܐ ܕܝܢ. ܠܐ ܡܬܚܒܠ

9. Cod. ܕܐܬܥܒܕܘ.

ܘܠܐ ܡܫܬܚܠܦ. ܘܠܐ ܡܬܚܙܝܐ. ܒܪ ܗܘ ܠܟܠ ܚܙܐ ܘܗܦܟ ܘܡܫܚܠܦ.

ܗܠܝܢ ܗܟܝܠ ܕܡܦܩܢܝܢ ܥܠ ܐܪܒܥܐ ܕܐܝܬܝܗܘܢ ܐܠܗܐ̈. ܡܢ ܒܪܘ ܠܓܘ ܠܗܘܢ. ܒܪ ܡܬܦܫܩܐ ܘܡܬܚܠܝܒܐ ܘܡܬܚܠܚܠܐ. ܘܒܪ ܡܦܩܠܐ ܝܐܬܐ ܕܐܬܬܒܥܐ ܕܒܢܝ ܐܢܫܐ. ܘܕܚܘܬܐ ܘܕܒܥܝܪܐ: ܘܒܪܡ ܒܪ ܗܘܝܐ ܕܠܐ ܫܡܫܘ: ܐܝܟ ܥܒܕ ܡܫܬܥܒܕܐ ܗܘܝܐ ܡܬܬܬܐ. ܡܢ ܚܙܩܐ ܒܪ ܢܫܐ ܘܠܐ ܡܕܡ. ܘܬܘܒ ܐܟ ܡܩܡ ܥܠܘܗܝ ܟܒܐ ܒܡ ܦܐܪܘܗܝ ܡܬܒܥܠܐ. ܘܗܘܐ ܡܬܕܥܐ ܡܢ ܟܫܘܢܐ ܘܒܟܝܪܐ ܘܡܦܩܠܐ ܠܡܐܘܬܐ ܕܕܡܐ ܕܟܠܠܐ. ܘܡܬܦܫܩܐ ܘܡܬܒܬܠܐ ܟܬܒܐ ܘܗܘܝܐ ܬܐܘܝܐ ܠܟܠܒܪܐ. ܗܪܐ ܕܠܐ ܡܫܡܫܐ ܕܒܢܝܐ ܗܘ ܒܪܫܐ ܘܡܗܡܢܪܐ ܘܠܒܬܘܢܐ ܘܠܐ ܡܬܒܥܠܢܐ ܢܦܠ ܚܙܐ ܡܢ ܗܠܝܢ ܀ ܘܡܒܝܢ ܕܗܪܐ ܐܬܒܝܫܬ ܠܝ. ܕܐܪܒܥܐ ܠܐ ܗܘܬ ܐܠܗܐ ܐܠܐ ܒܪܝܬܗ ܕܐܠܗܐ ܀

ܘܒܗ ܒܕܡܘܬܐ ܬܘܒ ܠܓܘ ܗܠܝܢ ܕܐܢܗܪܘ ܥܠ ܟܒܐ ܕܐܬܬܗܘܢ ܐܠܗܐ̈. ܟܒܐ ܓܝܪ ܠܚܡܫܬܗ ܕܒܪܝܫܐ ܐܬܒܪܝܘ. ܘܟܒܫܐ ܟܠܢܫܐ ܡܫܬܒܚܝܢ ܠܗ. ܡܫܬܢܢܝܢ ܓܝܪ ܘܡܚܡܠܝܢ ܝܐܘܬܐ. ܘܡܬܡܚܠܝܢ ܘܡܦܢܝܢ ܒܝܬܗܘܢ. ܒܪ ܒܡ ܝܩܘܬܐ ܗܟܝܪܬܐ ܡܬܚܪܟܝܢ. ܘܡܦܩܠܝܢ ܒܘܢܐ ܕܠܐ ܕܠܗܘܢ. ܗܠܝܢ ܕܐܝܟ ܡܢ ܒܪܢܫܐ ܡܬܠܒܫܝܢ. ܘܒܬܐܒܬܐ ܕܒܢܝܫܐ ܘܕܒܥܝܪܐ. ܘܒܕܡܘܬܐ ܕܟܠܠܐ ܡܬܒܪܝܢ ܘܡܬܦܫܩܝܢ. ܘܡܢ ܐܢܫܐ ܡܬܬܪܝܢ. ܕܒܗ

---

15. Cod. ܒܪܝܬܗ.

ܐܠܝܨܘܬܐ. ܕܫ̈ܒܒܬܐ: ܢܬܪܘܢ ܘܢܬܦܠܛܘܢ ܕܠܐ ܒܨܒܝܢܗܘܢ. ܘܢܬܠܘܢ ܠܚ̈ܝܐ. ܘܠܡ̈ܫܚܬܐ ܐܚܪ̈ܢܝܬܐ. ܐܝܟ ܕܢܬܩܢܘܢ ܘܢܦܫܘܢ ܕܠܐ ܕܒ̈ܢܝ ܐܢܫܐ. ܘܢܚܝܒܘܢ ܚܠܦ ܚܐܪܘܬܐ. ܘܢܫܟܚܘܢ ܫܘܠܛܢܗ ܕܟܝܢܐ ܕܚܐܪܘܬܗܘܢ. ܕܡܬܠܠܬܗ ܕܗܕܐ. ܠܐ ܕ... ، ܕܩܢܝܐ ܐܠܗܐ ܢܗܘܘܢ. ܐܠܐ ܐܝܬܝܗܘܢ ܒܟܪܗ ܕܐܠܗܐ ܘܡܢܬܐ ܕܒܠܚܘܕ܀

ܘܗܟܢܐ ܐܦ ܗܠܝܢ ܕܐܡܪܝܢ ܥܠ ܢܘܪܐ ܕܐܝܬܝܗ̇ ܐܠܗܐ ܠܗ ܕܠܐ ܒܪܝܐ. ܡܛܠ ܕܐܦ ܗܝ ܠܫܝܢܘܬܐ ܐܬܓܙܪܬ ܕܒ̈ܢܝ ܐܢܫܐ. ܘܩ̈ܢܝܢܐ ܦ̈ܠܚܐܐ ܠܗܘܢ ܡܫܬܒܚܐ ܒܡܘܕܝܢܐ ܕܡܫ̈ܠܬܬܐ ܘܦܘܪܩܢܐ ܕܫܠܝܬܐ: ܘܕܢܘܚܐ: ܐܝܠܝܢ ܕܡܓܘܫܐ ܒܫܡܗ̇ ܦܠܚܘܬܗܘܢ. ܒܗ ܗܝ ܗܕܐ ܩܢܝܐ ܦ̈ܠܚܐܐ. ܡܬܕܒܪܐ ܘܡܬܚܫܠܐ܀

ܘܬܘܒ ܐܝܠܝܢ ܕܐܡܪܝܢ ܥܠ ܡܫܟܐ ܕܚܘܝܐ ܕܐܠܗܐ ܐܝܬܘܗܝ ܐܦ ܗܢܘܢ ܗܠܝܢ ܠܗ. ܘܗܕܐ ܡܢܟܐ ܗܝ ܠܝ. ܕܗܢܘܢ ܚ̈ܘܝܐ ܠܐܢܫܐ ܡܫܬܒܚܝܢ. ܒܗ ܒܝܘܡ ܗܟܐ ܡܣܒܗܘܢ: ܘܒܝܘܡ ܒܪܐ ܘܩܛܠ: ܐܝܟ ܦܘܡܗ ܕܗܘ ܕܡܚܒܒ ܠܗܘܢ. ܡܛܠ ܒܪ ܐܢܫܐ ܓܒܪ ܐܬܒܪܝܘ ܡܢ ܐܠܗܐ: ܡܛܠ ܕܢܚܠܘܢ ܚܣܝܘܬܐ ܕܐܝܠܝܢ ܘܕܦܐܪܐ ܘܕܙܪ̈ܥܐ. ܘܠܡܫܬܠܛܘ ܒ̈ܠܫܐ ܒܚܝܐ. ܐܝܠܝܢ ܕܡܬܚܬܝܢ ܠܒ̈ܢܝ ܐܢܫܐ ܚܣܝܘܬܐ ܘܫܘܬܦܘܬܐ: ܡܢ ܐܝܟܐ ܕܚܝܘ̈ܬܐ ܠܐܝܟܐ ܕܠܐ ܚܣܝܢ. ܘܢܦܫܗܘܢ ܡܚܒܬܗ ܕܒܠܚܘܕ. ܗܘ ܗܢܐ ܒܝܘܡ ܒܗ ܦܓܥܐ ܘܒܗ ܒܪܐ. ܐܝܬ ܐܝܟܐ ܕܒܗܘܢ

---

20. Cod. ܕ.ܚܣܝܢ.

21. Cod. ܚܣܝܢ.—Read ܕܢܦܫܗܘܢ?

ܫܒܬܪ. ܘܒܕܘܟ ܡܫܚܠܦ. ܐܝܟ ܐܡܪܗ ܕܗܘܦ ܕܐܚܕܪܝ. ܘܐܦ ܒܢܝܢܫܐ ܡܫܡܫܝܢ. ܕܒܗ ܡܫܬܢܝܐ ܡܫܬܐ. ܢܦܩܘܢ ܘܡܫܬܘܕܥܝܢ. ܐܝܟ ܕܢܫܠܐ ܠܗܘܢ ܡܫܡܫܬܐ ܕܬܫܢܝܩ ܠܗ. ܘܟܠ ܢܦܫ ܫܘܠܛܢܐ ܠܝܬ ܠܗ ܐܦ ܠܐ ܚܕ. ܘܡܛܠ ܗܕܐ ܠܐ ܡܫܟܚܐ ܕܢܘܗܪܐ ܐܠܗܝܐ ܬܬܩܪܒܘܢ: ܐܠܐ ܒܒܪܗ ܕܐܠܗܐ ⁘

ܗܟܢܐ ܐܦ ܐܝܟ ܕܐܡܪܘܗܝ ܟܠ ܫܡܫܐ ܕܐܬܚܘܝܘ ܐܠܗܐ ܠܟܠ. ܗܘ ܟܕ ܚܙܝܬ ܠܗ: ܕܡܢ ܐܢܫܐ ܕܐܢܫܝܐ ܡܬܬܘܪܝܐ: ܘܡܬܗܦܟ ܘܪܕܐ. ܘܡܬܗܠܟ ܡܢ ܕܪܓܐ ܠܕܪܓܐ: ܟܕ ܒܟܠܝܘܡ ܢܪܚ ܘܢܚܬ. ܐܝܟ ܕܢܦܫ ܠܡܫܒܚܘܬܐ ܕܢܪܒܬܐ ܘܕܫܬܠܬܐ: ܘܢܘܒܠܐ ܒܐܐܪ ܕܡܬܡܪܟ ܒܗ ܬܕܐܐ ܒܠܗ ܕܟܠ ܐܪܒܐ. ܘܠܗ ܠܗܘܢܐ ܒܫܘܡܠܝ. ܫܬܐ ܐܝܬ ܠܗ. ܒܡ ܫܪܒܐ ܕܪܒܐ ܕܡܫܒܚܐ ܒܡܬܪܬܗ. ܘܒܗ ܗܘ ܚܕ ܐܬܘܗܝ ܒܢܝܗ. ܠܫܒܝܘܬܐ ܗܢܢܘܬܐ ܡܬܡܪܟܼ. ܠܗܘܬ ܘܬܪܝܢܐ ܕܫܡܫܘܬܗܘܢ ܕܩܠܠ ܐܢܫܐ. ܘܠܗ ܒܝܢܝܗ ܐܠܐ ܒܝܢܝܢܐ ܕܗܘܦ ܕܫܒܪ ܠܗ. ܘܡܛܠ ܗܕܐ. ܠܐ ܡܫܟܚܐ ܕܫܡܫܐ ܢܗܘܐ ܐܠܗܐ. ܐܠܐ ܒܪܗ ܕܐܠܗܐ ⁘⁘

ܘܒܗ ܒܕܡܘܬܐ. ܐܦ ܗܘܪܐ ܘܡܫܒܚܐ. ܐܝܟ ܕܡ ܕܐܬܘܕܝܘ ܒܠ ܒܢܝܫܐ ܡܫܬܢܝܐ. ܕܒܝܬܗܘܢ ܐܠܗܝܐ ܗܘܘ: ܗܝܢܘܢ ܗܠܝܢ ܗܟܝ ܠܚܘ. ܐܝܟ ܕܡܫܘܐ ܐܢܬ ܐܦ ܐܢܬ ܐܘ ܡܠܟܐ. ܕܟܕ ܐܢܫܐ. ܡܢ ܐܪܥܐ ܐܘܛܘܦܣܝܢ. ܘܡܢ

13. Cod. ܫܒܬܐ ܐܝܬ ܠܗ:

ܢܦܫܐ ܘܪܘܚܐ ܡܬܩܝܡ. ܘܡܛܠ ܗܕܐ ܐܦ ܥܠܡܐ ܡܬܩܪܐ. ܘܡܢ ܟܠܗ̇ ܚܕܐ ܡܢ ܗܠܝܢ ܡܢܘ̈ܬܐ ܠܐ ܦܐܫ. ܫܘܪܝܐ ܐܝܬ ܠܗ̇ ܘܫܘܠܡܐ. ܘܡܬܝܠܕ ܐܦ ܡܬܚܒܠ. ܐܠܗܐ ܕܝܢ ܐܝܟ ܕܐܡܪܬ. ܚܕܐ ܡܢ ܗܠܝܢ ܒܟܝܢܗ̇ ܠܝܬ ܠܗ. ܐܠܐ ܐܝܬܘܗܝ. ܠܐ ܒܪܝܐ ܘܠܐ ܡܬܚܒܠܢܐ. ܘܡܛܠ ܗܕܐ. ܠܐ ܡܫܟܚܐ ܕܒܪ ܐܢܫܐ ܡܢ ܟܝܢܐ ܢܣܝܡܘܗܝ ܕܐܠܗܐ. ܠܗܢܐ ܕܒܝܢ ܕܗ ܡܦܘܠܐ ܠܫܘܬܐ ܟܒܝܫܐ ܠܗ ܚܡܬܐ. ܘܠܒܘܫܐ ܘܢܟ̈ܒܐ ܠܗ ܟܐܒܐ. ܗܢܐ ܕܐܝܬܘܗܝ ܚܡܬܢܐ ܘܛܢܢܐ. ܘܡܫܬܚܠܦܢܐ ܘܡܬܚܒܠܢܐ. ܒܡ ܥܪ̈ܒܐ ܕܒܡܪ̈ܥܐ ܐܚܪ̈ܢܐ. ܘܒܥܝܪ̈ܐ ܦܓ̈ܥܐ ܡܬܚܒܠ ܡܢܗܘܢ ܕܐܣܛܘ̈ܟܣܐ. ܘܐܦ ܡܢ ܡܘܬܐ ܀

ܘܗܟܢܐ ܐܘ ܡܠܟܐ ܙܕܩ ܠܢ ܕܢܬܦܢܐ ܠܬܫܥܝܬܗܘܢ ܕܒܪ̈ܢܫܐ. ܕܢܚܘܐ ܕܠܐ ܒܡܕܡ ܥܠ ܐܠܗܐ ܫܪܝܪܐ. ܫܪ̈ܒܐ ܡܢ ܫܪܝܪ̈ܐ. ܘܐܝܠܝܢ ܒܬܪ ܙܒܢܬܐ ܕܬܪܝܢܗܘܢ ܕܗ ܦܠܫ ܠܐܣܛܘܟܣܐ ܡܫܬܪܝܢܐ ܘܠܨ̈ܠܡܐ ܡܝ̈ܬܐ. ܘܡܛܠ ܬܫܥܝܬܗܘܢ. ܠܐ ܝܕ̈ܥܝܢ ܕܡܢܘ ܐܠܗܐ ܫܪܝܪܐ ܀

ܢܬܦܢܐ ܗܟܝܠ ܐܦ ܥܠ ܝܘ̈ܢܝܐ: ܐܝܟܢܐ ܕܢܕܥ ܕܡܢܐ ܘܣܒܪܐ ܐܝܬ ܠܗܘܢ ܥܠ ܐܠܗܐ ܫܪܝܪܐ. ܝܘ̈ܢܝܐ ܗܟܝܠ ܡܛܠ ܕܚܟܝܡܝܢ ܡܢ ܒܪ̈ܒܪܝܐ: ܛܥܘ ܝܬܝܪ ܡܢܗܘܢ ܕܒܪ̈ܒܪܝܐ ܛܥܘ: ܟܕ ܐܥܠܘ ܐܠܗ̈ܐ ܣܓܝܐܐ ܥܒܝ̈ܕܐ. ܘܡܢܗܘܢ ܣܡܘ ܕܟܪ̈ܐ ܘܡܢܗܘܢ ܢܩܒ̈ܬܐ: ܘܕܐܝܟ ܕܡܢܗܘܢ ܡܢ

---

6. Cod. ܢܣܝܡܗܝ.

ܐܠܗ̈ܝܗܘܢ ܐܫܬܟܚܘ ܕܒܢ̈ܝܢ ܘܩ̈ܛܠܝܢ ܘܙܠܚܝܢ ܘܡܦ̈ܩܝܢ
ܘܙܟܝܢ ܘܡܬܢܨܚܝܢ. ܘܦܠܛܝܢ ܠܐܟ̈ܣܢܝܗܘܢ. ܘܟܢܫܝܢ
ܘܫܠܚܝܢ. ܘܡܬܐܡܪܘܢ ܐܚܝ̈ܕܝܢ ܕܫܘܠܛܢ̈ܐ ܘܫ̈ܘܟܢܐ ܗܘܘ.
ܘܡܬܐܡܪܘܢ ܒܢ̈ܝܐ. ܘܡܬܐܡܪܘܢ ܡܒܝܐ ܓ̈ܢܒܐ. ܘܡܬܐܡܪܘܢ
ܒܡܠܬ̈ܐ ܢܩܫܐ. ܘܡܬܐܡܪܘܢ ܒܠܘܪ̈ܐ ܡܬܬ̈ܪܝܢ ܗܘܘ.
ܘܡܬܐܡܪܘܢ ܒܚܕܐ ܡܢܬܐ. ܘܡܬܐܡܪܘܢ ܒܝܕ ܒܪ̈ܘܟܐ
ܐܬܡܟܢܘ. ܘܡܬܐܡܪܘܢ ܐܦ ܠܟ̈ܠܗ ܐܢܫܐ ܐܫܬܥܒܕܘ.
ܘܡܬܐܡܪܘܢ ܒܙܘܥܐ ܓ̈ܒܝܐ. ܘܡܬܐܡܪܘܢ ܒܝܕ ܟ̈ܠܗ ܐܢܫܐ
ܐܬܓܒܝܘ. ܘܡܬܐܡܪܘܢ ܗܐ ܡܬܬܟܢܝܢ ܘܡܬܬܐܠܝܢ ܡܢ ܟ̈ܠܗ
ܐܢܫܐ. ܘܡܬܐܡܪܘܢ ܐܚܪ̈ܢܝܢ ܠܥܘܠ ܢܨܚܘ. ܘܡܬܐܡܪܘܢ
ܡ̈ܬܕܒܪܢܐ ܐܬܕܒܪܘ. ܘܡܬܐܡܪܘܢ ܠܕܡܘܬܐ ܕܫ̈ܘܬܐ
ܐܫܬܘܠܛܘ: ܐܝܟ ܕܢܒ̈ܝܐ ܒܝܫܐ ܕܫܪܝܐ ܡܫ̈ܬܬܐ.
ܘܡܬܐܡܪܘܢ ܒܡܕܡܕܡܐ ܕܝܕܥ ܕܒܪ̈ܐ ܐܝܠܦܢܘ. ܘܡܬܐܡܪܘܢ
ܐܚܪ̈ܢܝܢ ܕܝܕܥ ܐܡ̈ܫܬܗܘܢ ܘܐܣ̈ܘܬܗܘܢ ܘܒܬ̈ܝܗܘܢ
ܐܘܕܘܠܐ. ܘܥܠ ܐܠܗ̈ܝܗܘܢ ܐܚܪ̈ܢܝܢ. ܕܝܕܥ ܟ̈ܠܗ ܐܢܫܐ
ܒܪܘ: ܘܐܬܡܠܟܘ ܡܠܟܝܢ ܒܠܥܕ ܡܕܡ ܕܐܦ ܗܘ
ܡ̈ܫܬܘܬܐ ܗܘ. ܘܥܠ ܡܠܟܝܢ ܐܚܪ̈ܢܝܢ ܕܥܠ ܥܘܦܪܐ
ܐܬܦܫܛ. ܘܡܕܡ ܟ̈ܠܗ ܐܢܫܐ ܒܕܝܢܐ ܚ̈ܠܝܢ. ܘܡ̈ܫܬܐ
ܗܘܐ ܕܡܫܝܚܐ: ܘܠܠܘܬܐ. ܐܘ ܡ̈ܠܟܐ: ܐܒܠܘ ܡ̈ܫܝܚܐ
ܥܠ ܐܠܗ̈ܝܗܘܢ ܘܥܠ ܢ̈ܦܫܗܘܢ: ܒܗܘ ܕܠܗܠܝܢ ܕܕܐܝܟ
ܗܟܢܐ ܐܢܬܘܢ ܐܡ̈ܪܘܬܗܘܢ ܡܢܗܘܢ. ܗܠܝܢ ܕܠܐ ܐܢܬܘܢ

---

1. For ܘܙܠܚܝܢ we should probably read ܘܙܠܝܢ.

17. For ܥܘܦܪܐ we should probably read ܥܦܘܪܐ.

18. Cod. ܒܠܗ.

ܐܠܗ̈ܝܐ. ܘܡܚܡܐ ܢܦܫܗ ܒܟ̈ܠ ܐܢܫܐ ܫ̈ܠܠܬܐ ܐܝܟ ܕܢܟܘܪܘܗܝ. ܘܢܬܢܘܢ. ܘܢܫܬܠܡܘܢ. ܘܕܢܦܫܪܘܢ ܥܠ ܕܥܒܕ ܘܗܘܝܐ ܘܢܕܘܕ. ܐܢܘܢ ܒܪ ܗܠܝܢ ܕܡܬܘܡ̈ܝܢ ܐܠܗ̈ܝܗܘܢ: ܒܠܗܘܢ ܗܠܝܢ ܕܡܬܟ̈ܢܫܝܢ ܡܢ ܟܠ ܦܢ̈ܝܢ. ܒܡܟܐ ܡܬܪܐܝܬ ܢܗܒ̈ܘܢ ܫ̈ܝܢ ܒܢ̈ܝ ܐܢܫܐ: ܐܝܠܝܢ ܕܒܗܘܢ ܒܗܠܝܢ ܡܗܝܡܢܝܢ ܕܗܦܟܘ ܗܠܝܢ. ܘܡܢ ܪܘܫܡܐ ܕܛܝܒܘܬܐ ܗܕܐ: ܗܐ ܟܕ ܝܗܒ ܠܒ̈ܢܝ ܐܢܫܐ: ܡܪܟܐ ܬܠܝܒܟܐ. ܘܡܩܒܠܐ ܪܘܪܒܐ ܘܡܥܒܕܐ ܡܕܝܢܬܐ. ܘܡܬܠܡܘܬܐ ܕܡܢ ܟܠ ܡܕܡ. ܘܗܘܐ ܡܦܝܣܝܢ ܘܥܕܡ ܟܠܗܘܢ ܗܠܝܢ ܟܠܗܝܢ. ܡܢ ܥܠܬܐ ܗܕܐ ܒܠܚܘܕ. ܘܥܕ ܡܦܝܣܝܢ ܠܗܝܢ. ܠܐ ܡܬܟܠܝܢ ܟܬܪܝܣܬܗܘܢ ܕܡܛܠ ܛܝܒܘܬܗܘܢ ܗܠܝܢ ܕܥܒܕ ܠܗܘܢ ܀ ܢܓܬܐ ܡܛܠ ܥܠ ܬܫܒܘܚܬܐ ܕܠܗܘܢ ܕܐܠܗ̈ܝܗܘܢ. ܐܡܟܢܐ ܕܢܗܘܐ ܫܬܬܐܝܬ ܥܠ ܟܠܗܝܢ ܕܐܡܬ̈ܝܗܘܢ ܡܢ ܠܟܠ. ܡܢ ܡܕܡ ܥܠ ܡܕܡ ܡܬܟܠܝܢ ܡܢܗܘܢ ܐܠܗܐ. ܠܡܪܢܘܣ ܗܘ ܕܡܬܦܫܩ ܒܦ̈ܢ ܘܥܠܝܗܘܢ ܕܗܢܐ: ܡܕܒ̈ܪܝܢ ܠܗ ܒ̈ܝܬܗܘܢ. ܘܡܢܗܘܢ ܟܕ ܚܝ̈ܝܢ ܡܩܘܡܝܢ ܠܗܘܢ ܒܠܗܘܢ ܥܠ ܗܢܝ. ܐܡܪܝܢ ܕܢܦܩ ܠܗ ܒܢ̈ܒܝܐ ܪܐܐ. ܘܡܟܢܫ ܐܘܠ ܒ̈ܢܝܐ ܩܕܡܝܐ: ܗܘ ܕܡܟܢܫ ܐܘܠ ܐܦ ܠܕܘܗ ܕܡܬܘܡܪܐ ܗܘܐ. ܗܢܐ ܕܠܫܪܬܐ ܥܒܕܐ. ܘܡܢ ܕܢܠܐ ܕܢܡܟܐ ܕܐܬܐܡܪ ܠܗ: ܥܕܐ ܗܘܐ ܠܡܬܐܠ ܒܝܘܡܗ. ܗܢܐ ܕܐܬܦܠܓ ܡܢܗ ܗܘܐ ܘܠܐ ܐܪܟܒ. ܕܠܗ ܠܗܢܐ ܠܫܪܬܐ ܦܪܫ ܗܘܐ ܘܦܫܛ ܒܟܪܘܬܗ ܘܥܕܐ ܒܢܟܐ: ܕܡܢ ܬܡܢ ܐܝܟ ܕܡܬܠܐ ܐܡܪܝܢ ܕܐܬܠܒܫܬ ܐܦܘܕܝܛܐ.

9. Cod. ܟܠܗܘܢ ܗܠܝܢ.

ܕܡܬܦܪܫܐ ܐܣܛܪܐ. ܘܠܗ ܠܦܠܛܘܢ ܒܪ ܫܢܝܢ ܫܒܥܣܪ ܫܢܥܘܒܐ. ܪܒܐ ܗܘܐ ܠܦܠܛܘܢ ܘܒܢܝܐ ܕܐܟܠܗ ܫ̈ܢܝܐ ܥܠ ܪܝܫܐ ܕܐܠܗ̈ܘܬܗܘܢ. ܟܬܒ ܕܥܠܡܝܢ ܡ̈ܠܝܢ ܐܚ̈ܪܢܐ ܥܠܗܘܢ. ܐܘ ܡ̈ܠܟܐ. ܠܐ ܡ̈ܫܡܫܢܐ ܕܐܠܗܐ ܢܛܦܪ ܐܘ ܢܛܦܘܢ. ܘܐܢ ܕܝܢ ܠܝ ܗܟܢ ܕܦܪܐ ܀

ܘܡܢ ܒܬܪ ܦܪܘܣܗ ܡ̈ܠܝܢ ܐܠܗܝܐ ܐܝܟܢܝ ܗܘܐ. ܘܐܡ̈ܪܝܢ ܥܠܘܗܝ ܕܗܘܝܐ: ܕܗܘ ܡܢ ܪܚܝܩܘܬܐ ܘܦܘܣܐ ܡ̈ܠܟܐ ܕܥܠܡ̈ܘܢ ܐܠܗ̈ܐ. ܘܐܡ̈ܪܝܢ ܥܠܘܗܝ ܕܐܪܣܛܘܛܠܝܣ ܠܟܬܒܘܗܝ ܘܠܡܡܪܐ ܐܚܪܝܢ: ܐܡܪܝܢ ܕܫܠܝܛ ܠܡ̈ܠܐ ܡܠܘܬܬܐ ܘܠܡܘܫ ܠܗ ܡܫܡܫ ܒܢ̈ܝܐ. ܒܪ ܟܕ ܐܡܪܝܢ ܕܐܪܣܛܘܛܠܝܣ ܠܐܪܟܘܣܐ. ܡܛܠ ܪܡܙܘܬܗ ܕܐܪܘܦܐ ܘܕܦܘܣܩܐ. ܘܬܘܒ ܐܪܣܛܘܛܠܝܣ ܠܡܘܬܐ ܕܗܘܝܐ ܡܛܠ ܪܡܙܘܬܗ ܕܕܝܢܐ. ܘܠܦܘܠܘܣ ܡܛܠ ܪܡܙܘܬܗ ܕܠܐܕܪܐ. ܘܠܟܪܘܢܐ ܡܛܠ ܪܡܙܘܬܗ ܕܐܦܘܠܘܢܐ. ܘܠܟܪܘܢܝ ܡܛܠ ܪܡܙܘܬܗ ܕܗܘܪܐ. ܐܡܪܝܢ ܕܡܢ ܐܠܝܢ ܐܘܠܐ ܒܢ̈ܝܐ ܦ̈ܝܠܣܦܐ ܡܢ ܐܦܠܘܛܐ ܒܬܪ ܐܡ̈ܪܝܢ ܕܐܘܠܐ ܗܘܠܝܦ ܘܐܡܬܘܣܝܢܐ. ܘܡܢ ܗܘܪܐ ܠܒܝܬܘܗܘܢ. ܡܢ ܐܠܡܬܢܝܐ ܠܡܪܘܠܝܘܣ. ܘܡܢ ܠܛܠ: ܠܐܦܠܘ ܘܠܐܦܠܝܛܘܢ. ܘܡܢ ܕܒܐܝܢ ܦܘܪܐܘܐ. ܘܡܢ ܠܒܝ ܗܘܦܛܪ ܘܦܠܕܘܢܘܣ. ܘܐܠܟܝܢ ܘܦܠܕܘܣ. ܘܡܢ ܦܘܬܘܡܣܦ ܐܘܠܐ ܬܢܝܢ ܦܪ̈ܘܬܐ: ܗܠܝܢ ܕܡܘܣܘܣ ܫܡܗ

3. Cod. ܪ̈ܝܫܐ. 14. Cod. ܪܡܙܘܬܗ ܕܗܘܪܐ.

17. For ܐܠܡܬܢܝܐ we should read ܐܠܡܬܢܝܐ or ܐܠܡܢܝܐ.

19. For ܘܐܠܟܝܢ we should read ܘܐܠܟܝ.

20. ܦܘܬܘܡܣܦ seems to be a corruption of ܡܢܡܘܣܘܢܝ (Μνημοσύνης).

ܙ̈ܝܬܘܣ. ܘܡܢ ܐܘܪܘܦܐ. ܡܝܢܘܐܣ ܘܪܘܕܡܢܘܐ. ܠܚܪܬܐ ܕܝܢ ܐܫܬܚܠܦ ܠܕܡܘܬܐ ܕܢܫܪܐ: ܡܛܠ ܪܚܡܬܗ ܕܓܢܘܕܡܘܣ ܪܥܝܐ ܀

ܡܢ ܬܠ̈ܠܬܐ ܕܗܠܝܢ ܬܫ̈ܥܝܬܐ ܐܘ ܡܠܟܐ. ܣܓ̈ܝܐܬ ܒ̈ܝܫܬܐ ܙܢ̈ܝܬܐ: ܠܒ̈ܢܝ ܐܢܫܐ ܕܒܥܕܢܐ ܗܢܐ. ܕܗ̣ ܡܬܕ̈ܡܝܢ ܒܐܠܗ̈ܝܗܘܢ. ܘܓܝܪܝܢ ܘܡܬܛ̈ܢܦܝܢ ܒܐܡܗ̈ܬܗܘܢ ܘܒܐܚܘ̈ܬܗܘܢ: ܘܒܡܕܡܟܐ ܕܕܟܪ̈ܐ. ܘܡܢܗܘܢ ܡܡܪ̈ܚܝܢ ܕܢܩܛܠܘܢ ܐܦ ܠܐܒܗ̈ܝܗܘܢ. ܐܦ ܓܝܪ ܗ̇ܘ ܕܡܬܐܡ̇ܪ ܪܫܐ ܘܡܠܟܐ ܕܐܠܗ̈ܝܗܘܢ ܗܠܝܢ ܥܒܕ. ܒܚܕܐ ܡܬܐܡܪ ܢܨ̈ܕܩܘܢ ܒܗ ܩ̈ܕܡܘܗܝ. ܘܪܒܐ ܥܘܠܬܐ ܕܐܟܘܬܗ ܬ̈ܘܒܐ ܒܥܒ̈ܕܝܗܘܢ ܕܟܠ ܗܢܐ. ܠܐ ܓܝܪ ܡܫܟܚܐ ܕܐܠܗܐ ܢܓܘܪ ܐܘ ܢܩܛܠ: ܐܘ ܢܬܦܪܥ ܠܡܕܡܟܐ ܕܥܡ ܕܟܪ̈ܐ. ܐܘ ܕܢܩܛܘܠ ܠܐܒܘܗ̈ܝ. ܘܐܦ ܕܝܢ ܠܗ ܗܟܢ ܒܚܝܫ ܡܢܗ ܕܗܘܐ ܡܚܒܠܢܐ ܀

ܬܘܒ ܡܥܠܝܢ ܐܠܗܐ ܐܚܪܢܐ ܐܦܣܛܘܣ. ܘܐܡܪܝܢ ܥܠܘܗܝ ܕܐܬܘܗܝ ܚܓܝܪܐ ܘܐܚܝܕ ܡܩܒܐ ܒܐܝܕܗ. ܘܠܓܒܝ ܒܐܝܕܗ ܥܠܬܐ ܘܦܘܪܢܣܐ. ܘܦܠܚ ܢܦܚܘܬܐ: ܐܝܟ ܕܒܚܝܠܗ ܢܦܩ ܣܢܩܬܐ ܕܡܦܪܢܣܬܗ. ܐܝܪܐ ܗܘ ܚܠܦ ܗܢܐ: ܣܢܝܩ ܐܠܗܐ ܗܢܐ: ܗܕܐ ܕܠܐ ܡܫܟܚܐ ܕܐܠܗܐ ܢܗܘܐ ܣܢܝܩܐ ܐܘ ܚܓܝܪܐ. ܘܐܦ ܕܝܢ ܠܐ ܣܓܝ ܡܣܟܠܐ ܀

ܬܘܒ ܡܥܠܝܢ ܐܠܗܐ ܐܚܪܢܐ. ܘܩܪܝܢ ܠܗ ܗܪܡܝܣ.

---

1. ܘܪܘܕܡܢܘܐ, a corrupt form. The Greek has καὶ Ῥαδάμανθυν.

3. ܕܓܢܘܕܡܘܣ for ܕܓܢܘܡܕܘܣ.

ܘܐܡܪܝܢ ܕܐܝܬܘܗܝ ܓܒܪܐ ܪܚܡ ܡܟܝܠܬܐ ܘܪܓܝܓ ܘܬܪ̈ܥܢܐ. ܘܡܟܫܦܢܐ ܘܦܫܝܓܐ ܘܕܪܪܐ. ܘܡܦܫܩܢܐ ܕܡ̈ܠܐ. ܗܕܐ ܕܠܐ ܡܫܟܚܐ ܕܐܠܗܐ ܢܗܘܐ ܡܟܫܦܢܐ ܐܘ ܡܚܒܠ ܐܘ ܦܫܝܓܐ: ܐܘ ܪܓܝܓ ܡܕܡ ܕܠܐ ܕܝܠܗ. ܐܘ ܕܐܪ̈ܪܐ. ܘܐܢ ܕܝܢ ܠܐ ܡܫܬܟܚ ܐܝܬܘܗܝ ܕܠܐ ܣܢܝܩܘ ⁘

ܘܡܢ ܒܬܪ ܗܢܐ ܡܥܠܝܢ ܐܠܗܐ ܐܚܪܢܐ: ܠܐܣܩܠܝܦܘܣ ܘܐܡ̈ܪܝܢ ܕܐܝܬܘܗܝ ܐܣܝܐ. ܘܡܬܩܢ ܣܡ̈ܡܢܐ ܘܐܣܦܠܝܢܘܬܐ ܡܛܠ ܕܢܬܠܐ ܣܢܝܩܘܬܐ ܕܡܣܒܪܬܗ. ܐܪܐ ܟܕ ܗܘܝܐ ܐܝܬܘܗܝ ܐܠܗܐ ܗܘܐ: ܗܘܐ ܕܠܚܪܬܐ ܟܠܒ ܒܪܘܩܐ ܡܢ ܕܝܘܣ: ܡܛܠ ܥܠܬܐ ܕܛܢܕܪܐܘܣ ܠܩܕܡܘܢܝܐ: ܘܗܟܢܐ ܡܝܬ: ܐܢ ܗܟܝܠ ܐܣܩܠܦܝܘܣ ܐܠܗܐ ܐܝܬܘܗܝ ܗܘܐ: ܘܟܕ ܟܠܒ ܒܒܪܘܩܐ ܠܐ ܐܫܟܚ ܕܢܥܕܪ ܢܦܫܗ. ܐܝܟܢܐ ܠܐܚܪ̈ܢܐ ܡܫܟܚ ܕܢܥܕܪ ܗܘܐ. ܗܢ ܕܠܐ ܡܫܟܚܐ ܕܗܢܐ ܐܠܗܐ ܢܗܘܐ ܗܘܝܐ: ܐܘ ܢܬܡܚܐ ܡܢ ܒܪܘܩܐ ⁘

ܘܬܘܒ ܡ̈ܥܠܝܢ ܐܠܗܐ ܐܚܪܢܐ ܘܩܪܝܢ ܠܗ ܐܪܝܣ. ܘܐܡܪܝܢ ܕܐܝܬܘܗܝ ܩܪܒܬܢܐ ܘܛܢܢܐ ܘܪܓܝܓ ܒܥܝܪ̈ܐ ܘܩܢܝܢܬܐ ܕܠܐ ܕܝܠܗ. ܘܗܢܐ ܡܣܬܓܐ ܒܗ ܐܢܘܢ. ܗܘܐ ܕܐܡܪܝܢ ܕܠܚܪܬܐ ܓܒܪ ܒܐܦܪܘܕܝܛܐ. ܘܐܬܐܣܪ ܡܢ ܛܠܝܐ ܕܒܘܪܐ ܐܪܘܣ. ܘܡܢ ܐܗܦܣܛܘܣ ܒܥܠܗ̇ ܕܐܦܪܘܕܝܛܐ.

---

1. ܓܒܪܐ seems to be a mistake for ܓܢܒܐ. The Greek has κλέπτην.

11. Cod. ܕܛܢܕܪܐܘܣ.

ܗ̇ܘ ܕܠܐ ܡܫܡܫܢܐ ܕܐܠܗܐ ܢܗ̇ܘܐ ܡܪܟܒܬܢܐ ܐܘ ܦܓܪܐ ܐܘ ܚ̈ܙܪܐ ܀

ܘܬܘ̇ܒ ܐܡܪ̇ ܠܗ ܕܢܗܘܘܢ. ܕܐܠܗܐ ܠܟ ܐܬܘܬܗܘܢ ܡܫܡܠܝܐ ܒܟ̈ܝܢܐ ܟܠܠܗܘܬ̈ ܘܟܠܗ ܪ̇ܘܚܬܐ. ܘܢ̇ܦܠ ܢܬ̈ܐ ܕܠܐ ܕܠܗ. ܘܠܫܪܬܐ ܐܡ̈ܪܝܢ ܕܒܝܫܐ. ܘܫܡܫ ܠܡܫܡ̈ܫܢܘܬܗ ܘܒܪܝܗ̇ ܠܡܒܕܪܐ. ܘܒܗ̇ ܒܫܘܬܗ ܐܟܠ ܗܘܐ ܫܘܬ̈ܦܐ. ܘܠܫܪܬܐ ܐܬܦܠܠ ܡܢ ܦܠܝܦܘܣ. ܐܟ̱ ܗܟܢ ܕܢܗܘܘܢ ܐܠܗܐ ܐܬܘܬܗܘܢ ܗܘܐ. ܘܟܕ ܐܬܦܠܠ ܠܐ ܐܫܟܚ ܕܢܬܕܪ ܠܦܬܓܡܗ. ܐܡܟܢܐ ܡܫܟܚ ܕܠܐܢܫ̈ܐ ܢܬܕܪ ܗܘܐ ܀

ܗܪܡܝܣ ܬܘܒ ܡܡܠܠ. ܘܐܡܪܝܢ ܠܘܬܗ ܕܐܬܘܬܗܘܢ ܐܠܗܐ. ܗ̇ܢܐ ܫ̈ܘܬܦܐ ܦܪܘܢܐ ܘܡܪܟܒܬܢܐ ܘܦ̇ܠܠ ܠܒܢ̈ܝܐ. ܘܟܠܗܘܢ ܕܗܢܐ ܐܡ̈ܪܝܢ. ܕܠܫܪܬܐ ܒܢܐ ܘܦܠܠ ܠܒܢܘܗܝ. ܘܒܪܐ ܢܦܫܗ ܒܗܘܪܐ ܘܡܚܝܬ. ܐܟ̱ ܗܟܢ ܗܪܡܝܣ ܐܠܗܐ ܐܬܘܬܗܘܢ: ܘܒܟܠܗܘܢ ܗܠܝܢ ܒܢ̈ܫܬܐ. ܠܐ ܐܫܟܚ ܕܢܗܘܐ ܠܦܬܓܡܗ. ܐܡܟܢܐ ܐܫܟ̈ܚܢܐ ܒܕܪ̈ܝܐ ܗܢܘܢ ܫܐܠܝܢ ܗܘܘ. ܗ̇ܘ ܕܠܐ ܡܫܡܫܢܐ ܕܐܠܗܐ ܢܗܘܐ ܫܒܝܐ. ܐܘ ܪܦܝܐ. ܐܘ ܦܠܠ ܠܒܢܘܗܝ. ܐܘ ܡܬܦܢܐ ܡܢ ܢܘܪܐ ܀

ܘܡܢ ܒܬܪ ܗܢܐ ܡܡܠܠ ܐܠܗܐ ܐܣܝܢܐ. ܘܐܡܪ ܠܗ ܐܦܠܐ̱. ܘܐܡܪܝܢ ܟܠܗܘܢ ܕܐܬܘܬܗܘܢ ܦܠܢܐ ܘܡܫܬܘܕܝܢܐ. ܘܒܗܘܢ ܠܒܢ̈ܝ ܡܫܬܐ ܘܦܠܐܘܪܐ. ܒܗܘܢ ܕܝܢ ܡܫܬܐ. ܘܢܘܡܘܣܐ. ܘܦܩܕ ܦܘܩܕܢܐ ܠܒܢ̈ܝ ܐܢܫܐ: ܐܝܟ ܕܢܦܩ ܡܢܗܘܢ ܐܟ̱ ܐܦܝܪܐ. ܐܘܪܐ ܒܗ: ܒܠ ܐܦܝܪܐ ܗܘܐ ܗܢܐ

4. Cod. ܪ̈ܘܗܬܐ.

ܐܠܗܐ܂ ܗܘ ܕܡܫܡܫܢܐ ܕܗܠܝܢ ܟܠܗܘܢ ܢܬܚܫܚܘܢ ܒܐܠܗܐ ܀

ܘܒܬܪܗ ܡܥܠܝܢ ܐܪܛܡܝܣ ܐܠܗܬܐ ܚܬܗ ܕܐܦܠܘ. ܘܐܡܪܝܢ ܕܐܝܬܝܗ̇ ܗܘܬ ܨܝܕܬܐ. ܘܗܝ ܗܕܐ܂ ܠܩܫܬܐ ܗܘܬ ܫܩܝܠܐ ܘܓܐܪ̈ܐ. ܘܡܬܪܗܛܐ ܗܘܬ ܒܛܘܪ̈ܐ. ܟܕ ܕܒܪܐ ܟܠܒ̈ܐ. ܐܘ ܕܬܨܘܕ ܐܝܠܐ ܐܘ ܚܙܝܪ̈ܐ ܕܒܪܐ. ܗܝ ܕܡܫܡܫܢܐ ܕܛܠܝܬܐ ܒܬܘܠܬܐ ܒܠܚܘܕܝܗ̇ ܬܬܟܪܟ ܒܛܘܪ̈ܐ. ܘܬܨܘܕ ܨܝܕܐ ܕܚܝܘܬܐ. ܡܛܠ ܗܕܐ ܠܐ ܡܫܟܚܐ ܕܐܪܛܡܝܣ ܐܠܗܬܐ ܬܗܘܐ ܀ ܀

ܬܘܒ ܐܡܪܝܢ ܥܠ ܐܦܪܘܕܝܛܐ ܕܐܠܗܬܐ ܠܗ̇ ܐܝܬܝܗ̇. ܘܒܙܒܢ ܠܗ̇ ܡܕܝܢܐ. ܥܡ ܐܠܗ̈ܘܬܐ. ܘܒܙܒܢ ܕܝܢ ܡܩܢܝܐ ܒܒܢ̈ܝ ܐܢܫܐ. ܘܒܙܒܢ ܕܝܢ ܗ̇ܘܐ ܠܗ̇ ܪܚܡܐ ܐܪܝܣ. ܙܒܢ ܕܝܢ ܐܕܘܢܝܣ ܕܐܝܬܘܗܝ ܬܡܘܙܐ. ܘܒܥܝܐ ܠܗ̇. ܗܝ ܐܦܪܘܕܝܛܐ ܐܠܗܐ ܗܘܬ ܘܒܟܝܐ ܠܡܘܬܗ ܕܠܗ ܕܬܡܘܙܐ. ܘܐܡܪܝܢ ܕܢܚܬܬ ܠܫܝܘܠ ܐܝܟ ܕܬܦܪܘܩܝܘܗܝ ܠܐܕܘܢܝܣ ܡܢ ܦܪܣܦܘܢܝ ܕܐܝܬܝܗ̇ ܒܪܬ ܫܝܘܠ. ܐܢ ܗܟܝܠ ܐܦܪܘܕܝܛܐ ܐܠܗܬܐ ܐܝܬܝܗ̇. ܘܠܐ ܐܫܟܚܬ ܕܬܥܕܪܝܘܗܝ ܠܪܚܡܗ̇ ܒܡܘܬܗ. ܐܝܟܢܐ ܡܨܝܐ ܕܠܐܚܪ̈ܢܐ ܬܥܕܪ. ܘܗܕܐ ܠܐ ܡܫܟܚܐ ܕܬܫܬܡܥ ܕܟܝܢܐ ܐܠܗܝܐ ܠܒܟܝܐ ܘܠܐܒܠܐ ܘܠܓܘܪܐ ܢܐܬܐ ܀

ܘܬܘܒ ܐܡܪܝܢ ܥܠ ܬܡܘܙܐ ܕܐܝܬܘܗܝ ܐܠܗܐ. ܘܐܝܬܘܗܝ ܠܗ ܨܝܕܐ ܘܓܢܒܪܐ. ܘܐܡܪܝܢ ܕܗܘ ܗܢܐ ܐܬܩܛܠ ܡܢ ܡܚܘܬܐ ܕܚܙܝܪ ܒܪܐ. ܘܠܐ ܐܫܟܚ ܕܢܥܕܪ

13. Cod. ܐܕܘܢܝܣ.

ܠܢܦܫܗ. ܘܐܢ ܠܢܦܫܗ ܠܐ ܐܫܟܚ ܕܢܟܪ. ܐܡܝܢܐ ܠܓܘܫܡܐ ܐܝܟܢܐ ܡܫܟܚ ܕܢܦܪܘܩ. ܘܗܕܐ. ܠܐ ܡܫܟܚܐ ܕܐܠܗܐ ܚܢܝܪܐ ܐܘ ܓܕܫܐ ܐܘ ܡܟܐܒ ܐܢܬ ܟܒܝܫܘܬܐ ܢܗܘܐ ܀

ܬܘܒ ܐܡܪܝܢ ܥܠ ܙܗܘܐ. ܕܐܝܬܘܗܝ ܠܡ ܐܡܬܐ ܕܐܠܗܘܬܗܘܢ. ܘܐܡܪܝܢ ܥܠܘܗܝ ܕܗܘܐ ܠܗ ܒܪܡ ܙܗܘܐ ܐܦܠܛܘ. ܘܗܘ ܗܕܐ ܚܕܐ ܗܘܬ ܒܥܒܕܐ ܡܫܬܥܠܐ. ܠܣܘܪܛܐ ܕܡܢ ܐܢܫܘܬ ܡܪܕܘܬܐ ܘܐܠܗܐ ܗܘܬ ܠܗ ܠܐܦܠܛܘ ܙܗܘܐ. ܐܢ ܗܟܝܠ ܐܡܬܐ ܕܐܠܗܘܬܗܘܢ ܠܐ ܐܫܟܚܬ ܕܬܥܒܕ ܠܙܗܘܐ. ܘܬܥܒܕܘܗܝ ܡܢ ܡܬܘܬܐ. ܐܝܟܢܐ ܡܫܟܚܐ ܕܠܐܢܫܘܬܐ ܬܥܒܕ. ܡܫܟܚܐ ܗܟܝܠ ܕܐܠܗܘܬܐ ܬܥܒܕ ܘܬܥܒܕܐ: ܘܫܪܘܬܐ ܥܠ ܡܫܬܥܠܐ ܬܗܘܐ ܠܗ ܀

ܬܘܒ ܡܢܬܝܢ ܗܘܪܐ. ܘܐܡܪܝܢ ܕܐܝܬܘܗܝ ܐܠܗܘܬܐ. ܘܗܘ ܗܕܐ ܐܬܒܝܠܬ ܡܢ ܦܠܛܘܢ. ܘܠܐ ܐܫܟܚܬ ܕܬܥܒܕ ܢܦܫܗ. ܐܢ ܗܟܝܠ ܐܠܗܘܬܐ ܐܝܬܘܗܝ. ܘܠܢܦܫܗ ܠܐ ܐܫܟܚܬ ܕܬܥܒܕ. ܐܝܟܢܐ ܡܫܟܚܐ ܕܠܐܢܫܘܬܐ ܬܥܒܕ. ܐܠܗܐ ܓܝܪ ܕܡܬܢܫܐ ܗܘ ܡܫܒܠ.܀.

ܘܠܡ ܗܟܝܠ ܥܠܗܘܢ ܐܘ ܡܠܟܐ. ܐܟܠܘ ܡܩܝܡܐ ܥܠ ܐܠܗܝܗܘܢ. ܘܟܕܘ ܘܐܡܬܪܘ ܥܠܝܗܘܢ. ܕܡܢܗܘܢ ܢܦܩܘ ܥܠܝܗܘܢ ܒܢܝ ܐܢܫܐ ܥܠܬܐ: ܕܢܣܒܪܘܢ ܥܠ ܙܘܥܝܢ ܘܟܠ ܙܠܝܦܘܢ. ܘܗܕܐ ܐܬܡܫܠܬ ܐܪܥܐ ܥܠܘܗܝ܀

---

5. Cod. ܗܪܐܐ.

6. Cod. ܠܗ.

ܡܨܪ̈ܝܐ ܕܝܢ ܡܛܠ ܕܒܨ̈ܝܪܝܢ ܘܗܕܝ̈ܘܛܝܢ ܝܬܝܪ ܡܢ ܟܠܗܘܢ ܥܡ̈ܡܐ ܕܐܝܬ ܥܠ ܐܪܥܐ. ܗ̇ܢܘܢ ܛܥܘ ܝܬܝܪ ܡܢ ܟܠܗ ܥܡܐ. ܠܐ ܓܝܪ ܣܦܩܬ ܠܗܘܢ ܕܚܠܬܗܘܢ ܕܟܠܕ̈ܝܐ ܘܕܝ̈ܘܢܝܐ. ܐܠܐ ܐܝܬܝܘ ܐܦ ܡܢ ܚܝܘܬܐ ܕܝܒܫܬܐ. ܘܐܡܪܘ ܟܠܗܘܢ: ܕܐܝܬܝܗܘܢ ܐܠܗ̈ܐ. ܘܐܦ ܡܢ ܪ̇ܚܫܐ ܕܡܬܪܚܫ ܒܝܒܫܐ ܘܒܡ̈ܝܐ: ܘܥܠ ܢܨ̈ܒܬܐ: ܘܥܠ ܩܝ̈ܣܐ. ܐܡܪܘ ܕܐܝܬܝܗܘܢ ܐܠܗ̈ܐ ܐܢܘܢ. ܘܐܬܛܥܝܘ ܒܟܠܗ̇ ܫܢܝܘܬܐ ܘܦܠܚܢܘܬܐ. ܝܬܝܪ ܡܢ ܟܠܗܘܢ ܥܡ̈ܡܐ ܕܐܝܬ ܥܠ ܐܪܥܐ. ܡܢ ܩܕܝܡ ܓܝܪ ܦܠܚܝܢ ܗܘܘ ܠܐܝܣܝܣ. ܘܐܡܪܝܢ ܕܐܠܗܬܐ ܠܡ ܐܝܬܝܗ̇. ܕܐܝܬ ܗܘܐ ܠܗ̇ ܠܡ ܒܥܠܐ ܐܘܣܝܪܝܣ ܐܚܘܗ̇. ܟܕ ܕܝܢ ܠܡ ܐܬܩܛܠ ܐܘܣܝܪܝܣ ܡܢ ܛܝܦܘܢ ܐܚܘܗܝ. ܥܪܩܬ ܐܝܣܝܣ ܥܡ ܐܘܪ ܒܪܗ̇ ܠܓܒܠܘܣ ܕܒܣܘܪܝܐ. ܘܗܘܬ ܬܡܢ ܙܒܢܐ ܡܙܒܢܐ ܥܕܡܐ ܕܪܒܐ ܒܪܗ̇. ܘܐܬܟܬܫ ܥܡ ܛܝܦܘܢ ܕܩܛܠܗ ܘܩܛܠܗ. ܘܗܝܕܝܢ ܠܡ ܐܝܣܝܣ ܥܒܕܬ ܘܡܬܟܪܟܐ ܗܘܬ ܥܡ ܐܘܪ ܒܪܗ̇: ܘܒܥܝܐ ܗܘܬ ܠܦܓܪܗ ܕܐܘܣܝܪܝܣ ܒܥܠܗ̇. ܘܠܡܬܒܥܘܬܗ ܡܪ̈ܝܪܬܐ ܫ̇ܩܠܐ ܗܘܬ. ܐܢ ܡܟܝܠ ܐܝܣܝܣ ܐܠܗܬܐ ܐܝܬܝܗ̇: ܘܠܐ ܐܫܟܚܬ ܕܬܥܕܪ ܠܐܘܣܝܪܝܣ ܐܚܘܗ̇ ܘܒܥܠܗ̇. ܐܝܟܢܐ ܡܫܟܚܐ ܕܠܐܢܫ̈ܐ ܬܥܕܪ. ܗ̇ܝ ܕܠܐ ܡܫܟܚܐ ܕܚܒܝܐ ܐܠܗܝܐ ܢܦܠ ܘܢܦܪܘܫ: ܐܘ ܢܦܩܐ ܘܠܐܐ. ܘܐܢ ܕܝܢ ܠܐ ܗܟܢ ܗܘܐ.

ܘܟܠܗܘܢ ܕܝܢ ܕܐܘܣܝܪܝܣ ܐܡܪܝܢ. ܕܐܠܗܐ ܐܝܬܘܗܝ ܡܬܚܪܝܢܐ. ܘܐܬܩܛܠ ܡܢ ܛܝܦܘܢ ܘܠܐ ܐܫܟܚ ܕܢܥܕܪ ܢܦܫܗ. ܘܗܕܐ ܝܕܝܥܐ. ܕܥܠ ܐܠܗܘܬܐ ܠܐ ܡܬܐܡܪܐ: ܘܬܘܒ ܐܡܪܝܢ ܥܠ ܛܝܦܘܢ ܐܚܘܗܝ: ܕܐܝܬܘܗܝ

ܐܠܗܐ ܦܠܓ ܐܝܬܘܗܝ. ܘܡܬܦܠܓ ܡܢ ܒܪ ܐܝܬܘܗܝ ܘܡܢ ܟܠܬܗ. ܕܐܠܐ ܡܫܟܚ ܕܢܥܕܪ ܠܢܦܫܗ: ܘܐܝܟܢܐ ܟܝ ܗܘ ܕܠܢܦܫܗ ܠܐ ܡܥܕܪ ܐܝܬܘܗܝ ܐܠܗܐ܀

ܡܨܪ̈ܝܐ ܗܟܝܠ: ܡܛܠ ܕܣ̈ܟܠܝܢ. ܡܢ ܥܡܡܐ ܕܒܥܠܡܐ: ܠܐ ܣܦܩ ܠܗܘܢ ܗܠܝܢ ܘܕܐܝܟ ܗܠܝܢ ܐܠܗ̈ܐ: ܐܠܐ ܐܦ ܥܠ ܚ̈ܝܘܬܐ ܕܒܠܚܘܕ ܢܦܫܐ ܠܝܬ ܒܗܘܢ: ܣܡܘ ܫܡܐ ܕܐܠܗ̈ܐ. ܐܢܫܐ ܓܝܪ ܡܢܗܘܢ ܦܠܚܝܢ ܠܥܢܐ: ܐܚܪ̈ܢܐ ܕܝܢ ܠܥܓܠܐ. ܘܡܢܗܘܢ ܠܚܙܝܪܐ. ܘܐܚܪ̈ܢܐ ܠܫܠܘܪܐ. ܘܡܢܗܘܢ ܠܩܪܩܘܕܝܠܘܣ ܘܠܒܙܐ. ܘܠܢܘܢܐ. ܘܠܐܒܝܬܐ. ܘܠܟܘܕܪܐ ܘܠܢܫܪ̈ܐ ܘܠܥܘܪܒܐ. ܡܢܗܘܢ ܦܠܚܝܢ ܠܫܘܢܪܐ. ܘܐܚܪ̈ܢܐ ܠܢܘܢܐ ܥܒܘܬܐ. ܡܢܗܘܢ ܠܟܠܒܐ. ܡܢܗܘܢ ܠܚܘܪܐ. ܘܡܢܗܘܢ ܠܐܣܦܣ. ܘܐܚܪ̈ܢܐ ܠܐܪܝܐ. ܘܐܚܪ̈ܢܐ: ܠܬܘܡܐ ܘܠܒܨ̈ܠܐ ܘܠܟܘ̈ܒܐ. ܘܐܚܪ̈ܢܐ ܠܢܡܪܐ: ܘܠܫܪܟܐ ܕܐܝܟ ܗܠܝܢ. ܘܠܐ ܡܣ̈ܬܟܠܝܢ ܕܘܝ̈ܐ: ܕܟܠܗܝܢ ܗܠܝܢ ܕܠܘ ܡܕܡ ܐܢܝܢ. ܟܕ ܟܠܝܘܡ ܚܙܝܢ ܠܐܠܗ̈ܝܗܘܢ ܕܡܬܐܟܠܝܢ ܘܐܒܕܝܢ ܡܢ ܒ̈ܢܝ ܐܢܫܐ. ܐܦ ܡܢ ܚ̈ܒܪܝܗܘܢ: ܘܡܢܗܘܢ ܟܕ ܡܘܩܕܝܢ. ܘܡܢܗܘܢ ܟܕ ܡܝܬܝܢ ܘܡܬܡܣܝܢ ܘܗܘܝܢ ܥܦܪܐ. ܘܠܐ ܡܣܬܟܠܝܢ ܕܐܝܟܢ ܒܢ̈ܝܐ ܩܛܝܠܐ..܀

ܘܠܐ ܐܣܬܟܠܘ ܗܟܝܠ ܡܨܪ̈ܝܐ: ܕܗܠܝܢ ܕܐܝܟ ܗܠܝܢ: ܠܐ ܐܝܬܝܗܘܢ ܐܠܗ̈ܐ: ܗܠܝܢ ܕܠܝܬ ܒܐܝ̈ܕܝܗܘܢ ܦܘܪܩܢܗܘܢ. ܘܐܦܠܐ ܗܘ ܥܠ ܦܘܪܩܢܐ ܕܢܦܫܗܘܢ ܡܬܒܠܝܢ. ܥܠ ܦܘܪܩܢܐ ܕܐܠܗ̈ܝܗܘܢ ܗܢܝܢ. ܡܢ ܐܝܟܐ ܐܝܬ ܒܗܘܢ ܚܝܠܐ ܕܢܥܕܪܘܢ. ܛܥܝܘܬܐ ܗܟܝܠ ܪܒܬܐ

ܠܓܘ ܡܢ̈ܝܢܐ܆ ܡܛܠ ܕܡܢ ܟܠܗܘܢ ܒܒܪ̈ܝܬܐ܆ ܕܐܝܬ ܟܠ ܨ̈ܒܘܬ ܕܐܪ̈ܥܐ. ܕܕܘܡܝܢܐ ܕܝܢ ܐܝܬܝܗ̇ ܐܘ ܡܠܟܐ. ܟܠ ܡ̈ܢܝܢܐ܆ ܕܗܢ ܡܬܚ̈ܙܝܢ ܡܢ ܥܒܕܐ ܕܟܠܗܘܢ ܒܒܪ̈ܝܬܐ܆ ܒܗܘ̈ܦܟܝܗܘܢ ܘܒܡܫܠܡܢܘܬܗܘܢ܆ ܐܡܝܢܐ ܠܓܘ ܒܬܪ ܒܬܪ̈ܐ ܡܬܢ̈ܝܬܐ ܘܡܠܦ̈ܢܐ ܕܠܐ ܢܦܫܐ. ܗܢ ܚܙܝܢ ܠܐܠܗ̈ܝܗܘܢ ܕܡܢ ܒܥܒ̈ܕܝܗܘܢ ܡܬܢܛܪܝܢ ܘܡܫܬܟܚܝܢ܆ ܘܡܬܓܒܠܝܢ ܘܡܬܦܣܠܝܢ܆ ܘܡܬܬܚܬܟܝܢ ܘܡܬܢܣܪ̈ܝܢ܆ ܘܥܠ ܕܡܚܒ ܠܗܘܢ ܡܬܥܬܩܝܢ. ܘܟܕ ܚܠܦܝܢ ܘܡܢ ܢܚܫܘܬܐ ܕܒܢܝܐ ܡܬܦܟܝܢ. ܘܟܕ ܡܬܚܫܒܝܢ ܘܟܕ ܡܬܕܩܩܝܢ. ܐܡܝܢܐ ܟܕ ܠܐ ܐܬܬܘܥܠܘ ܒܠܒܗ̈ܘܢ ܕܠܐ ܐܝܬܝܗܘܢ ܐܠܗ̈ܐ܆ ܘܗܠܝܢ ܕܦܘܪܩܢܐ ܕܢܦܫܗܘܢ ܠܐ ܐܬܡܨܝܘ. ܐܡܝܢܐ ܝܩܝܪܘܬܐ ܕܒ̈ܢܝ ܐܢܫܐ ܡܥܒܕܝܢ ܕܢܥܒܕܘܢ܆ ܐܠܗܐ ܐܦ ܗܘ̈ܡܟܐ ܘܦܠܚ̈ܘܬܐ. ܕܒܗ̈ܘܢ ܒܗ ܠܓܒܝܢ ܐܟܠܘ ܒܠܒܗܘܢ ܕܐܠܗ̈ܐ ܐܢܘܢ܆ ܗܠܝܢ ܕܐܝܟ ܗܘ ܕܡܬܥܒܕܝܢ ܠܐܝܩܪܗ ܕܐܠܗܐ ܐܚܝܕ ܟܠ. ܘܟܕ ܚܙܝܢ ܒܟܢ ܕܢܕܡܘܢ ܠܐܠܗܐ ܗܘ ܕܡܬܥܒܕܘܬ ܐܝܟ ܠܐ ܚܙܘܗܝ ܕܠܟܝ ܕܟܐ. ܘܠܐ ܒܚܟܡ ܕܚܙܝܗܘܢ. ܘܒܗܠܝܢ ܡܟܠܝܢ ܟܠ ܐܠܗܘܬܐ. ܐܝܟ ܗܘ ܕܒܢ̈ܝܘܬܐ ܡܫܚܠܦܐ ܢܐܕܘܢ. ܟܕ ܕܐܬܡܪ̈ܝܢ܆ ܕܡܦܟܠ ܕܟܝܢܬܐ ܘܡܫܠ ܟܠܗܝܢ ܘܢܗܘܝܢܐ. ܘܦܠܚ̈ܐ ܕܒ̈ܢܐ ܐܢܫܐ ܘܫܘܚܠܦܐ. ܐܠܗܐ ܕܝܢ ܠܐ ܫܘܚܠܦܐ ܐܝܬܘܗܝ. ܘܡܢ ܗܠܝܢ ܡܕܡ ܠܐ ܡܬܚܒܠܐ ܠܗ. ܘܡܕܡܐ ܗܘ ܕܠܟܝܢ ܒܢ̈ܝ ܐܢܫܐ ܒܗܠܝܢ ܕܡܬܚܫܒܝܢ. ܘܦܬܟܪ̈ܝܗܘܢ ܕܝܢ

10. Cod. ܐܬܬܘܥܠ.

22. Cod. ܐܠܗ̈ܝܗܘܢ ܕܝܢ ܘܦܬܟܪ̈ܝܗܘܢ.

ܘܦܝܠܘܣܘܦܘܗܝ ܣܟܠܝܢ ܘܐܡܪܝܢ. ܕܒܢܝܐ ܕܟܠܗܘܢ ܐܠܗ̈ܝܗܘܢ ܐܝܬܝܗܘܢ ܚܕ. ܘܠܐ ܐܣܬܟܠܘ ܠܐܠܗܐ ܡܛܠ ܕܗ̣ܘ ܚܕ ܐܝܬܘܗܝ. ܒܟܠ ܐܝܬܘܗܝ. ܚܙܝܢ ܗܟܝܠ. ܐܢ ܓܝܪ ܦܓܪܗ ܕܒܪܢܫܐ ܚܕ ܗ̣ܘ ܒܡܢܘܬܐ: ܠܐ ܕܚܠ ܗܕܡܐ ܡܢ ܚܒܪܗ: ܐܠܐ ܟܕ ܐܝܬܘܗܝ ܦܓܪܐ ܡܫܬܘܝܐ: ܟܠܗ ܥܡܐ ܥܡ ܟܠܗ. ܗܟܢܐ ܗܟܝܠ ܐܦ ܐܠܗܐ ܕܐܝܬܘܗܝ ܚܕ ܒܟܝܢܗ: ܚܕܐ ܐܝܬܘܬܐ ܙܕܩ ܠܗ ܥܡ ܥܡܐ ܒܟܝܢܗ ܘܐܝܬܘܬܗ: ܘܠܐ ܕܚܠ ܗܘ ܡܢܗ. ܐܢ ܗܟܝܠ ܒܢܝܐ ܕܐ̈ܠܗܐ ܚܕ ܐܝܬܝܗܘܢ: ܠܐ ܙܕܩ ܕܐܠܗܐ ܠܐܠܗܐ ܢܪܕܘܦ. ܐܦܠܐ ܕܢܩܛܘܠ ܐܦ ܠܐ ܕܢܚܒܠ ܠܗ ܕܒܝܫ ܀

ܐܢ ܗܟܝܠ ܐܠܗܐ ܡܢ ܐܠܗ̈ܐ ܐܬܝܠܕܘ ܘܐܬܒܪܝܘ. ܘܡܢܗܘܢ ܐܬܒܠܥܘ: ܘܡܢܗܘܢ ܒܪ̈ܘܩܐ ܐܬܚܢܩܘ. ܡ̈ܕܡܐ ܗܢܝ. ܕܠܘ ܚܕ ܗ̣ܘ ܒܢܝܐ ܕܐܠܗ̈ܝܗܘܢ. ܘܡ̈ܕܡܐ ܡ̈ܕܡܐ ܗܢܝ ܐܦ ܡܫܠܡܐ: ܕܓܒܪܘܬܐ ܗܝ ܗܢ ܕܡܫܥܒܕܝܢ ܒܢ̈ܝܐ ܕܐܠܗ̈ܝܗܘܢ: ܘܡܢܗܘܢ ܠܗܘܢ ܠܚܕ ܚܒܪܐ. ܐܢ ܗܟܝܠ ܙܢܐ ܕܡܬܪܕܦܝܢ ܒܐܠܗܐ: ܕܡܬܚܙܝܐ ܘܠܐ ܚܙܐ. ܒܡܕܡ ܡܬܪܐܡܐ ܥܡܝܐ ܠܕܡܘܬܐ: ܗܢܘ ܕܢܦܫܩܘܢ ܐܝܟ ܒܢܝܐ ܠܐ ܡܬܚܙܝܐ ܘܚܙܐ ܠܟܠ. ܘܐܢ ܗܘܐ ܦܠܐ ܕܢܬܦܬܟܪܐ ܐܝܟ ܒܒܢ̈ܝܬܗ ܕܐܘܡܢܐ. ܚܕ ܒܢܝܐ ܦܠܐ ܕܢܩܒܠ ܐܝܟ ܠܟܡܘܕܐ ܕܐܘܡܢܐ ܀

ܗܐ ܓܝܪ ܚܕ ܗܘܐ ܡܢܝܢܐ ܢܡܘܣܐ. ܠܐ ܐܫܬܟܚܘ ܕܒܢܝ̈ܚܘܗܝܗܘܢ ܠܐܠܗ̈ܝܗܘܢ ܡܫܬܥܝܢ. ܐܢ ܓܝܪ

22. Cod. ܐܫܬܟܚ.

ܡܕܝܢ ܢܚܘܘܬܗܘܢ ܒܗܠܝܢ ܐܠܟܣܢܕܪܘܣ. ܕܥܒܕܘ ܥܒܪ ܢܚܘܘܐ: ܟܕ ܡܦܠܠܝܢ ܠܬܪܥܐ ܘܦܬܚܝܢ ܫܢܝܘܬܐ: ܘܒܬܝܢ ܘܫܠܡܝܢ ܘܒܬܒܝܢ: ܘܕܡܟܝܢ ܒܗ ܕܒܪܐ: ܒܗ ܫܪܒܐ ܕܗܘܒܪܝܫܗܘܢ ܐܚܪܢܐ. ܐܦ ܕܝܢ ܐܠܟܣܢܕܪܘܣ: ܫܦܝܪ ܘܐܝܟ ܕܡܒܠܒܠܝܢ ܗܦܟܘ ܗܠܝܢ ܒܠܗܝܢ. ܒܗܠܝܢ ܢܚܘܘܬܗܘܢ ܕܡܠܝܢܐ: ܕܠܐ ܐܬܬܗܘܝܘ ܐܝܟ ܒܢܝܢܐ ܕܐܠܟܣܢܕܪܘܣ: ܘܒܗ ܒܗܕܐ ܢܨܒܐ ܒܠܒܐ ܒܠܗ. ܀܀

ܬܫܒܘܚܬܐ ܒܪܢ ܕܐܠܟܣܢܕܪܘܣ. ܡܒܗܝܢ ܡܬܠܐ. ܘܡܒܗܝܢ ܒܝܢܬܐ. ܘܡܒܗܝܢ ܙܡܪܬܐ ܘܩܝܢܬܐ ܐܬܬܗܝܡ. ܙܡܪܬܐ ܗܘܝܠ ܘܡܝܢܬܐ: ܡܠܐ ܗܦܩܬܐ ܘܙܡܟܐ. ܗܠܝܢ ܕܝܢ ܒܝܢܬܐ: ܐܦ ܐܬܗܘܬܪ ܐܝܟ ܕܐܡܬܝܢ. ܠܐ ܡܠܗܐ ܐܢܘܢ: ܡܛܠ ܕܗܠܝܢ ܗܒܪܘ ܘܗܠܝܢ ܫܥܘ ܘܦܓܪܘ. ܘܗܠܝܢ ܡܬܠܐ: ܡܠܐ ܬܐܝܢ ܦܢܝܬܐ: ܕܠܒܓܪ ܚܠܐ ܠܝܬ ܒܗܝܢ܀

ܢܬܪܬܐ ܡܛܠ ܐܘ ܡܠܒܐ. ܐܦ ܒܠ ܫܪܒܐ ܕܡܘܕܝܐ: ܘܫܪܝܐ ܐܝܢܐ ܚܫܒܢܐ ܐܝܬ ܠܗܘܢ ܒܠ ܐܠܗܐ. ܡܘܕܝܐ ܗܘܠ ܐܡܪܝܢ. ܕܚܕ ܗܘ ܐܠܗܐ ܒܪܘܝܐ ܕܟܠ ܘܐܚܝܕ ܒܠ. ܘܕܠܐ ܙܕܩ ܕܢܬܦܠܓ ܡܕܡ ܐܚܪܝܢ: ܐܠܐ ܐܢ ܗܢܐ ܐܠܗܐ ܒܠܚܘܕܘܗܝ. ܘܒܗܕܐ ܡܬܚܙܝܢ ܕܡܙܡܪܝܢ ܠܫܪܪܐ ܛܒܪ ܡܢ ܒܠܗܘܢ ܒܢܟܡܐ. ܒܗܝ ܕܡܬܪܐܡܬ ܠܐܠܗܐ ܦܟܕܝܢ ܘܠܗ ܠܒܪܘܗܝ. ܘܡܬܕܡܝܢ ܒܐܠܗܐ: ܟܕ ܙܢܚܐ ܐܢܫܐ ܕܐܝܬ ܠܗܘܢ ܟܕ ܡܪܚܡܝܢ ܒܠ ܡܘܡܢܐ. ܘܦܪܩܝܢ ܢܚܝܐ: ܘܡܒܪܝܢ ܡܪܥܬܐ ܘܡܒܪܕܝܢ ܕܕܚܝܢ ܠܗܠܝܢ. ܗܠܝܢ ܕܡܩܒܠܝܢ ܒܠ ܐܠܗܐ. ܘܫܦܝܪ ܐܦ ܠܒܝܫܫܐ. ܗܠܝܢ ܕܦܒܠܘ ܡܢ ܐܒܫܘܢܗܘܢ ܘܕܡܚܐ.

ܒܪܡ ܕܝܢ ܐܦ ܗܢܘܢ ܛܥܘ ܡܢ ܝܕܥܬܐ ܫܪܝܪܬܐ. ܘܒܬܪܥܝܬܗܘܢ ܣܒܪܝܢ ܕܠܐܠܗܐ ܗܘ̇ ܦܠܚܝܢ. ܒܛܘܣܐ ܕܝܢ ܕܥܒ̈ܕܝܗܘܢ: ܠܡܠܐ̈ܟܐ ܗܘ̇ ܘܠܐ ܠܐܠܗܐ ܗܘ ܦܘܠܚܢܗܘܢ. ܟܕ ܢܛܪܝܢ ܫܒ̈ܬܐ ܘܪܝܫ ܝܪ̈ܚܐ. ܘܦܛܝܪ̈ܐ ܘܨܘܡܐ ܪܒܐ. ܘܨܘܡܐ ܘܓܙܘܪܬܐ. ܘܕܘܟܝܐ ܕܡ̈ܐܟܘܠܬܐ. ܗܠܝܢ ܕܐܦ ܠܐ ܗܟܢܐ ܡܫܡܠܝܐܝܬ ܢܛܪܝܢ ܠܗܝܢ ܀

ܟܪ̈ܣܛܝܢܐ ܕܝܢ ܐܘ ܡܠܟܐ. ܟܕ ܡܬܟܪܟܝܢ ܘܒܥܝܢ ܐܫܟܚܘܗ̇ ܠܫܪܪܐ. ܘܐܝܟ ܕܐܕܪܟܢ ܡܢ ܟܬܒܝܗܘܢ. ܗܠܝܢ ܩܪܝܒܝܢ ܠܗ ܠܫܪܪܐ ܘܠܝܕܥܬܐ ܫܪܝܪܬܐ. ܝܬܝܪ ܡܢ ܫܪܟܐ ܕܥܡ̈ܡܐ. ܝܕܥܝܢ ܓܝܪ. ܘܡܗܝܡܢܝܢ ܒܗ ܒܐܠܗܐ: ܒܪܘܝܐ ܕܫܡܝܐ ܘܕܐܪܥܐ: ܗܘ̇ ܕܟܠ ܒܗ ܘܟܠ ܡܢܗ: ܗܘ̇ ܕܠܝܬ ܠܗ ܫܘܬܦܐ ܐܠܗܐ ܐܚܪܢܐ. ܗܘ̇ ܕܩܒܠܘ ܡܢܗ ܦܘܩ̈ܕܢܐ ܗܠܝܢ ܕܥܠ ܬܪܥܝܬܗܘܢ ܪܫܝܡܝܢ ܐܢܘܢ. ܗܠܝܢ ܕܢܛܪܝܢ ܠܗܘܢ ܥܠ ܣܒܪܐ ܘܣܘܟܝܐ ܕܥܠܡܐ ܕܥܬܝܕ. ܡܛܠܗܕܐ ܕܗܢܐ: ܠܐ ܓܝܪܝܢ ܘܠܐ ܙܢܝܢ. ܘܠܐ ܡܣܗܕܝܢ ܣܗܕܘܬܐ ܕܓܠܬܐ. ܘܠܐ ܚܡܣܝܢ ܥܠ ܓܘܥܠܢܐ. ܘܠܐ ܪ̈ܓܝܢ ܕܠܐ ܕܝܠܗܘܢ. ܠܐܒܐ ܘܠܐܡܐ ܡܝܩܪܝܢ. ܘܠܐܝܠܝܢ ܕܩܪ̈ܝܒܝܢ ܠܗܘܢ ܡܛܐܒܝܢ. ܘܕܝܢܐ ܕܩܘܫܬܐ ܕ̈ܝܢܝܢ. ܘܠܦܬܟܪ̈ܐ ܕܒܕܡܘܬ ܒܪܢܫܐ ܠܐ ܣܓܕܝܢ. ܘܡܕܡ ܕܠܐ ܨܒܝܢ ܕܢܥܒܕܘܢ ܠܗܘܢ ܐܚܪ̈ܢܐ: ܠܐܢܫ ܠܐ ܥܒܕܝܢ. ܘܡܢ ܡܐܟܘܠܬܐ ܕܕܒܚ̈ܐ ܕܦܬܟܪ̈ܐ ܠܐ ܐܟܠܝܢ. ܕܕܟ̈ܝܐ ܓܝܪ ܐܢܘܢ. ܘܠܐܝܠܝܢ ܕܥܨܝܢ ܠܗܘܢ

1. Cod. ܫܪܪܬܐ.

ܡܒܝܐܝܢ. ܘܪ̈ܚܡܐ ܠܗܘܢ ܥܒܕܝܢ ܠܗܘܢ. ܘܠܒܥܠܕܒܒ̈ܝܗܘܢ ܡܛܐܒܝܢ. ܘܢ̈ܫܝܗܘܢ ܕܝܢ ܐܘ ܡܠܟܐ ܐܝܟ ܒܬܘܠܬܐ. ܘܒ̈ܢܬܗܘܢ ܢܟ̈ܦܢ. ܘܓܒ̈ܪܝܗܘܢ ܡܬܢܟܦܝܢ ܡܢ ܟܠ ܙܘܘܓ ܕܠܐ ܢܡܘܣ ܘܡܢ ܟܠܗ̇ ܛܢܦܘܬܐ: ܥܠ ܣܒܪܐ ܕܦܘܪܥܢܐ ܕܥܬܝܕ ܒܥܠܡܐ ܐܚܪܢܐ. ܥܒ̈ܕܐ ܕܝܢ ܘܐܡ̈ܗܬܐ ܐܘ ܒܢ̈ܝܐ ܐܢ ܐܝܬ ܠܚܕ ܚܕ ܡܢܗܘܢ. ܡܦܝܣܝܢ ܠܗܘܢ ܕܢܗܘܘܢ ܟܪ̈ܣܛܝܢܐ ܡܛܠ ܚܘܒܐ ܕܐܝܬܝܗܘܢ. ܘܡܐ ܕܗܘܘ. ܐܚ̈ܐ ܩܪܝܢ ܠܗܘܢ ܕܠܐ ܦܘܠܓ. ܠܐܠܗ̈ܐ ܢܘܟܪ̈ܝܐ ܠܐ ܣܓܕܝܢ. ܘܒܟܠܗ̇ ܡܟܝܟܘܬܐ ܘܒܒܣܝܡܘܬܐ ܡܗܠܟܝܢ. ܘܕܓܠܘܬܐ ܠܐ ܡܫܬܟܚܐ ܒܝܢ̈ܬܗܘܢ. ܘܠܚܕ̈ܕܐ ܡܚܒܝܢ. ܘܡܢ ܐܪ̈ܡܠܬܐ ܠܐ ܡܗܦܟܝܢ ܐܦ̈ܝܗܘܢ. ܘܠܝܬܡܐ ܡܦܨܝܢ. ܡܢ ܡܢ ܕܕܒܪ ܠܗ ܒܩܛܝܪܐ. ܘܡܢ ܕܐܝܬ ܠܗ ܠܡܢ ܕܠܝܬ ܠܗ ܝܗܒ ܕܠܐ ܫܘܒܗܪܐ. ܘܠܐܟܣܢܝܐ ܡܐ ܕܚܙܝܢ ܠܒܝܬ̈ܝܗܘܢ ܡܥܠܝܢ ܠܗ. ܘܚܕܝܢ ܒܗ ܐܝܟ ܕܒܐܚܐ ܫܪܝܪܐ. ܠܘ ܓܝܪ ܐܚ̈ܐ ܕܒܦܓܪ ܩ̈ܪܝܢ ܠܗܘܢ ܐܠܐ ܐܚ̈ܐ ܕܒܪܘܚ ܘܕܒܐܠܗܐ. ܐܡܬܝ ܕܝܢ ܕܚܕ ܡܢ ܡܣ̈ܟܢܝܗܘܢ ܥܒܪ ܡܢ ܥܠܡܐ. ܘܚܙܐ ܠܗ ܟܠ ܚܕ ܡܢܗܘܢ: ܐܝܟ ܚܝܠܗ ܢܦܩ ܕܩܒܘܪܬܗ. ܘܐܢ ܫ̈ܡܥܝܢ ܕܚܕ ܡܢܗܘܢ ܚܒܝܫ ܐܘ ܐܠܝܨ ܡܛܠ ܫܡܗ ܕܡܫܝܚܗܘܢ: ܟܠܗܘܢ ܢܨܦܝܢ ܕܢܫܡܫܘܢܗ. ܘܐܢ ܡܫܟܚܐ ܕܢܬܦܪܩ ܦܪܩܝܢ ܠܗ. ܘܐܢ ܐܝܬ ܒܗܘܢ ܐܢܫ ܕܡܣܟܢ ܐܘ ܕܣܢܝܩ: ܘܠܗܘܢ ܠܝܬ ܝܬܝܪܬܐ ܕܬܘܪܣܝܐ: ܨܝܡܝܢ ܬܪ̈ܝܢ ܐܘ ܬܠܬܐ ܝܘ̈ܡܝܢ. ܐܝܟ ܕܠܡܣ̈ܟܢܐ ܢܣܦܩܘܢ ܣܝܒܪܬܐ ܕܡܐܟܘܠܬܗܘܢ. ܘܦܘ̈ܩܕܢܘܗܝ ܕܡܫܝܚܗܘܢ ܒܝܨܝܦܘܬܐ ܪܒܬܐ ܢܛܪܝܢ ܠܗܘܢ. ܒܟܐܢܘܬ ܘܒܢܟܦܘܬ ܚܝܝܢ: ܐܝܟ

ܕܦܩܕ ܐܢܘܢ ܡܪܝܐ ܐܠܗܗܘܢ. ܒܟܠܗܘܢ ܨܦܪ̈ܐ ܘܒܟܠ ܫ̈ܥܝܢ. ܥܠ ܛܝ̈ܒܘܬܗ ܕܐܠܗܐ ܕܥܡܗܘܢ ܡܘܕܝܢ ܘܡܫܒܚܝܢ ܠܗ. ܘܥܠ ܡܐܟܘܠܬܗܘܢ ܘܥܠ ܡܫܬܝܗܘܢ ܡܩܒܠܝܢ ܛܝܒܘܬܗ. ܘܐܢ ܐܢܫ ܙܕܝܩܐ ܡܢܗܘܢ ܢܦܩ ܡܢ ܥܠܡܐ: ܚܕܝܢ ܘܡܩܒܠܝܢ ܛܝܒܘܬܗ ܕܐܠܗܐ. ܘܡܠܘܝܢ ܠܦܓܪܗ ܐܝܟ ܕܡܢ ܐܬܪܐ ܠܩܪܝܒ ܫܢܐ. ܘܐܡܬܝ ܕܡܬܝܠܕ ܠܚܕ ܡܢܗܘܢ ܛܠܝܐ: ܡܘܕܝܢ ܠܐܠܗܐ. ܘܐܢ ܬܘܒ ܢܫܢܐ ܘܡܛܐܬ ܒܛܠܝܘܬܗ. ܡܘܕܝܢ ܠܐܠܗܐ ܝܬܝܪܐܝܬ. ܐܝܟ ܡܢ ܕܥܒܪܗ ܠܥܠܡܐ ܕܠܐ ܚ̈ܛܗܐ. ܘܐܢ ܬܘܒ ܚܙܝܢ ܕܡܝܬ ܚܕ ܡܢܗܘܢ ܒܪܘܫܥܗ ܐܘ ܒܚ̈ܛܗܘܗܝ: ܥܠ ܗܢܐ ܒܟܝܢ ܡܪܝܪܐܝܬ ܘܡܬܬܢܚܝܢ. ܐܝܟ ܡܢ ܕܥܬܝܕ ܕܢܐܙܠ ܠܬܫܢܝܩ ܕܝܢܐ.

ܗܢܘ ܦܘܩܕܐ ܕܢܡܘܣܗܘܢ ܕܟܪ̈ܣܛܝܢܐ ܐܘ ܡܠܟܐ ܘܕܘܒܪ̈ܝܗܘܢ. ܐܝܟ ܐܢܫܐ ܕܝܕܥܝܢ ܠܐܠܗܐ ܫܐܠܝܢ ܡܢܗ ܫܐ̈ܠܬܐ: ܕܦܐ̈ܝܢ ܠܗ ܠܡܬܠ ܘܠܗܘܢ ܠܡܣܒ. ܘܗܟܢܐ ܡܫܡܠܝܢ ܙܒܢܐ ܕܚܝܝܗܘܢ. ܘܡܛܠ ܕܝܕܥܝܢ ܛܝ̈ܒܘܬܗ ܕܐܠܗܐ ܕܥܡܗܘܢ: ܗܐ ܡܛܠܬܗܘܢ ܪ̈ܕܝܢ ܫܘܦܪ̈ܐ ܕܐܝܬ ܒܥܠܡܐ. ܘܫܪܝܪܐܝܬ ܕܗܠܝܢ ܐܢܘܢ ܕܐܫܟܚܘܗ ܠܫܪܪܐ: ܟܕ ܡܬܟܪ̈ܟܝܢ ܘܒܥܝܢ ܠܗ. ܘܡܢ ܡܕܡ ܕܐܣܬܟܠܢ ܐܕܪܟܢ. ܕܗܠܝܢ ܒܠܚܘܕ ܩܪ̈ܝܒܝܢ ܠܝܕܥܬܐ ܕܫܪܪܐ. ܛܝܒܘܬܐ ܕܝܢ ܕܥܒ̈ܕܝܢ ܠܐ ܡܟܪ̈ܙܝܢ ܒܐܕ̈ܢܝܐ ܕܣܓܝܐܐ. ܘܙܗܝܪܝܢ ܕܠܐ ܢܪܓܫ ܒܗܘܢ ܐܢܫ. ܘܡܛܫܝܢ ܠܗ̇ ܠܡܘܗܒܬܗܘܢ. ܐܝܟ ܡܢ ܕܡܫܟܚ ܣܝܡܬܐ

23. Cod. ܠܗ.

ܘܡܫܠܡܐ ܠܗ. ܘܡܫܟܚܝܢ ܕܢܗܘܘܢ ܙܕܝ̈ܩܐ: ܐܝܟ ܦܡ ܕܚܫܝܢ ܕܢܦܫܗܘܢ ܠܡܫܝܚܗܘܢ: ܘܢܦܠܘܢ ܡܢܗ ܣܘ̈ܕܪܐ ܕܠܘܬܗܘܢ ܒܬܚܘܒܬܐ ܪܒܬܐ. ܬܠ̈ܡܝܕܝܗܘܢ ܕܝܢ ܘܦܘܩ̈ܕܢܝܗܘܢ ܐܘ ܦܠܚܐ. ܘܡܫܒܚܝܢ ܠܡܪܝܐ ܕܦܘܠܚܢܗܘܢ. ܘܗܘܘܢ ܐܝܟܢܐ ܕܦܩܕܝܢܗܘܢ: ܐܝܟ ܗܘ ܡܢܗܘܢ ܕܡܫ ܚܕ ܡܢܗܘܢ. ܕܡܫܟܚܝܢ ܠܗ ܒܥܠܡܐ ܐܚܪܢܐ. ܡܢ ܒ̈ܢܬܗܘܢ ܦܫܛܝܢ ܐܝܟ ܕܐܦ. ܘܦܫ ܠܗ ܕܝܢ ܕܒܣ̈ܪܬܐ ܐܘܕܝܢ ܠܡܠܘܟܗܘܢ: ܒܠ ܗܘ̈ܦܟܝܗܘܢ ܘܫܪ̈ܪܝܗܘܢ ܕܟܪܣܛܝܢܐ. ܫܪܝܪܐܝܬ ܓܝܪ. ܕܝܢ ܘܬܘܕܝܢܗ ܘܠܫܝܢܗܘܢ: ܠܗܢ ܕܢܓܒܐ ܕܢܬܒܥܐ ܘܢܬܦܠ ܒܗ. ܘܫܪܝܪܐܝܬ ܚܕܬܐ ܐܝܬܝܗܘܢ ܒܥܡܐ ܗܢܐ. ܘܡܫܘܬܦܬܐ ܐܠܗܝܬܐ ܐܝܬ ܒܗ. ܗܟܢ ܡܚܝܠ ܒܬܪ̈ܥܝܗܘܢ. ܘܩܪܘ ܒܗܘܢ. ܘܗܘܐ ܕܡܫܟܚܝܢ ܐܝܬܝܗܘܢ ܕܠܘ ܡܢ ܢܫܐ ܗܠܝܢ ܐܦܢܘܬ: ܐܘ ܐܝܟ ܗܘܢܐ ܕܟܬܒܝܗܘܢ ܗܠܝܢ ܐܡܪܬ. ܐܠܐ ܐܝܟ ܡܢ ܕܩܪܝܬ ܒܟܬ̈ܒܝܗܘܢ ܠܗܠܝܢ ܐܡܪܬ: ܘܐܦ ܠܗܠܝܢ ܕܒܬ̈ܪܗ. ܘܡܛܠ ܗܕܐ ܐܬܬܐܠܝܨܬ ܠܡܫܘܘ ܫܪܪܐ: ܠܐܝܠܝܢ ܕܢܓܥܝܢ ܒܗ ܘܦܫܝܢ ܠܥܠܡܐ ܕܥܬܝܕ. ܘܐܝܬ ܠܝ ܦܠܚܘܬܐ: ܕܠܐ ܡܛܠ ܬܫܡܫܬܗܘܢ ܕܟܪ̈ܣܛܝܢܐ ܘܢܚܐ ܒܡܚܝܢܬܐ. ܫܪܝܪܐ ܕܝܢ ܕܒܟ̈ܬܒܐ ܢܦܫܝܢ ܘܦܚܠܝܢ. ܕܐ ܡܬܒܪܟܝܢ ܘܢܣܡ ܐܦܘܠܘܓܝܣܡܘܢ ܕܟܪ̈ܣܛܝܢܐ: ܐܝܟ ܦܡ ܕܠܐ ܢܓܒܐ ܚܢܝܐ ܕܬܪ̈ܥܝܬܗܘܢ ܕܟܬܒܝ ܐܢܘܢ. ܘܡܚܝܒܝܢ ܐܝܟ ܕܡܫܘܕܥܐ. ܡܛܠ ܕܠܐ ܢܓܒܝܢ ܕܢܬܚܫܘܢ ܠܒܪܝܐ. ܘܐܝܟ ܐܪܘ̈ܥܐ ܚܙܝܢ ܘܡܗܘܫܟܝܢ ܚܕ ܠܚܕ ܘܢܦܠܝܢ. ܒܕܡܘܬܐ ܠܡܪܕܐ ܦܠܚܝ ܐܠܗܐ ܐܫܟܚܬ. ܒܠ ܕܫܪܪܐ ܒܢܝ: ܐܝܟ

7. Cod. ܕܐܘܕܝܢ.

ܕܐܡܝܪ̈ܢ ܡܢ ܠܒܪ ܡܫ̈ܬܡܥܝܢ ܒܟܬ̈ܒܝܗܘܢ ܐܚܪ̈ܢܐ: ܡ̈ܠܐ ܕܒܥܝܢ ܠܡܬܡܠܠܘ ܐ̈ܢܫ: ܐܦ ܕܢܬܒܐ ܐܚܪ̈ܢ ܐܢܫ. ܗܠܝܢ ܕܠܐ ܟܠܗܘܢ ܡܐܡܪ ܐܡܪ̈ܢ. ܐܠܐ ܐܦ ܡܫܬܒܪ̈ܘ ܐܫܬܒܪ̈ܢ܀

ܡܩܘܢܐ ܕܝܢ ܐܘ ܡܠܟܐ. ܡܛܠ ܕܗܒܪ̈ܝܢ ܓ̈ܡܘܬܐ ܡܫܪ̈ܪܬܐ ܒܡܕܡܟܟܐ ܕܒܡ ܕܒܪ̈ܐ: ܘܕܒܡ ܐܡܟܐ ܘܣܘܬܐ ܘܒܪ̈ܬܐ: ܠܚܘܒܐ ܕܢܦܫܬܗܘܢ ܟܠ ܟܪ̈ܣܛܝܢܐ ܡܫܦ̈ܩܝܢ ܠܗ. ܟܪ̈ܣܛܝܢܐ ܕܝܢ. ܟܐܢ̈ܝܢ ܘܢܟܦ̈ܝܢ. ܘܫܪܪܐ ܗܝܡܢ ܡܕܡ ܒܬ̈ܠܘܬܗܘܢ. ܘܢܛܪ̈ܝܢ ܪܘܚܗܘܢ. ܘܡܛܠ ܗܕܐ ܟܕ ܥܒܕܝܢ ܠܟܝܢܘܬܗܘܢ ܘܡܬܢܟܦܝܢ ܡܢܗܘܢ: ܠܟ̈ܢܝܢ ܘܡܫܡܫܝܢ ܠܗܘܢ. ܘܡܬܪܐܡܝܢ ܚܫܝܢ ܟܠܗܘܢ. ܐܝܟ ܐܚܐ ܕܡܫܝܢ ܡܢ ܥܕܬܐ. ܘܠܥܠܝܗܘܢ ܡܩܪܒܝܢ ܓܠܘܬܐ ܐܝܟ ܕܢܬܘܟܠܘܢ ܡܢ ܟܢܘܬܗܘܢ. ܡܟܐ ܕܝܢ ܕܐܡܪ ܘܬܒ ܚܕ ܡܢܗܘܢ. ܡܬܚܫܒ ܡܢ ܟܪ̈ܣܛܝܢܐ: ܡܢ ܗܘܝܘ ܒܪ̈ܝܐ ܕܗܘܝܢ ܠܗ. ܘܡܘܕܐ ܠܐܠܗܐ ܟܕ ܐܡܪ. ܕܕܠܐ ܒܐܝܕܥܬܐ ܗܠܝܢ ܫܒܪܬ. ܘܡܘܕܐ ܠܗܘ ܘܡܫܬܒܚܝܢ ܠܗ ܡܝܬ̈ܪܘܬܗ. ܡܛܠ ܕܕܠܐ ܒܐܝܕܥܬܐ ܫܒܪ ܐܢܝܢ. ܒܐܒܠܐ ܘܒܡܚܬܐ: ܟܕ ܡܚܝܒ ܗܘܐ ܘܡܢܥܐ ܗܘܐ ܠܐܝܕܥܬܗܘܢ ܥܪܝܪܬܐ ܕܟܪ̈ܣܛܝܢܐ. ܘܥܪܝܪܐܝܬ ܕܩܪܒܘܬܗܘܢ ܠܡܫܐ ܕܟܪ̈ܣܛܝܢܐ ܡܢ ܟܠܗܘܢ ܠܗܘܢ ܟܕܝ ܐܢܫܐ ܕܐܝܬ ܟܠ ܦ̈ܘܫ ܕܐܪܟܐ. ܢܫܬܬܘܢ ܡܛܠ ܠܬܝ̈ܣܗܘܢ ܕܡܡܠܠܝܢ ܩܘܫܬܐ ܘܒܥ̈ܝܢ ܠܟܪ̈ܣܛܝܢܐ.

---

1. Cod. ܡܫܬ̈ܡܥܝܢ.

ܘܢܫܬܠܠܘܢ ܡܛܠ ܥܙܪܐ. ܦܫܝܩܐ ܗܘ ܠܗܘܢ ܓܝܪ ܕܢܗܦܟܘܢ ܠܐܠܗܐ ܫܪܝܪܐ: ܘܬܢܝ ܡܢ ܕܢܗܦܟܘܢ ܠܡܬܟܚܐ ܕܠܐ ܦܘܪܫ. ܘܫܪܝܪܐܝܬ ܕܐܠܗܐ ܗܘ ܡܕܡ ܕܡܬܡܠܠ ܒܦܘܡܗܘܢ ܕܟܪܣܛܝܢܐ. ܘܝܘܠܦܢܗܘܢ ܬܪܥܐ ܐܝܬܘܗܝ ܕܢܘܗܪܐ. ܢܬܩܪܒܘܢ ܠܗ ܡܛܠ ܟܠܗܘܢ ܐܝܠܝܢ ܕܠܐ ܝܕܥܘ ܠܐܠܗܐ. ܘܢܩܒܠܘܢ ܡ̈ܠܐ ܠܐ ܡܬܚܒܠܢܝܬܐ: ܐܝܠܝܢ ܕܐܝܬܝܗܝܢ ܡܢ ܡܬܘܡ ܘܡܢ ܥܠܡ. ܢܩܕܡܘܢ ܗܟܝܠ ܗܟܝܠ ܠܕܝܢܐ ܕܥܬܝܕ: ܗܘ ܕܒܝܕ ܝܫܘܥ ܡܫܝܚܐ ܥܬܝܕ ܕܢܗܘܐ ܥܠ ܟܠܗ ܓܢܣܐ ܐܢܫܝܐ ܀

ܫܠܡ: ܡܦܩ: ܒܪܘܚܐ: ܕܐܪܣܛܝܕܝܣ: ܦܝܠܘܣܘܦܐ:

THE SYRIAC TEXT OF THE

APOLOGY OF ARISTIDES.